Merrell's Strong Kids—Grades 3-5

Second Edition

 **STRONG KIDS**™

Other programs in **Strong Kids™:**
A Social & Emotional Learning Curriculum

Merrell's Strong Start—Pre-K:
A Social & Emotional Learning Curriculum,
Second Edition

Merrell's Strong Start—Grades K–2:
A Social & Emotional Learning Curriculum,
Second Edition

Merrell's Strong Kids—Grades 6–8:
A Social & Emotional Learning Curriculum,
Second Edition

Merrell's Strong Teens—Grades 9–12:
A Social & Emotional Learning Curriculum,
Second Edition

Merrell's Strong Kids—Grades 3-5

A Social & Emotional Learning Curriculum

Second Edition

by

Dianna Carrizales-Engelmann, Ph.D.
University of Oregon
Eugene

Laura L. Feuerborn, Ph.D.
University of Washington, Tacoma

Barbara A. Gueldner, Ph.D.
Successful Kids Today
Steamboat Springs, Colorado

and

Oanh K. Tran, Ph.D.
California State University
Hayward

·P·A·U·L·H·
BROOKES
PUBLISHING Co®

Baltimore • London • Sydney

Paul H. Brookes Publishing Co.
Post Office Box 10624
Baltimore, Maryland 21285-0624
USA

www.brookespublishing.com

Typeset by Absolute Service, Inc., Towson, Maryland.
Manufactured in the United States of America by
Sheridan Books, Inc., Chelsea, Michigan.

The individuals described in this book are composites or real people whose situations are masked and are based on the authors' experiences. In all instances, names and identifying details have been changed to protect confidentiality.

Cover image © istockphoto/Christopher Futcher.
Stock photos and clip art are © istockphoto.com and Jupiterimages Corporation.

Source for Chapter 1 extract: From "Enhancing school-based prevention and youth development through coordinated social, emotional, and academic learning," by M.T. Greenberg, et al., *American Psychologist*, 2003, 58, pp. 466–474.

Library of Congress Cataloging-in-Publication Data

The Library of Congress has cataloged the print edition as follows:

Names: Carrizales-Engelmann, Dianna, author. | Merrell, Kenneth W. Strong start.
Title: Merrell's strong kids, grades 3-5 : a social and emotional learning curriculum / by Dianna Carrizales-Engelmann,
     Ph.D., University of Oregon, Eugene; Laura L. Feuerborn, Ph.D., University of
     Washington, Tacoma; Barbara A. Gueldner, Ph.D., Successful Kids Today, Steamboat Springs, Colorado; and
     Oanh K. Tran, Ph.D., California State University, East Bay.
Description: Second edition. | Baltimore, Maryland : Brookes Publishing, 2016. | Series: Strong kids | Revised edition
     of: Strong start / Kenneth W. Merrell. c2007. | Includes bibliographical references and index.
Identifiers: LCCN 2015038445 | ISBN 9781598579536 (paperback)
Subjects: LCSH: Affective education. | Education, Elementary. | Social learning. | Child development. | Emotional
     intelligence. | Education--Social aspects.
Classification: LCC LB1072 .C365 2016 | DDC 370.15/34--dc23 LC record available at http://lccn.loc.gov/2015038445

British Library Cataloguing in Publication data are available from the British Library.

2020   2019   2018   2017   2016

10   9   8   7   6   5   4   3   2   1

Contents

About the Downloadable Material

Purchasers of this book may download, print, and/or photocopy the ancillary material for educational use. These materials are included with the print book and are also available at www.brookespublishing.com/downloads, keycode: 36rrAnJ3n

CONTENTS OF THE DOWNLOADABLE MATERIAL

Lesson 1

Supplement 1.1: The Limbic System
Supplement 1.2: *Strong Kids* Rules
Supplement 1.3: Comment Slip
Supplement 1.4: *Strong Kids* Lessons
Supplement 1.5: Key Terms and Definitions
Supplement 1.6: List of Emotions
Supplement 1.7: My Emotions

Lesson 2

Supplement 2.1: Picture of a Roller Coaster
Supplement 2.2: Key Terms and Definitions
Supplement 2.3: Practice Scenarios
Supplement 2.4: Emotions Thermometer
Supplement 2.5: Identifying and Measuring My Emotions

Lesson 3

Supplement 3.1: Thoughts, Emotions, and Behaviors
Supplement 3.2: Key Terms and Definitions
Supplement 3.3: Cartoon Example
Supplement 3.4: Practice Situations
Supplement 3.5: Ways of Showing Emotions

Lesson 4

Supplement 4.1: Key Terms and Definitions
Supplement 4.2: List of Emotions
Supplement 4.3: Small-Group Student Role-Play Scenarios
Supplement 4.4: Empathy Assignment

Lesson 5

Supplement 5.1: Key Terms and Definitions
Supplement 5.2. What Problem Does My Anger Want Me to Solve?
Supplement 5.3: Not-So-Good First Choices
Supplement 5.4: Anger Model
Supplement 5.5: Tamika's Problem
Supplement 5.6: Anger Management Skills and Strategies
Supplement 5.7: Anger Management Worksheet

Lesson 6

Supplement 6.1: Picture of a Frog
Supplement 6.2: Picture of a Scientist
Supplement 6.3: Key Terms and Definitions
Supplement 6.4: Picture of a Thought Bubble
Supplement 6.5: Picture of a Man Trapped in a Hole
Supplement 6.6: Common Thinking Traps
Supplement 6.7: Example Situations
Supplement 6.8: Practice Situations Worksheet

Lesson 7

Supplement 7.1: Thinking Traps
Supplement 7.2: Picture of a Snowball
Supplement 7.3: Key Terms and Definitions
Supplement 7.4: Picture of Looking for Evidence
Supplement 7.5: Evidence for or Against
Supplement 7.6: Looking for Evidence to Reframe
Supplement 7.7: Reframing Thinking Traps Examples
Supplement 7.8: Reframing Thinking Traps Using Evidence
Supplement 7.9: Reframing Thinking Traps Worksheet

Lesson 8

Supplement 8.1: Picture of Two Students Fighting Over a Laptop
Supplement 8.2: Key Terms and Definitions
Supplement 8.3: Conflict Resolution: What Can I Do?
Supplement 8.4: A Four-Step Problem-Solving Model for Conflict Resolution
Supplement 8.5: Using a Problem-Solving Model to Resolve Conflicts

Lesson 9

Supplement 9.1: Pictures of Stressful Situations
Supplement 9.2: Key Terms and Definitions
Supplement 9.3: Stress Symptoms and Example Situations
Supplement 9.4: Personal Triggers and Stress Identification
Supplement 9.5: Relaxation Techniques
Supplement 9.6: Letting Go of Stress

Lesson 10

Supplement 10.1: Key Terms and Definitions
Supplement 10.2: Feeling Good Activities
Supplement 10.3: Healthy Habits
Supplement 10.4: Weekday Habits and Routines
Supplement 10.5: Weekend Habits and Routines
Supplement 10.6: Example Situation: Helping Tamika Make Healthy Choices
Supplement 10.7: What Did You Do Toward Positive Living This Week?

Lesson 11

Supplement 11.1: Your Younger Self
Supplement 11.2: Key Terms and Definitions
Supplement 11.3: Healthy Living Domains
Supplement 11.4: Examples and Nonexamples of Goal Setting
Supplement 11.5: Setting SMART Goals
Supplement 11.6: Steps to Setting and Attaining Goals
Supplement 11.7: Personal Goal Organizer

Lesson 12

Supplement 12.1: *Strong Kids* Lesson Review and Discussion Questions
Supplement 12.2: Resilience Scenarios
Supplement 12.3: Steps to Perseverance
Supplement 12.4: Helping Resources Handout
Certificate of Achievement

Appendix A

Strong Kids Knowledge Test for Students in Grades 3–5

Appendix B

Basic Fidelity Checklist

About the Authors

Dianna Carrizales-Engelmann, Ph.D., College of Education, 230Q HEDCO, 1215 University of Oregon, Eugene, OR 97403

Dianna Carrizales-Engelmann is currently an instructor at the University of Oregon in Eugene specializing in performance assessment for teacher preparation. Over the course of her career in the field of education, Dr. Carrizales-Engelmann has maintained a consistent focus in the development, research, and troubleshooting of educational assessments. Dr. Carrizales-Engelmann's assessment development experience includes state assessments, nationally standardized assessments, and classroom and curriculum-based assessments. In addition to her role in the field of educational assessment, Dr. Carrizales-Engelmann has had several years of policy-related experience in the areas of education and assessment at the Oregon Department of Education.

Laura L. Feuerborn, Ph.D., Associate Professor, Department of Education, University of Washington, Tacoma, 1900 Commerce Street, Box 35835, Tacoma, Washington 98402

Dr. Feuerborn is Associate Professor at the University of Washington, Tacoma, and is a nationally certified school psychologist. She received her Ph.D. in school psychology with an emphasis in emotional and behavioral supports from the University of Oregon. Since joining the faculty at the University of Washington, Tacoma, in 2006, she has taught graduate-level courses for educators in both general and special education. Her areas of teaching expertise include classroom management, systems of prevention and supports, and collaborative consultation. She developed and now leads a course that focuses on social and emotional learning (SEL) for teachers. Dr. Feuerborn's research centers on the science of implementing systems change. She is an author of the Staff Perceptions of Behavior and Discipline (http://spbdsupport.com), an assessment tool that helps leadership teams understand the needs and perceptions of school staff in the implementation of positive behavior interventions and supports (PBIS). Dr. Feuerborn has been presenting her work in regional, national, and international conferences for more than 15 years. She serves as a reviewer for scholarly journals and publishes peer-reviewed research in the fields of SEL and schoolwide PBIS.

Barbara A. Gueldner, Ph.D., Licensed Psychologist, Successful Kids Today, P.O. Box 772748, Steamboat Springs, Colorado 80477

Dr. Gueldner is a licensed psychologist and nationally certified school psychologist who works with children and families in Steamboat Springs, Colorado. She obtained her doctorate in school psychology from the University of Oregon and has worked in educational, medical, and community settings for 20 years. Dr. Gueldner specializes in promoting wellness and resilience through social and emotional learning (SEL) program development and implementation, parent education and support, integrating mental health care into primary care and schools, and early detection and intervention with developmental, behavioral, social, and emotional problems. She has published in the areas of SEL and general childhood mental health issues, coauthoring journal articles, book chapters, the first editions of *Strong Kids* and *Strong Teens*, and a book on implementing SEL in schools. Dr. Gueldner is involved in a variety of public outreach and educational initiatives in her community.

Oanh K. Tran, Ph.D., Professor, Department of Educational Psychology, California State University, East Bay, 25800 Carlos Bee Boulevard, Hayward, California 94542

Dr. Tran teaches in the Child Clinical/School Psychology (CCSP) Program at California State University, East Bay. The CCSP program is approved by the National Association of School Psychologists (NASP). Dr. Tran also practices as a school psychologist in the San Francisco Bay Area and consults with school districts and mental health agencies. Dr. Tran's direct experience includes working with diverse and at-risk populations in public and nonpublic schools as well as residential, foster care, outpatient, and in-home settings. Her research and professional interests include psychoeducational assessments, special education, social and emotional learning, academic and behavioral consultation, response to intervention, positive behavior supports, cognitive behavioral therapy, and parent training. She has presented locally and nationally and has published articles, chapters, and prevention curricula in the area of children's mental health. Dr. Tran continues her research and mentoring of her graduate students in social-emotional development and learning for students in Grades K–12.

Foreword

This remarkable curricular program is a fitting tribute to Ken Merrell's legacy as one of the foremost scholar–innovators in the realm of emotional literacy and social and emotional learning (SEL). This work, along with its authors, are clearly reflective of the superb contributions that Ken made to our field of practice and research inquiry in teaching our school-age students, from preschool through high school, how to manage their emotions and attitudes in a healthier, more competent manner. I am honored to write this foreword as a means of acknowledging the work that Ken contributed and inspired in a career that was cut short so tragically.

Children and youth today are exposed constantly to so much toxicity in our national discourse about all manner of societal issues, not to mention the potential abuses of pervasive social media use that so dominates their lives. We do not provide them with competent models of interpersonal behavior nor with the tools for evaluating and making sense of what they hear and see. Nor do we model and teach healthy strategies for problem solving difficult social and interpersonal situations. Far too many youth today do not have the means to access material such as that provided in the *Strong Kids*™ curriculum. I can think of no other current innovation deliverable within the schooling context that holds greater importance for our youth's future than this one.

Mastery of the content of this curricular program has so many uses in a student's daily life that are manifested in one's self-management as well as in relating to others. This content holds substantial potential for improving student mental health and social relationships throughout one's social network. This program revision introduces "emotion identification" that allows students to better cope with complex and concurrent emotions, and students are taught how to confront their emotions in a proactive manner rather than as something to simply change or fix. Students are taught about emotional expression in contextual terms that include not only how they are expressed but with whom and where. The scenarios provided as teaching aids are authentic and carefully referenced to the problems and social situations today's students are likely to experience within their respective social networks. In terms of useful content, there seems to be very little that the authors have overlooked. I am especially impressed with the material on selecting smart, achievable goals and strategies for integrating SEL content across social settings and the generalizability–sustainability of key concepts.

The new content added to this revision passes the logic test for me in that it encompasses exactly what I think students of today need to cope effectively with the challenges and stresses of their daily life. These include units on understanding your emotions, understanding the emotions of others, dealing with anger, clear thinking, solving people problems, letting go of stress, positive living, behavior change, and finishing UP. These essential competencies are embedded within five lessons focused respectively on self-awareness, self-management, social awareness, relationship skills, and responsible decision making. Exposure to and mastery of this material through a universal curricular teaching approach would go a long way toward enhancing the socialization process for many of our stressed out and anxious students. I am also impressed with the section on mindfulness and frankly did not expect such a unit in a curriculum of this type. However, as the authors present it, this material appears to fit seamlessly with the other content.

I have long believed that best practices in the SEL domain involve use of the most effective principles of academic instruction to teach this content. There are two types of mastery that should be addressed in this regard: *conceptual and behavioral*. This curriculum addresses both types of mastery and also provides for the universal and small group/individualized teaching of the content for those students who struggle with mastery in a group context. I applaud the authors for their accommodation of this important task in their work.

Over 20 years of research and development have been invested in this program to date. It is also grounded in a strong practitioner feedback loop that has provided invaluable information on the best ways to teach this content in a user-friendly fashion that students find appealing and acceptable. More than anything I can think of, the *Strong Kids* curriculum holds the potential to realize schools' role in promoting the emotional literacy and mental health of today's students. The *Strong Kids* curriculum program is very well designed, meets the best standards of curricular development, is easy to teach, and—best of all—students seem to like it, which, in my view, is the ultimate test of such a product. The *Strong Kids* curriculum is indeed a seminal contribution to our knowledge and practice base on social-emotional development. We owe Ken Merrell and the authors a huge debt!

Hill M. Walker, Ph.D.
Professor Emeritus
College of Education
University of Oregon

Acknowledgments

This second edition of *Strong Kids* and *Strong Teens* is published in memory of and dedication to Dr. Kenneth W. Merrell: teacher, mentor, friend, advisor, and inspiration (1957–2011). These programs would not exist without his vision and commitment to the mission of the Oregon Resiliency Project. Through these revised programs, we aim to honor and extend his legacy of supports for children, adolescents, and school communities. He was on our minds and in our hearts at every step of this process.

We continue to acknowledge the foundational research, development, and support of the Oregon Resiliency Project members (2001–2011): Leah Benazzi, Sara Castro-Olivo, Erin Chaparro, Christine Davis, Keith Herman, Duane Isava, Travis Laxton, Verity Levitt, Kelly McGraw, Kent McIntosh, Jean Mercier, Nicole Nakayama, Christiane Oilar, Kristin Orton, Wendy Reinke, Scott Ross, and Lisa Sterling.

SECTION I

Introduction and Overview

CHAPTER 1

About *Strong Kids*

Strong Kids™: A Social and Emotional Learning Curriculum is a social and emotional learning curriculum that consists of five brief and practical social and emotional learning (SEL) programs designed for the purpose of teaching social and emotional skills and assets that promote resilience and mitigate risk in children and adolescents. These introductory chapters provide information on the following:

- The importance of promoting children's mental health and doing so in the context of social and emotional learning

- The design of the *Strong Kids* program

- Evidence of the program's effectiveness

- Tips for using the curriculum effectively and with confidence

- Updates to the second edition

Strong Kids—Grades 3–5 is designed specifically for use with children in Grades 3–5 or those who are approximately ages 8–12 years. Because *Strong Kids—Grades 3–5* is designed to be both a prevention and an early intervention (EI) program, it has a wide range of applications and may be used effectively with children who are high functioning, typically developing, at risk for social and emotional problems, or struggling with social and emotional difficulties. *Strong Kids—Grades 3–5* can be implemented in a variety of settings: general and special education classrooms, group counseling settings, and youth treatment facilities that have an educational component.

For younger students in the early elementary grades, the *Strong Kids* curriculum also offers *Strong Start—Pre-K* and *Strong Start—Grades K–2*. For older students in higher grades, the curriculum also offers *Strong Kids—Grades 6–8* for use with students in middle school and *Strong Teens—Grades 9–12* for use with high school–age students.

Children in the *Strong Kids—Grades 3–5* range experience a host of changes during this time in their development. Academic task demands increase, along with expectations for increased independence and organization. Social relationships become more complex, emotional experiences may feel confusing, and students become increasingly aware of issues of which they may have been previously unaware or only partially aware. Stressors such as family problems, parents' marital conflict, peer acceptance or rejection, and expectations at school and in their community suddenly gain weight and relevance. *Strong Kids—Grades 3–5* is designed to help increase children's awareness of their social and emotional worlds and teach skills to manage both effectively while having fun and engaging in activities that support their academic, social, and emotional learning.

PROMOTING CHILDREN'S MENTAL HEALTH

As many researchers, writers, and public officials have noted, changes in the structure of society and families have resulted in an increasing percentage of children and families who are at risk for developing a variety of behavioral, social, and mental health problems (e.g., Costello & Angold, 2000; Doll & Lyon, 1998; Farmer & Farmer, 1999; Hoagwood & Erwin, 1997; Satcher, 1999). The numbers of children and youth affected by these problems are surprisingly high. Greenberg, Domitrovich, and Bumbarger (2001) asserted that between 12% and 22% of children and adolescents younger than age 18 experience mental health problems of sufficient severity to be in need of mental health services. These percentages represent a staggering figure of up to 1 out of every 5 children and adolescents in some instances. The Centers for Disease Control and Prevention (2013) estimated that among adolescents within a 12-month period, 8% will attempt suicide and 20% will have been bullied, and during a 30-day period, 41.4% texted or e-mailed while driving a car and 34.9% consumed alcohol. Without question, effective responses early on to these problems, including mental health prevention and EI curricula in educational settings, must occur if these challenges are to be stemmed.

Despite sincere and well-meaning attempts to offer real solutions to social, emotional, and mental health problems of students in school settings, many of the programs or interventions that have been implemented are simply ineffective. Walker stated that "educators are notorious for embracing programs that look good but do no actual good" (2001, p. 2). In these educators' defense, we should note that school personnel who work on the front lines of serving children and youth who have significant mental health issues are often overworked and not provided with sufficient resources with which to make the impact they desire. Furthermore, some developers and publishers of mental health prevention programs tend to overwhelm educators and clinicians with claims of effectiveness, even when there is little or no supporting evidence. Worse yet are reactionary school policies, such as the perennial "get tough" approaches that are not only ineffective in the long term but also contribute to the development of systems that are hostile, aversive, socially toxic, and incompatible with optimal development of academic skills and mental health (Hyman & Perone, 1998; Skiba & Peterson, 1999).

Despite these problems and challenges, there is reason for optimism regarding our ability to positively affect the social and emotional health and resilience of children and adolescents, even those from very adverse life circumstances. One reason for this optimism is the accumulation of a large body of scientific evidence regarding what has been termed *developmental resilience* (Doll & Lyon, 1998). This notion of resilience concerns the ability of individuals to cope successfully with adversity, risk factors, and severe life stress and for young people to develop into competent and happy adults despite these problems.

Central to this notion of developmental resilience is the idea that some characteristics of resilience—the cognitive, behavioral, and affective skills that enable one to cope effectively with adversity—may be systematically taught and learned. Although some aspects of resilience or developmental hardiness may be innate or biologically based, the evidence shows that learning plays a crucial role in developing the ability to cope effectively with problems and challenges. Stated simply, the ability to be resilient and to cope effectively in the face of adverse circumstances and challenges in life is something that can be acquired in great measure through systematic and effective instruction in the critical requisite skills involved.

Although the primary mission of public education has traditionally been perceived as promoting the development of academic skills, there is growing support and advocacy for the systematic inclusion of skills that may be considered "nonacademic" but are, in fact, key to supporting students' overall development (Pellegrino & Hilton, 2013). Critical thinking, problem solving, creativity, communication, and responsible thinking are necessary for students to succeed in the 21st century (Partnership for 21st Century Skills, 2008), and a growing body of evidence demonstrates that social and emotional skills are particularly relevant (see Durlak, Dymnicki, Taylor, Weissberg, & Schellinger, 2011, for a meta-analytic review) and believed to be a "missing piece" (Elias, 2006, p. 6). There is no question that most educators, parents, students, and the general public also support and expect a broader mission for schools (Greenberg et al., 2003). Some examples of this expanded agenda include character education, development of good work habits, promotion of good citizenship, development of social and emotional competence, and promotion of a healthy and productive lifestyle. Commenting on the need for this broader agenda, Greenberg and his colleagues stated

> High-quality education should teach young people to interact in socially skilled and respectful ways; to practice positive, safe, and healthy behaviors; to contribute ethically and responsibly to their peer group, family, school, and community; and to possess basic competencies, work habits, and values as a foundation for meaningful employment and citizenship. . . . We consequently assert that school-based prevention programming—based on coordinated social, emotional, and academic learning—should be fundamental to preschool through high school education. (2003, pp. 466–467)

We emphatically agree with this statement. In addition, we propose that teaching young people positive social, emotional, and behavioral skills is not only an essential mission for educators and mental health professionals but also one of the most critical challenges facing our society in the 21st century. Students are placed under so many stressors at times during their young development that teaching resilience is critical for academic and life success.

SOCIAL AND EMOTIONAL LEARNING

A framework, aptly named *social and emotional learning*, has guided efforts to effectively teach the social and emotional health and resilience of young people. Drawing from the fields of child and adolescent development, health promotion, principles of instruction, affective neuroscience, positive psychology, cognitive therapy, behavioral theory and application, and prevention science (Zins, Bloodworth, Weissberg, & Walberg, 2004), specific skills are ideally taught over the course of students' academic tenure (i.e., preschool through high school). These skills also should be taught with coordination and strategy in mind (Devaney, O'Brien, Resnik, Keister, & Weissberg, 2006; Greenberg et al., 2003). That is, how will the skills be infused throughout a busy school day? How will we know students are learning and applying the information? What kind of support is needed and is this support feasible? The goal is to provide *all* students with effective instruction and support to mitigate risk behaviors and outcomes and enhance protective factors known to affect positive overall development (Greenberg et al., 2003). Achieving this goal is possible by applying current evidence and continuing to investigate ways in which we can improve.

The efforts of the Collaborative for Academic, Social, and Emotional Learning (CASEL) at supporting SEL in youth have been instrumental in understanding the key areas for social and emotional development and best practices in facilitating this process. CASEL has endorsed five person-centered and interrelated competency areas that are essential to cognitive, social, and emotional development: self-awareness, self-management, social awareness, relationship skills, and responsible decision making (CASEL, 2014; Zins et al., 2004). There is growing evidence that SEL programming, highlighting these competency areas, is effective (e.g., Durlak et al., 2011; Durlak & Wells, 1997; Payton et al., 2008; Sklad, Diekstra, De Ritter, Ben, & Gravesteijn, 2012). Improvements have been measured in areas such as identifying emotions, resolving conflict, self-efficacy, attitudes toward school, positive social behaviors, and academic performance. Conduct problems, as well as emotional distress, have been reduced. In addition to benefits for youth, teachers view SEL to be a priority (Bridgeland, Bruce, & Hariharan, 2013), and school staff are able to implement SEL effectively and without mental health training (Durlak et al., 2011).

Since the early 1990s, many SEL programs have been developed and used in education and mental health settings. The type of program ultimately selected will depend on a variety of factors such as the needs of the setting, financial considerations, training and resource requirements, and time constraints. *Strong Kids* was designed with these variables in mind and, we believe, offers an affordable and relatively low-resource option, using principles of effective instruction and evidence-based strategies for promoting mental health, to effectively teach SEL skills.

MODEL FOR PREVENTING BEHAVIORAL AND EMOTIONAL PROBLEMS

Education researchers have adapted a public health prevention model for use in school systems (e.g., Merrell & Buchanan, 2006; U.S. Department of Education,

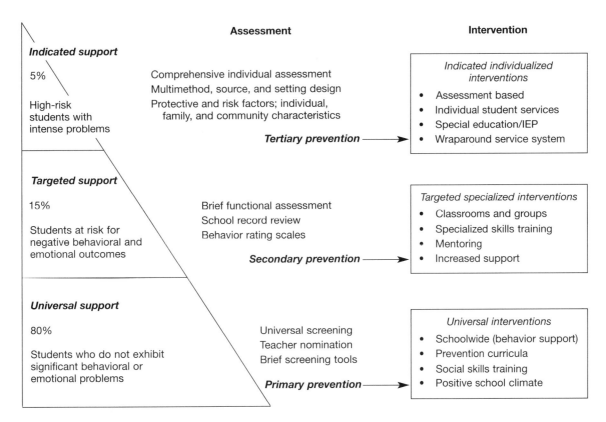

Figure 1.1. The prevention triangle model, specifically adapted for how to make systems work for assessing, identifying, and serving students with behavioral, social, and emotional problems. (*Key:* IEP, individualized education program.)

2004; Walker et al., 1996). We believe that this three-tiered model (see Figure 1.1) has great importance for promoting SEL and for school-based promotion of children's mental health in general. Sometimes referred to as the "triangle," this model of prevention and intervention includes service delivery at three levels of prevention: students who currently are not experiencing learning or social/behavior difficulties (*primary prevention*); students who are considered to be at risk for the development of learning or social/behavior difficulties (*secondary prevention*); and students who currently are experiencing significant learning or social/behavior difficulties (*tertiary prevention*).

We can visualize this model and its three levels of prevention as a triangle. The entire triangle represents all students within a school setting, the majority of whom are not experiencing difficulties (i.e., the bottom portion of the triangle), some of whom are at risk of developing significant problems (i.e., the middle portion), and an even smaller percentage who are currently experiencing significant difficulties (i.e., the top portion). Typical practice is to focus on those students who are at the top of the triangle—those who are currently experiencing significant learning or social-emotional difficulties. Practitioners tend to spend the majority of their time and effort providing tertiary prevention (i.e., individualized assessment and intervention services) to these students on a case-by-case basis. These students make up the smallest percentage of the school population, but because of the significance of their problems, they often require the majority of time and resources from school personnel (Walker et al., 1996). Figure 1.1 illustrates the prevention triangle model, specifically adapted for how to make systems work for assessing, identifying, and serving students with behavioral, social, and emotional problems.

Shifting to a systemwide prevention model requires looking at the "big picture" by considering the needs of *all* students, not just those who are referred because they are currently experiencing significant difficulties. The foundation of a prevention approach is the use of universal interventions (i.e., primary prevention) designed to enhance the delivery of effective instruction and improved school climate to promote the academic, social, and behavioral resilience of *all* students in the school. This idea requires that educators begin to move some resources and energy toward those children and adolescents who are not currently experiencing significant difficulties in order to promote skills to provide a sort of inoculation for the developmental challenges that may occur. The premise is to reduce the probability that these youth will eventually rise to the "top of the triangle" where more resources are required. More specifically, primary prevention for students who are not currently experiencing learning or social/behavior difficulties is accomplished through schoolwide and classwide efforts that involve the consistent use of research-based effective practices, ongoing monitoring of these practices and student outcomes, staff training, and professional development. The goal of primary prevention is to create school and classroom environments that promote student learning and health and decrease the number of students at risk for learning or social/behavior problems.

As important as it is to focus on primary prevention, we also know that not all students respond similarly to these efforts. Thus, it is important to monitor student progress and to assess whether students are at risk (i.e., in need of secondary prevention efforts) or are experiencing significant difficulties (i.e., in need of tertiary prevention efforts). Identifying students at risk for learning, social-emotional, and behavior difficulties is an important aspect to comprehensive prevention efforts. For students identified as at risk and in need of secondary prevention efforts, the focus is on the delivery of specialized interventions (often at a small-group level) to prevent the worsening of problems and to prevent the development of more significant concerns. The focus on early identification and EI is important.

With respect to mental health and social-emotional problems of children and adolescents, we believe that this prevention model is an ideal way to think about providing SEL programs and other services. Thinking in this way about the challenges faced in promoting social-emotional wellness and mental health among children and adolescents makes these challenges more manageable. Instead of waiting until students have developed severe problems and require extensive time and effort to simply be managed, you can continually focus a portion of your resources on prevention activities that will ultimately reduce the number of students at the "top of the triangle."

DESIGN OF THE *STRONG KIDS* CURRICULUM: BACKGROUND

The *Strong Kids* curriculum was developed by the Oregon Resiliency Project (ORP) at the University of Oregon and under the direction of the late Kenneth W. Merrell, Ph.D. Several goals led the research and development efforts to

1. Target each of the five pathways to wellness advocated by Cowen (1994), a pioneer in the modern science of mental health and wellness promotion:

   • Forming wholesome early attachments

   • Acquiring age-appropriate competencies

   • Having exposure to settings that favor wellness outcomes

   • Having the empowering sense of being in control of one's fate

   • Coping effectively with stress

2. Make available a program that was prevention oriented, practical, cost-effective, and feasible for teachers to implement in the classroom and within the course of a typical class period

3. Design the program to be useful across grade levels, thereby providing a means to provide a more cohesive and collaborative approach to SEL programming (Zins, 2004)

As we revised this curriculum, we envisioned *Strong Kids* as a carefully designed SEL program to prevent the development of certain mental health problems and promote social and emotional wellness among young people (see Chapter 4 for more information on the revisions). *Strong Kids* is not the right SEL program for all types of problems. We especially targeted the domain of internalizing behavioral and emotional problems (e.g., depression, anxiety, social withdrawal, somatic problems), using a largely cognitive-behavioral theoretical orientation given its evidence of effectiveness with youth in these areas (Weisz, Hawley, & Doss, 2004), to promote *social and emotional resilience. Strong Kids* should not be considered a comprehensive program for preventing school violence or antisocial behavior, even though it may play a role in supporting these aims as part of a comprehensive program of effective behavior support.

The advantage of this programming approach is that *Strong Kids* follows the recommendations outlined by Durlak and DuPre (2008) for skill training by being sequenced, active, focused, and explicit. One disadvantage of this approach is that the program is not designed to be a complete mental health treatment package for children and youth with severe mental health problems. Although our research to date has shown that the curriculum can make a meaningful difference with these populations, it should be used as one component of a comprehensive, intensive intervention program in such cases.

IMPLEMENTATION GUIDELINES AND LESSON STRUCTURE

The *Strong Kids* and *Strong Teens* programs were designed to circumvent common barriers to implementation such as time, resources, and training while upholding criteria for effective instructional design and delivery (Carnine, Silbert, Kame'enui, & Tarver, 2009; Coyne, Kame'enui, & Carnine, 2006). Thus, this curriculum was developed with both time feasibility and ease of implementation as high priorities. Even an exceptionally strong intervention program will fail to make an impact if its time requirements and difficulty of implementation result in few people being able to use it within the time and training constraints of a school system or other youth-serving agency. We recommend teaching the *Strong Kids—Grades 3–5* lessons once per week for 12 weeks, although there is evidence to support implementation at a more accelerated tempo such as two lessons per week for 6 weeks with similar effective outcomes (Tran, 2008). The one lesson per week format may allow students sufficient time to complete any homework that may be assigned, internalize the concepts taught, and practice the new skills they learn, both at school and outside of school.

Each lesson takes between 60 and 80 minutes to complete. All lessons can be shortened by stopping at the end of an activity and finishing up with the Closure activity, found at the end of the lesson. When continuing the lesson, teachers simply resume by starting with the Mindfulness-Based Focusing Activity found in the Introduction section, followed by the point in the lesson where the lesson was stopped during the previous instructional period and, again, ending with the Closure activity. For each lesson, we have suggested a stopping point. Please refer to the Running Short on Time? section, found at the beginning of each lesson, for these suggestions. Lessons also can be lengthened, using additional activities found at the end of each lesson, at the instructor's discretion.

Each lesson includes instructional scaffolding (e.g., optional scripting and explicit directions) to eliminate the need for intensive preparation, a review and introduction of the lesson and key concepts, a range of examples to define the concept, and opportunities to practice and integrate skills through activities such as modeling, guided practice and role play, and independent practice. Generalization and maintenance of skills are promoted by providing strategies for practice throughout the school day, in other academic areas, and across settings.

We specifically designed *Strong Kids* as a low-cost, low-technology program that can be implemented in a school or related educational setting with minimal professional training and resources. It is not necessary to be a licensed mental health professional to learn and implement this curriculum. General and special education teachers, speech-language pathologists, school counselors, social workers, psychologists, and other education or mental health professionals may serve as effective group leaders. The program may be taught in a general education classroom or in selected small-group settings. One of the advantages of the *Strong Kids* curriculum is that it is designed to support academic skills and to be integrated within an instructional program. The activities in this curriculum not only promote SEL and resilience but also support literacy, language arts, social studies, and health.

Strong Kids—Grades 3–5 is highly structured and semiscripted, designed to cover very specific objectives and goals. We developed the objectives and goals for each lesson, as well as the implementation guidelines, based on current research findings in education and psychology, aiming for a prevention and intervention program that is built on a solid base of empirical evidence. Each lesson follows a similar format with the following sections:

Social and Emotional Competency Areas: CASEL (2014) endorsed five key areas necessary in building SEL skills (self-awareness, self-management, social awareness, relationship skills, and responsible decision making); skills categories are assigned to each lesson where content reflects these areas.

Purpose and Objectives: Describes the skills students will learn

Materials Needed: Lists the materials needed for advance preparation

Running Short on Time?: Suggests an optional stopping point to segment the lesson

Instructor Reflection: Provides an opportunity for instructors to reflect on the content of the lesson to increase knowledge and personalize the application

Review: Lists topics covered in the previous lesson

Introduction: Introduces the concepts for the lesson

Mindfulness-Based Focusing Activity: Helps students focus and prepare for the lesson

Key Terms and Definitions: Provides an introduction to any relevant vocabulary

Instructional Content and Practice Activities: Provides content and activities specialized to each lesson's theme

Putting It All Together: Reviews the key concepts practiced in the lesson

Closure: Provides a brief breathing and reflection activity

In addition, each lesson provides optional scripts to aid content delivery, sample situations and examples to better illustrate the content, and opportunities for guided and independent practice. Group leaders can follow the script and examples directly or modify the sample script to present the lesson's main ideas using language that is most appropriate for their group(s). At the end of each of the 12 lessons is a section titled Tips for Transfer Training and Homework. This section includes optional homework assignments and take-home handouts, tactics that are further designed to reinforce learning outside of the *Strong Kids— Grades 3–5* instructional setting. This section also prompts instructors to precorrect (i.e., anticipate students' errors and difficulties in learning the skills), remind (i.e., provide verbal or visual prompts of the steps and actions needed to use the skills), and reinforce (i.e., provide social reinforcement, such as praise, when students use the skills) the lesson objectives. These instructional principles are known to improve skills maintenance over time and generalization across settings (e.g., Langland, Lewis-Palmer, & Sugai, 1998; Sugai, Bullis, & Cumblad, 1997). Ideas for making the content especially relevant to students are included in each lesson, typically within each practice activity. Additional suggestions for activities are listed at the end of each lesson and are provided to encourage practice that is embedded throughout the course of the school day, to make the lesson content relevant to students, and to allow additional opportunities to practice and reinforce the concepts. Lesson 12 can be used as a "booster lesson" to provide an opportunity to reteach and reemphasize critical *Strong Kids* content and skills after a period of time—usually several weeks to a few months—and following the completion of the 12 lessons.

EVIDENCE

The *Strong Kids* curriculum, from *Strong Start—Pre-K* to *Strong Teens*, has been evaluated and continues to be studied within a multitiered model (universal and tertiary prevention and intervention programming), across age and grade levels (elementary through high school–age individuals), and in a variety of settings. The strongest evidence exists for a unilateral increase in knowledge of social and emotional content across studies. Some studies have also found significant decreases in internalizing problem symptoms and increases in social and emotional skills and assets. Teachers and students have found the program worthwhile and feasible, thereby providing evidence for the social validity of the program. A reference section at the end of this chapter provides relevant sources for these studies. If you are conducting research or a program evaluation of the *Strong Kids* curriculum, we would be very interested in hearing from you.

SUMMARY

We are at a pivotal point in history whereby our youths' social and emotional resilience is developing through direct instruction and application, with the use of materials developed from years of research and practice across multiple relevant disciplines. The *Strong Kids* curriculum offers one way of helping our youth develop into socially and emotionally healthy individuals. Together, we can prepare today and tomorrow's global citizens for 21st century stressors and opportunities.

Strong Start, Strong Kids, and *Strong Teens*: Research

Barker, E.S., Marcotte, A.M., & Whitcomb, S.A. (2015). Promoting positive teacher–child interactions through implementation of a social emotional learning curriculum with performance feedback. Manuscript in revision.

Berry-Krazmien, C., & Torres-Fernandez, I. (2007, March 27–31). *Implementation of the Strong Kids curriculum in a residential facility.* Poster presentation at the Annual Convention of the National Association of School Psychologists, New York, NY.

Caldarella, P., Christensen, L., Kramer, T.J., & Kronmiller, K. (2009). Promoting social and emotional learning in second grade students: A study of the *Strong Start* curriculum. *Early Childhood Education Journal, 37*, 51–56. doi:10.1007/s10643-009-0321-4

Castro-Olivo, S. (2014). Promoting social-emotional learning in adolescent Latino ELLs: A study of the culturally adapted Strong Teens program. *School Psychology Quarterly, 29*, 567–577.

Faust, J.J. (2006). *Preventing anxiety and depression: An evaluation of social-emotional curriculum* (Unpublished educational specialist's thesis). University of Wisconsin, Whitewater.

Feuerborn, L.L. (2004). *Promoting emotional resiliency through classroom instruction: The effects of a classroom-based prevention program* (Unpublished doctoral dissertation). University of Oregon, Eugene.

Gueldner, B.A., & Merrell, K.W. (2011). The effectiveness of a social and emotional learning program with middle school students in the general education setting and the effect of consultation on student outcomes. *Journal of Educational and Psychological Consultation, 21*, 1–27. doi:10.1080/10474412.2010.522876

Gunter, L., Caldarella, P., Korth, B. B., & Young, K. R. (2012). Promoting social and emotional learning in preschool students: A study of Strong Start Pre-K. *Early Childhood Education, 40*, 151–159.

Harlacher, J.E., & Merrell, K.W. (2009). Social and emotional learning as a universal level of support: Evaluating the follow-up effect of Strong Kids on social and emotional outcomes. *Journal of Applied School Psychology, 26*(3), 212–229. doi:10.1080/15377903.2010.495903

Isava, D.M. (2006). *An investigation of the impact of a social emotional learning curriculum on problem symptoms and knowledge gains among adolescents in a residential treatment center* (Unpublished doctoral dissertation). University of Oregon, Eugene.

Kramer, T.J., Caldarella, P., Christensen, L., & Shatzer, R.H. (2010). Social and emotional learning in the kindergarten classroom: Evaluation of the *Strong Start* curriculum. *Early Childhood Education Journal, 37*, 303–309. doi:10.1007/s10643-009-0354-8

Kramer, T.J., Caldarella, P., Young, R., Fischer, L., & Warren, J.S. (2014). Implementing Strong Kids school-wide to reduce internalizing behaviors and increase prosocial behaviors. *Education and Treatment of Children, 37*, 659 680.

Levitt, V. (2009). *Promoting social-emotional competency through quality teaching practices: The impact of consultation on a multidimensional treatment integrity model of the Strong Kids Program* (Unpublished doctoral dissertation). University of Oregon, Eugene.

Marchant, M., Brown, M., Caldarella, P., & Young, E. (2010). Effects of Strong Kids curriculum on students at risk for internalizing disorders: A pilot study. *Journal of Empirically Based Practices in Schools, 11*(2), 123–143.

Merrell, K.W., Juskelis, M.P., Tran, O.K., & Buchanan, R. (2008). Social and emotional learning in the classroom: Impact of Strong Kids and Strong Teens on students' social-emotional knowledge and symptoms. *Journal of Applied School Psychology, 24*, 209–224. doi:10.1080/15377900802089981

Meyer, K.M. (2014). *Program evaluation of the Strong Start curriculum as a selected intervention for early elementary students* (Unpublished doctoral dissertation). University of Massachusetts, Amherst.

Nakayama, N.J. (2008). *An investigation of the impact of the Strong Kids curriculum on social-emotional knowledge and symptoms of elementary aged students in a self-contained special education setting* (Unpublished doctoral dissertation). University of Oregon, Eugene.

Sicotte, J.L. (2013). *Effects of Strong Start curriculum on internalizing, externalizing behaviors, and emotion knowledge among kindergarten and first grade students* (Unpublished doctoral dissertation). University of Massachusetts, Amherst.

Tran, O.K. (2008). *Promoting social and emotional learning in schools: An investigation of massed versus distributed practice schedules and social validity of the Strong Kids curriculum in late elementary aged students* (Unpublished doctoral dissertation). University of Oregon, Eugene.

Whitcomb, S.A., & Merrell, K.W. (2012). Understanding implementation and effectiveness of Strong Start K–2 on social-emotional behavior. *Early Childhood Education Journal, 40*, 63–71. doi:10.1007/s10643-011-0490-9

White, N.J., & Rayle, A.D. (2007). Strong Teens: A school-based small group experience for African American males. *The Journal for Specialists in Group Work, 32*, 178–189. doi:10.1080/01933920701227224

REFERENCES

Bridgeland, J., Bruce, M., & Hariharan, A. (2013). *The missing piece: A national survey on how social and emotional learning can empower children and transform schools*. Washington, DC: Civic Enterprises.

Carnine, D.W., Silbert, J., Kame'enui, E.J., & Tarver, S.G. (2009). *Direct instruction reading* (5th ed.). Upper Saddle River, NJ: Pearson/Prentice Hall.

Centers for Disease Control and Prevention. (2013). Youth risk behavior surveillance—United States, 2013. *Surveillance Summaries, 63*, 1–168. Retrieved from http://stacks.cdc.gov/view/cdc/23483

Collaborative for Academic, Social, and Emotional Learning. (2014). *What is SEL? Skills and competencies*. Chicago, IL: Author. Retrieved from http://www.casel.org/social-and-emotional-learning/core-competencies

Costello, E.J., & Angold, A. (2000). Developmental psychopathology and public health: Past, present, and future. *Development and Psychopathology, 12*, 599–618.

Cowen, E.L. (1994). The enhancement of psychological wellness: Challenges and opportunities. *American Journal of Community Psychology, 22*, 149–179.

Coyne, M.D., Kame'enui, E.J., & Carnine, D.W. (2006). *Effective teaching strategies that accommodate diverse learners* (3rd ed.). Upper Saddle River, NJ: Pearson/Prentice Hall.

Devaney, E., O'Brien, M.U., Resnik, H., Keister, S., & Weissberg, R.P. (2006). *Sustainable schoolwide social and emotional learning: Implementation guide and toolkit.* Chicago, IL: Collaborative for Academic, Social, and Emotional Learning.

Doll, B., & Lyon, M.A. (1998). Risk and resilience: Implications for the delivery of educational and mental health services in schools. *School Psychology Review, 27*, 348–363.

Durlak, J.A., & DuPre, E.P. (2008). Implementation matters: A review of research on the influence of implementation on program outcomes and the factors affecting implementation. *American Journal of Community Psychology, 41*(3 4), 327 350.

Durlak, J.A., Dymnicki, A.B., Taylor, R.D., Weissberg, R.P., & Schellinger, K.B. (2011). The impact of enhancing students' social and emotional learning: A meta-analysis of school-based universal interventions. *Child Development, 82*, 405–432. doi:10.1111/j.1467-8624.2010.01564.x

Durlak, J.A., & Wells, A.M. (1997). Primary prevention mental health programs for children and adolescents: A meta-analytic review. *American Journal of Community Psychology, 25*, 115–152. Retrieved from http://hmprg.org/assets/root/PDFs/2012/07/prevention_meta_analysis_durlak_wells_1997.pdf

Elias, M.J. (2006). The connection between academic and social-emotional learning. In M.J. Elias & H. Arnold (Eds.), *The educator's guide to emotional intelligence and academic achievement* (pp. 4–14). Thousand Oaks, CA: Corwin Press.

Farmer, E.M.Z., & Farmer, T.W. (1999). The role of schools in outcomes for youth: Implications for children's mental health services research. *Journal of Child and Family Studies, 8*, 377–396.

Greenberg, M.T., Domitrovich, C., & Bumbarger, B. (2001, March 30). The prevention of mental health disorders in school-aged children: Current state of the field. *Prevention and Treatment, 4*(Article 1). Retrieved from http://www.researchgate.net/profile/Brian_Bumbarger/publication/216458565_The_prevention_of_mental_disorders_in_school-aged_children_Current_state_of_the_field/links/0fcfd50d20aaf66cf7000000.pdf

Greenberg, M.T., Weissberg, R.P., O'Brien, M.U., Zins, J.E., Fredericks, L., Resnick, H., et al. (2003). Enhancing school-based prevention and youth development through coordinated social, emotional, and academic learning. *American Psychologist, 58*, 466–474. doi:10.1037/0003-066X.58.6-7.466

Hoagwood, K., & Erwin, H. (1997). Effectiveness of school-based mental health services for children: A 10-year research review. *Journal of Child and Family Studies, 6*, 435–451.

Hyman, I.A., & Perone, D.C. (1998). The other side of school violence: Educator policies and practices that may contribute to student misbehavior. *Journal of School Psychology, 36*, 7–27. Retrieved from http://youthjusticenc.org/download/education-justice/suspension-and-expulsion/The%20Other%20Side%20of%20School%20Violence:%20Educator%20Policies%20and%20Practices%20That%20May%20Contribute%20to%20Student%20Misbehavior.pdf

Langland, S., Lewis-Palmer, T., & Sugai, G. (1998). Teaching respect in the classroom: An instructional approach. *Journal of Behavioral Education, 8*, 245–262.

Merrell, K.W., & Buchanan, R.S. (2006). Intervention selection in school-based practice: Using public health models to enhance systems capacity of schools. *School Psychology Review, 35*, 167–180.

Partnership for 21st Century Skills. (2008). *21st century skills, education, and competitiveness: A resource and policy guide.* Washington, DC: Author. Retrieved from http://www.p21.org/storage/documents/21st_century_skills_education_and_competitiveness_guide.pdf

Payton, J., Weissberg, R.P., Durlak, J.A., Dymnicki, A.B., Taylor, R.D., Schellinger, K.B., & Pachan, M. (2008). *The positive impact of social and emotional learning for kindergarten to eighth-grade students: Findings from three scientific reviews (Technical report).* Chicago, IL: Collaborative for Academic, Social, and Emotional Learning.

Pellegrino, J.W., & Hilton, M.L. (Eds.). (2013). *Education for life and work: Developing transferable knowledge and skills in the 21st century.* Washington, DC: National Academies Press. Retrieved from http://www.leg.state.vt.us/WorkGroups/EdOp/Education%20for%20Life%20and%20Work-%20National%20Academy%20of%20Sciences.pdf

Satcher, D. (1999). *Mental health: A report of the Surgeon General, 1999.* Washington, DC: U.S. Department of Health and Human Services. Retrieved from http://dx.doi.org/10.1037/0735-7028.31.1.5

Skiba, R., & Peterson, R. (1999). The dark side of zero tolerance: Can punishment lead to safe schools? *Phi Delta Kappan, 80,* 372–376, 381–382. Retrieved from http://curry.virginia.edu/uploads/resourceLibrary/dark_zero_tolerance.pdf

Sklad, M., Diekstra, R., De Ritter, M., Ben, J., & Gravesteijn, C. (2012). Effectiveness of school-based universal social, emotional, and behavioral programs: Do they enhance students' development in the area of skill, behavior, and adjustment? *Psychology in the Schools, 49*(9), 892–909. doi:10.1002/pits.21641

Sugai, G., Bullis, M., & Cumblad, C. (1997). Provide ongoing skill development and support. *Journal of Emotional and Behavioral Disorders, 5,* 55–64.

Tran, O.K. (2008). *Promoting social and emotional learning in schools: An investigation of massed versus distributed practice schedules and social validity of the Strong Kids curriculum in late elementary aged students* (Unpublished doctoral dissertation). University of Oregon, Eugene.

U.S. Department of Education, Office of Special Education Programs (OSEP), Center on Positive Behavioral Interventions and Supports. (2004). *School-wide PBIS.* Retrieved from http://www.pbis.org/school

Walker, H.M. (2001). "Preventing mental disorders in school-aged children: Current state of the field": Commentary. *Prevention and Treatment 4*(1).

Walker, H.M., Horner, R.H., Sugai, G., Bullis, M., et al. (1996). Integrated approaches to preventing antisocial behavior patterns among school-age children and youth. *Journal of Emotional and Behavioral Disorders, 4,* 194–209. Retrieved from http://idahotc.com/Portals/6/Docs/Tier%20Training/Preventing%20Antisocial%20Behavior%20Patterns.pdf

Weisz, J.R., Hawley, K.M., & Doss, A.J. (2004). Empirically tested psychotherapies for youth internalizing and externalizing problems and disorders. *Child and Adolescent Psychiatric Clinics of North America, 13*(4), 729–815. Retrieved from http://web.missouri.edu/~hawleyk/pdfs/WeiszHawleyJensenDoss2004.pdf

Zins, J.E., Bloodworth, M.R., Weissberg, R.P., & Walberg, H.J. (2004). The scientific base linking social and emotional learning to school success. In J. Zins, M. Wang, & H. Walberg (Eds.), *Building academic success and social-emotional learning: What does the research say?* New York, NY: Teachers College Press.

CHAPTER 2

Preparing Your Lessons and Your Students

To implement *Strong Kids—Grades 3–5*, you should have access to a projector, a copy machine, chart paper, chalk, color markers, or a marker board and a means of showing occasional Internet videos or images when the lesson requires. Many of the lessons also include reproducible templates for in-class handouts or worksheets for students, also available for download (refer to About the Downloadable Material for download information). Materials are made easily accessible via download, so you can project lesson supplements, handouts, and other images from a laptop or desktop computer or share the hard copy material directly. However, if a computer with an accompanying projector is not available for implementation, you can choose another option available at your site where materials can be projected or shown on the board (e.g., overhead projector) for the lesson materials. Although it is not essential to project the images or other materials, we have found that doing so provides the advantage of being able to go over a graphic illustration or chart in front of the class while you introduce the critical concepts that are connected to them. Alternatively, some teachers and group leaders have found that they prefer to make paper copies of the supplements and provide each student with a copy of these materials rather than presenting the materials with a projector.

SUPPLEMENTARY MATERIALS

Each *Strong Kids—Grades 3–5* lesson includes supplementary materials needed for each lesson. The supplementary materials can be found at the end of the lesson and are available for download. These materials are labeled throughout the text with a "reminder" symbol (a finger with a string tied to it). For the sake of consistency, we refer to these materials as "supplements" and have titled them that way. These supplements are available as online downloads for use as in-class handouts, worksheets, and homework handouts. Each supplement is labeled with its intended use and indicates whether it should be used as a handout for students, as a visual aid for you to display as you discuss a section, or both. Prior to teaching the lesson, review the Materials Needed section at the beginning of each lesson and make copies of downloads or handouts before lesson implementation as needed. These supplements are all reproducible for users of the curriculum. Although we have made suggestions regarding how to use the supplementary materials, you should feel free to adapt them to your own needs and situation. In addition, some lessons will require the use of online videos or images to help illustrate the content. When a video or image is recommended, a description is provided to help in locating these videos or images online. More supplemental materials and resources can be found by visiting our companion web site: www.strongkidsresources.com.

PROVIDING AN AGENDA

During the course of teaching *Strong Kids—Grades 3–5*, we recommend that you make use of a visual schedule to provide students with some predictability regarding the lesson for the day. It may be helpful to outline the lesson agenda briefly in a bulleted list or flow chart format before the class begins in order to establish a visual reference that you can refer to with your students. In this case, an outline of the topics included in the curriculum may be useful, as well as an agenda for each individual lesson.

STATING EXPECTED BEHAVIORS

Because of the nature of the lessons in *Strong Kids—Grades 3–5*, behavior expectations for students or group members must be very clear and discussed at the very start of *Strong Kids*. Some of the units revolve around sensitive issues, and every opportunity should be taken to provide instruction and subsequent reinforcement for appropriate behavior. Students should feel free to share their beliefs and feelings on the targeted topics but must not feel pressured into revealing anything that makes them feel uncomfortable or makes others in the group feel uncomfortable. You should state expected behaviors before instruction, before modeling examples, and before the practice sections of lessons. In some cases, you may need to teach and reinforce behavioral expectations more frequently than at these suggested times, or you may choose to remind students before each lesson.

As a general recommendation for promoting appropriate behavior in school and related settings, we recommend that teachers and group leaders develop and teach a few simple rules for appropriate behavior. There are three guidelines in Lesson 1 that you may use as examples. When making rules, be sure to state expectations clearly and positively. For example, if it is necessary to make a rule around fighting, instead of saying "no fighting," we might say "respect your classmates, which means being friendly, keeping hands to self, looking for nice things to say, and no arguing or fighting." Rules should be simple and appropriate to the developmental level of the children for whom they are intended. In addition, the list of rules should be kept to a minimum. Usually, no more than five general rules are needed. You will find that rules are more effective when you teach them to students and then find frequent opportunities to reinforce them through reminders, examples, and so forth. In addition, the literature suggests giving positive praise to any negative statement in a five-to-one ratio (Fredrickson & Losada, 2005). This way, students feel more supported and encouraged to engage in the prosocial behaviors. You also may want to post these rules in your classroom as a reminder for students and to offer opportunities for practice.

PLANNING FOR SMOOTH TRANSITIONS

Time is one of the most precious commodities in your classroom or center. In a brief curriculum such as *Strong Kids—Grades 3–5*, the element of time is especially critical. To make the best use of your limited time in teaching the curriculum, use your transition time wisely before and during the lessons. We recommend that you have all materials prepared and organized for easy distribution to students. Make sure that equipment is in working order before you start the lessons. *Explicitly state directions before and during transitions.* If possible, precorrect for any possible behavioral difficulties. If, due to student discussion or other scheduling restraints, you find you need to end the lesson before it is complete, we recommend completing at a natural transition such as the end of an activity and then concluding the lesson with the Closure activity.

PHYSICAL ARRANGEMENTS

For the lessons in this curriculum, all students must have a clear view of you, the group leader. It is recommended that students are situated in forward-facing seats or a horseshoe shape. You may want to preassign students to groups of two or three because some activities in certain lessons will require small-group discussion or a mini-project. This practice not only will save time but also will give you control of how your students are grouped. Always use movement around the classroom and around the student groups, voice level, and voice intonation to increase the interest of your students and, consequently, increase active participation.

ADAPTATIONS FOR UNIQUE NEEDS AND DISABILITIES

In many of the lessons, you will be encouraged to create scenarios pertaining to a certain topic. To facilitate and encourage student participation, think of situations that would best reflect the interests, abilities, and level of understanding of the students in your class or group. You may choose to use current situations relevant to your classroom and school or global current events to illustrate the concepts. The situations provided in the units are to be considered examples and can be modified extensively to best fit the unique needs of your students. Making appropriate adaptations for the needs of your students not only will make the delivery of lessons go more smoothly but also will aid with generalization and maintenance of new skills. Before starting the program, it is important to consider whether your students have behavioral needs, learning difficulties, or developmental disabilities so you can prepare for any adaptations or modifications. Also, many of the Mindfulness-Based Focusing Activities include engaging the senses, such as touch and hearing. If students use wheelchairs or have sensory impairments, these activities will need to be adapted according to their needs. For low-functioning groups, adapt lessons by creating simpler examples and by breaking the lessons into shorter sessions. For high-functioning groups, introduce complexity in the form of concurrent emotions and involved situations. For mixed groups, be sure to provide opportunities for questions, and allow peer interaction when appropriate so that students with a stronger grasp of the emotions can stay engaged by participating in explanations and/or skits for students who need extra support. The following are suggested modifications and adaptations:

- Work with fewer items per page or line and/or materials in a larger print size.

- Have a designated reader or group leader.

- Use a larger desk for group work, if available.

- Set up a buddy system to identify students who may be higher functioning.

- If assistive technology is used, identify key words/concepts to be programmed into the device.

- Use various and combinations of sensory modalities.

In the second edition of *Strong Kids—Grades 3–5*, an Instructor Reflection section is included to encourage the group leader to consider the lesson topic from a personal perspective. Use this opportunity for reflection to come up with appropriate examples from your own experiences and/or to generate empathy for how your students may experience the subject matter.

ADAPTATIONS FOR CULTURALLY AND LINGUISTICALLY DIVERSE LEARNERS

As our society becomes increasingly diverse, researchers and practitioners are recognizing the need to address cultural issues in curriculum development and implementation. Efforts to address cultural issues have ranged from ignoring or dismissing the need for cultural adaptations to arguing the need for culture-specific research and curricula tailored for each cultural subgroup. Between these two extreme positions has emerged a set of criteria and recommendations for making cultural adaptations to existing curricula. The cultural adaptation approach retains the core assumptions and skill domains of the existing curriculum but recommends tailoring the teaching of these concepts to the specific needs of particular groups of interest. Research supports the success of making cultural adaptations to existing social and emotional curricula for specific groups (see Castro-Olivo, 2014; Muñoz et al., 2002; Yu & Seligman, 2002).

We began the development of *Strong Kids* with the assumption that no single curriculum could meet the learning needs of all students. By focusing on teaching a set of key ideas related to SEL and resilience, however, we believe that the curriculum can successfully meet the needs of a wide range of students when appropriate adaptations are made. Some particular cultural variables that may require attention in curriculum adaptation processes include language, race/ethnicity, acculturation, socioeconomic status, sexual orientation, religion, gender, disability status, and nationality.

GENERALIZATION AND MAINTENANCE OF SKILLS

Instructors often find it difficult to help students generalize social and emotional skills to different settings and to ensure that these skills are maintained over time. To increase sustainability and generalizability of skills learned in the *Strong Kids* and *Strong Teens* programs, look for opportunities to use the Tips for Transfer Training and supplemental activities that are found at the end of each lesson. We have included prompts for precorrecting errors in learning the expected skills, reminding students of the concepts being learned, and reinforcing students for demonstrating the skills that have been introduced and taught in the program. Reinforce *Strong Kids* and *Strong Teens* skills both within and outside the teaching setting as much as possible. Make sure that parents, teachers, administrators, and other staff are aware of the skills you are instructing, because your students will require frequent feedback in several settings in order for the skills to be durable and generalized. After the program has been completed, Lesson 12, Finishing UP!, can be adapted and used as a "booster lesson" to reteach and reinforce the major objectives from all the lessons. Also, specific lessons may be chosen to target skills in need of reteaching. For example, after completing the *Strong Kids* or *Strong Teens* program, if you notice that your students are having increasing difficulty resolving conflicts, you might choose to reteach Lesson 8, Solving People Problems, and implement the supplemental activities offered at the end of that lesson.

SUGGESTIONS FOR SUCCESS

As you teach the lessons in *Strong Kids—Grades 3–5*, you will increase your likelihood of success by observing and following a few additional suggestions for successful implementation of the curriculum. We have developed these suggestions through piloting the program in numerous settings and through the feedback we have received from our associates who have used it in their schools and treatment centers.

- *Practice your lessons* before implementing them. Each lesson is slightly different and will require advance preparation in the form of photocopying and generating examples, grouping, and in some cases considering actors for a skit. Each lesson also will require your own personal involvement and understanding of the subject matter. Each lesson builds on the previous, so the more prepared you are, the more successful and efficient the lesson instruction will be.

- Be sure to give the students an *overview* of each lesson's purpose. Explain that a different topic/unit will be taught each week (or as frequently as possible), because students may come to expect a continuation of a certain topic as opposed to a new topic each lesson.

- In our experience, folders that are specifically designated for students to store their handouts, notes, and homework assignment sheets will help *keep materials organized* and will reduce the amount of time needed by the teacher or group leader to start the weekly lessons. We suggest that you consider having all of your students keep a special *Strong Kids* folder for this purpose. However, use the system that works best for your students to organize their *Strong Kids* handouts.

- Ensure that you allow sufficient time to *review the topics* from prior lessons and integrate concepts when at all possible.

- Introduce or reintroduce a *behavior management technique*, such as a token economy, to reinforce prosocial behaviors during the unit. Remind students of your school and classroom rules as well as the rules associated with this curriculum.

- This curriculum involves teaching a wide range of skills in a relatively short period of time. In order to use your time most effectively, *directly teach these skills.* Place your priority on instruction and allowing your students to ask questions. During the lessons, you may need to keep discussion and activity time to a minimum. However, we encourage you to have in-depth discussions with your students as much as possible during class meetings or as you integrate the concepts in other settings or in other classes.

- Be prepared to *include a "twist"* to a scenario from your own experience or something the class may recognize from recent experiences. Many lessons include references to twists in which a scenario is presented from a different perspective or with additional context. Understand your students and determine how much complexity you can add to the lessons to strengthen their interaction with the content.

- *Complete at least one homework example* with the entire class or group to help them understand the assignment and be prepared to complete it. It is recommended to complete the homework handouts from the beginning lessons as a way to provide a model early on.

- As a general practice, we suggest that you *do not add new students to the group once the program has already started.* Particularly when the program is taught to small groups of students rather than entire classrooms, we have found that having new students join the group once it has started can be disruptive to the group process and may result in a slowing of the flow of training as well as a reduction in the willingness of group members to participate. If you do find that that you need to add students, look for an opportunity to brief the new student or students separately in advance, and bring them up to speed on the topics presented so far and how your group interacts and shares information. It may be important for you also to brief the existing group so they are aware of the change and aware of how the new student(s) will be incorporated into grouping and other activities.

- Be on the lookout for signals from your students that they may need more support than the curriculum can provide. Check the comment box regularly; students in immediate social and emotional need may seek indirect routes to request help. Remember that these lessons are not intended for students in crisis or for students who have more significant mental health needs. Lessons 1 and 12 include reminders about connecting students to their larger network of supports for specific needs. Be prepared to provide these contacts to students throughout the curriculum. Prior to starting *Strong Kids*, it is recommended that you talk to your school psychologist or counselor about your implementation plans and learn more about the mental health resources available at your school or site. As applicable, consider inviting your school's primary mental health practitioner (school psychologist, counselor, or other affiliated mental health provider) into your class to introduce him- or herself to your students.

The Big Ideas of *Strong Kids—Grades 3–5*

As noted previously, a successful curriculum adaptation process requires particular innovations and modifications to meet the needs of specific individuals and groups. At the same time, these adaptations must retain the general concepts, or big ideas, on which the curriculum is based. With this notion in mind, we list the most important features of *Strong Kids—Grades 3–5*, with the hope that these ideas will be taken into account when making any type of adaptation to the curriculum. With the underlying goals of improving SEL curriculum and resilience in children and adolescents; preventing and reducing depression, anxiety, and other internalizing disorders; and promoting awareness of moods and symptoms of internalizing disorders, these big ideas include the following:

- To teach children and youth to understand their own and other people's feelings

- To teach children and youth to understand the link between thoughts and emotions and to learn to monitor and modulate them appropriately

- To teach children and youth to identify thinking traps that may interfere with healthy decision making

- To help students learn strategies for increasing habits for positive living

- To help children and youth learn to identify stress and cognitive and behavioral strategies to manage stress

- To teach children and youth problem-solving skills, effective communication skills, and the anger model in order to be more successful in social contexts (e.g., listening, being assertive)

- To teach children and youth to set appropriate and realistic goals based on their own values and to monitor their behavior in order to reach their goals using SMART goals (specific, measurable, attainable, relevant, and timely)

- To help students identify comfortable and uncomfortable feelings and distinguish healthy and unhealthy ways to express emotions

Specific Strategies for Making Cultural Adaptations

Keeping these big ideas in mind, *Strong Kids—Grades 3–5* may be adapted to better fit the needs of diverse children. It is critical to be culturally sensitive because often there are cultural differences in expressing emotions. For this purpose, we propose a few guidelines for making cross-cultural adaptations. These suggestions are based on our own experiences in attempting to adapt the *Strong Kids* curriculum with specific cultural groups. They are also based in great measure on the premises of the American Psychological Association's Guidelines for Providers of Psychological Services to Ethnic, Linguistic, and Culturally Diverse Populations (available at http://www.apa.org/pi/oema/resources/policy/provider-guidelines.aspx).

1. Get to know your students.

   • Ask students about their cultural identities, activities, and rituals.

   • Reflect on the dominant cultural variables in your classroom and how these aspects of culture affect the way your students behave and think.

   • Identify common success and failure experiences, problem situations, and challenging life circumstances confronted by your students.

   • Encourage students to share aspects of their culture with the larger group.

2. Get to know your students' communities.

   • Visit the families and, as appropriate, the homes of students in your class or group.

   • Identify a cultural liaison to help you with your research about your students' culture.

   • Ask the cultural liaison to assist with the cultural adaptation process.

3. Deliver the curriculum in a manner that your students can understand.

   • Modify the language of each lesson so that your students can easily understand the key ideas.

   • Use examples and situations that match the lives of your students (e.g., change characters' names, include extended family, include children with disabilities, use problem examples that your students have experienced).

4. Encourage tolerance and establish a climate in which differences are viewed as resources, not deficits.

   • Teach students ways to show respect for different cultural groups.

   • Encourage and reinforce students for respecting the examples and comments made by their peers.

   • Establish and enforce a classroom rule that teasing and name calling are not allowed.

5. Adapt assessment tools.

- Adapt the assessment materials so that students can understand (e.g., language, context).

- Pilot test some of the assessment materials with small groups of students prior to implementing the curriculum to ensure that students understand the questions.

6. Become aware of variations within cultures. For example, some cultures tend to be more expressive and value the discussion of individual emotions and beliefs, whereas others tend to be more reserved and value privacy.

- Do not assume too much about a student's culture or ethnicity.

- Avoid making overgeneralizations about cultural groups. Not all members of a culture act the same way.

- Examine your own values, assumptions, and worldviews and how these are the same and different from those of your students.

- Continually examine the accuracy and fairness of your assumptions about the beliefs and behaviors of different cultural groups.

7. Seek feedback.

- View the adaptation process as an ongoing process.

- Consult with students, your colleagues, and community members about the relevance and accuracy of the adaptation efforts.

- Ask students how well the curriculum is matching their needs and life experiences (see Castro-Olivo, 2010).

In sum, adapting *Strong Kids—Grades 3–5* or any other SEL curriculum for use with culturally and linguistically diverse learners may be challenging, but it is essential if the curriculum is to have the most meaningful impact on the learners. The suggestions we have offered in this section may be useful as a guide to making the flexible *Strong Kids—Grades 3–5* program appropriate for children and youth from a variety of cultural backgrounds.

REFERENCES

Castro Olivo, S. (2010). One size does not fit all: Adapting SEL programs for use in our multicultural world. In K.W. Merrell & B.A. Gueldner (Eds.), *Social and emotional learning in the classroom: Promoting mental health and academic success.* New York, NY: Guilford.

Castro-Olivo, S. (2014). Promoting social-emotional learning in adolescent Latino ELLs: A study of the culturally adapted Strong Teens program. *School Psychology Quarterly, 29,* 567–577.

Fredrickson, B., & Losada, F. (2005). Positive affect and the complex aspects of human flourishing. *American Psychologist, 60*(7), 678–686.

Muñoz, R.F., Penilla, C., & Urizar, G. (2002). Expanding depression prevention research with children of diverse cultures. *Prevention and Treatment, 5.* doi:10.1037/1522–3736.5.1.513c

Yu, D.L., & Seligman, M.E.P. (2002). Preventing depressive symptoms in Chinese children. *Prevention and Treatment, 5.* doi.org/10.1037/1522-3736.5.1.59a

CHAPTER 3

Overview of the Lessons

The *Strong Kids* programs consist of 12 carefully sequenced lessons that are designed for maximum impact on cognitive, affective, and social functioning within a relatively brief period of time. This chapter provides an overview of each lesson. Read the descriptions carefully prior to preparing your first lesson so that you will understand the lesson sequencing and the big ideas behind the *Strong Kids* programs.

LESSON 1: ABOUT *STRONG KIDS:* EMOTIONAL STRENGTH TRAINING

In the first lesson, About *Strong Kids:* Emotional Strength Training, students are introduced to the program. Behavioral expectations—including respectful listening to others, participation, and maintaining confidentiality—are reviewed and discussed. A general overview of the overall curriculum and individual lessons is presented, providing students with information regarding what they can expect over the course of the program. Emotions and critical terms such as *resilience, adversity,* and *perseverance* are defined for the first time, and students are encouraged to seek adult assistance if they are experiencing difficulties. If optional student assessments are administered as part of the curriculum, they should be given to students for completion during this first lesson.

LESSONS 2 AND 3: UNDERSTANDING YOUR EMOTIONS

The second and third lessons, Understanding Your Emotions (1 and 2), are intended to improve students' emotional vocabulary and awareness. Being able to understand and recognize one's emotions is an important skill for all individuals during all stages of their lives because people experience emotions at school, at home, at work, and at play. Being able to recognize one's emotions and react in a helpful way, even when the feeling is uncomfortable, will allow students to create and sustain positive relationships in school and throughout their lives.

In Understanding Your Emotions 1, students learn to identify different emotions and the physical feelings that occur with emotions and to distinguish feelings as being comfortable or uncomfortable. Students also learn to measure the intensity of emotions and begin to identify what the emotion may be communicating about themselves or the situation they are experiencing. The goal of this lesson is to apply the skills learned to different situations at different times and in different settings. In Understanding Your Emotions 2, students learn that thoughts and behaviors are linked to emotions, and by identifying thoughts and behaviors, one can better understand emotions and learn how to express oneself in a way that is helpful. Students also learn that emotions are expressed differently, depending on the situation. Students then have the opportunity to use their new skills in application exercises, making it more likely that they will be able to generalize the new skills to other situations.

LESSON 4: UNDERSTANDING OTHER PEOPLE'S EMOTIONS

The purpose of the fourth lesson, Understanding Other People's Emotions, is to introduce students to the concept and practice of empathy and thus help them better understand other people's feelings. Although the previous three lessons have focused on students' own feelings, Lesson 4 covers the ability to recognize the emotions of others and share their perspectives, an essential skill in conflict resolution and compassion. Students who can identify the feelings of others are more likely to be tolerant of people with different views. Students will learn to see clearly how their actions can affect the emotions of other people.

Children with antisocial tendencies often experience what is called *hostile attribution*, in which they misperceive others' emotions as anger. This misperception can lead to aggression and violence. Students who practice empathy skills are more able to see a variety of emotions other than anger. By learning to look for physical cues (sometimes referred to as *clues*), they may be more likely to discern the true feelings of others.

Lesson 4 first explains key concepts and then moves into identifying clues about the emotions other people are feeling. Once students are able to identify the potential clues and what they might mean, the lesson progresses to a role play in which students will experience how people may perceive the same situation differently. The children will be asked to take the perspectives of others in order to gain a greater understanding of empathy. Finally, the homework handout provides opportunities for students to apply these skills to their own life experiences.

LESSON 5: DEALING WITH ANGER

The fifth lesson, Dealing with Anger, teaches students that everyone experiences anger in his or her life. Many students, however, are not able to appropriately understand and effectively deal with their anger. Misunderstanding anger, and an inability to appropriately manage it, can often manifest itself in inappropriate behaviors such as arguments and fights, depression, and severe frustration, each of which can have unfortunate consequences.

This lesson teaches students to understand their anger through a multistep anger model and teaches skills for helping them manage their anger. Anger is introduced as one of many normal emotions that serve a purpose in helping people understand and adapt to the world. It is important that students understand two basic concepts: 1) that anger is a normal emotion and 2) that anger serves the important function of protection and motivation in our lives. Students are taught to understand anger using the sequential anger model to improve their ability to recognize what anger looks like in action. In this lesson, students learn that anger does not "just happen." It is triggered by predictable events and progresses through a series of steps within which individuals can play an active role. Students are taught to understand their active roles in the anger process and the fact that they are not helpless "victims" of their anger but are active participants in choosing how to respond to anger.

LESSONS 6 AND 7: CLEAR THINKING

Individuals who are depressed and anxious are very likely to develop or have previously developed patterns of unrealistic, distorted, and otherwise maladaptive cognitions or thoughts. The Clear Thinking lessons are designed to help students to be more aware of their thought patterns and recognize how these patterns can contribute to their moods, choices, and actions. The lesson is divided into two parts: Clear Thinking 1 and Clear Thinking 2. Clear Thinking 1 teaches students strategies that are helpful in recognizing unhelpful or maladaptive thought patterns by providing descriptions of some of the more common "thinking traps" that individuals use. When possible, the thought patterns such as "binocular vision," "dark glasses," and "black-and-white thinking" are depicted both as visual icons and in simplified language to facilitate comprehension and retention. Clear Thinking 2 uses the information provided in Clear Thinking 1 to teach students techniques such as how to use evidence to proactively identify thinking traps and then how to apply strategies to reframe unhelpful thoughts and attributions. Practice exercises and vignettes are used for discussion.

LESSON 8: SOLVING PEOPLE PROBLEMS

The eighth lesson, Solving People Problems, is designed to promote awareness of useful strategies for resolving social conflict. Interpersonal conflict provides one of the most fertile breeding grounds for depression, anxiety, and negative thinking. Thus, learning appropriate and effective ways to resolve these conflicts may be a strong preventive factor for deterring emotional problems as well as social problems.

Because conflicts may occur daily and can be a source of stress and frustration for students, step-by-step outlines for resolving conflicts are presented. This lesson details the use of a problem-solving model for managing day-to-day social conflicts and presents techniques for its use and application. The lesson is predominantly organized to address conflicts with peers; however, application of various strategies—such as deal-making, compromising, discussion, and brainstorming—are presented in situations that involve hierarchical relationships as well. Students will learn from this lesson that conflict is often a natural part of social interaction and that, with the tools to address conflict, more social interactions can be approached with awareness, respect, openness, sensitivity, and confidence. Practice exercises and role-play situations also are used as examples and teaching tools.

LESSON 9: LETTING GO OF STRESS

Using appropriate techniques to manage stress is an important strategy to promote emotional resilience and prevent physical and emotional problems. Lesson 9, Letting Go of Stress, provides the foundation for teaching students about stress and relaxation. Through the lesson and activities, the students will learn how to identify stress in their lives. An opportunity is provided for students to learn a few relaxation techniques that have been proven to be effective with many people as well as to generate their own ways of coping with stress. The homework assignment allows students to apply the discussed techniques.

Students begin to learn about themselves and how to deal with stress in an effective and healthy manner. Stress is a fact of every person's life. Stress can be healthy to some degree; however, too much stress or not dealing with it effectively can lead to long-term problems. The sooner students learn how to identify it and deal with this aspect of being human, the better their chances are for a healthy existence. Learning how to let go of stress is an integral skill in the development of a strong and resilient kid.

LESSON 10: POSITIVE LIVING

Lesson 10, Positive Living, is new to the second edition of *Strong Kids— Grades 3–5*. It provides students with strategies to incorporate positive habits into day-to-day life to offset negative habits that can affect health and emotion. For students prone to negative thinking, positive feelings are promoted through a discussion of lifestyle choices that involve physical health (eating and sleeping), emotional and mental health (TV time vs. productive time), community connections (helping others and being involved), and family and social connections (maintaining healthy relationships). Encouraging positive choices and thoughts about healthy options in our daily activities is intended to generate habits toward long-term well-being.

The Positive Living lesson is designed to arm all students, not just those who may be prone to pessimism and spirals of negativity, with ways to think about day-to-day behaviors with intention so that healthy choices can be made. The method includes training students to spot the difficult situations that may be changed by altering the areas of their lives in which they have more control.

LESSON 11: CREATING STRONG AND SMART GOALS

Throughout life, people are asked to achieve many goals. Frequently, they are not taught the steps that are necessary to achieve these goals. Research supports the idea that students who are able to set and achieve goals independently perform better than students who are told what goals to achieve. This evidence also confirms that learning how to engage more consistently in appropriate positive activities can help to reduce symptoms of depression and anxiety. The steps outlined in this lesson are all necessary in order for students to attain their goals as well as to identify values in the different domains of their lives. Learning these steps and having immediate success by implementing them is crucial to the success of this lesson. If students set a short-term goal first and are successful in the goal-attainment process, then they will be more likely to use the process again in other applications. These steps are beneficial for students' academic achievement, and when individuals set realistic and attainable goals, they begin taking control of their lives, which leads to an increase in the number of positive activities in which they participate. This lesson teaches students the skills necessary to set realistic short- and long-term goals, to identify the key steps in attaining their goals, and to apply the procedures to their own lives by increasing the amount of positive activities in which they are engaged. Developing skills for increasing positive activities through setting and attaining positive goals is of critical importance in sustaining positive mental health.

To this end, in this lesson students learn the skill of goal setting and increasing positive activity as a means to a healthy life. This lesson addresses the importance of increasing and maintaining positive activities and helps students develop an awareness of their own strengths and limitations across major life domains such as physical, mental, and emotional health and engagement in school, family, and community. Students also set SMART goals (those that are specific, measurable, attainable, relevant, and timely), develop action plans for goal attainment, and learn strategies for monitoring their progress and persevering after setbacks.

LESSON 12: FINISHING UP!

The title of the final lesson, Finishing UP!, has a double meaning. It implies that this lesson is the final one in the curriculum, but also it shows how we are striving to end on a positive or upbeat note, integrating the learned concepts, and celebrating the accomplishments that have been made through involvement with the *Strong Kids* curriculum. This lesson provides the opportunity for students to review key points and terms from the lessons presented throughout the program. Issues of confidentiality are revisited, and information for handling more critical emotional issues (using appropriate resources) is covered. The Finishing UP! lesson also provides an opportunity for teachers to assess students using follow-up measures. These results can be compared with the information gained from the optional preassessments that may be administered at the time the first lesson is presented.

CHAPTER 4

What's New

Updates to Strong Kids and Strong Teens

We have made some exciting and progressive changes to the *Strong Kids* and *Strong Teens* programs in light of recent advances in the field of SEL and in response to user feedback. The following section describes the major changes in content within the programs, changes across the levels of programs, and changes to the lesson components.

CHANGES TO THE CONTENT

In the revised versions of *Strong Kids* and *Strong Teens*, you will find substantive improvements to the content. These changes are delineated as follows and in Table 4.1. First, the revisions better reflect the dynamic nature of emotions and interpersonal relationships and promote cognitive flexibility and problem solving. Because emotions are not always easy to identify, and they may not fall neatly into simple categories such as *happy, sad,* or *mad,* we introduce emotion identification, including complex and concurrent emotions, earlier in the program in order to develop more advanced emotional literacy. We have deemphasized the use of judgmental terms such as *appropriate* and reduced the amount of dichotomies such as *okay-not okay* and *positive-negative,* also allowing for the experience of emotions on a continuum of intensity. We use "twists" in examples, which change a small aspect of the example, thereby altering the way students perceive the situation and the outcome. We also include more modern graphics to pique the interest of students and help ground the more abstract ideas. The updated scenarios better capture the more challenging and realistic situations that students experience.

In addition, the experience of distressing emotions such as anger or sadness is discussed in this edition using a slightly different orientation. Rather than conveying only the message that uncomfortable feelings are something to change or fix, we emphasize the value of simply listening to what our bodies are communicating through these emotions. The intention is to build a tolerance for discomfort and thereby reduce reactivity. Also, in keeping with a major impetus of the original programs—to address SEL issues associated with students who internalize their emotions—we discuss both the potential negative consequences of acting out *and* withdrawing, hiding, and repressing emotions.

Table 4.1. New content by lesson

Lesson and topic	Summary of new content
1. About *Strong Kids: Emotional Strength Training*	The concept of emotions is introduced in Lesson 1 rather than in Lesson 2. Introduces emotion names, including a broader scope of emotional vocabulary and images of children modeling emotions Introduces the concept of concurrent emotions Introduces mindfulness-based focusing activities
2. Understanding Your Emotions 1	Lesson 2 introduces the concept of physical feelings associated with emotions. Normalizes feelings of discomfort Includes strategies to promote mindfulness regarding emotions, thoughts, and physical feelings
3. Understanding Your Emotions 2	Lesson 3 introduces the concept of emotions, thoughts, and behaviors interacting. Includes discussion of the ways in which behaviors communicate emotions, including helpful and unhelpful behaviors Includes discussion of avoidance or repression of feelings Considers the context in the expression of emotions: The way we show how we are feeling depends on where we are, who we are with, what we want/need in the situation.
4. Understanding Other People's Emotions	In the revised programs, this lesson is sequenced before the lesson on anger to provide more instruction on empathy and alternative perspectives first. Introduces enhanced distinctions between empathy and sympathy Includes enhanced discussion and role play regarding perspective taking
5. Dealing with Anger	Lesson 5 frames the reaction to anger as a range of choices. Introduces the option of not reacting when experiencing anger Includes concepts pertaining to complex and concurrent emotions: Anger can be experienced along with emotions like sadness or jealousy.
6. Clear Thinking 1	"Thinking errors" are now defined as "thinking traps." Introduces two new cognitive distortions or thinking traps: "All alone," the feeling that one's experiences are so unique that no one else could possibly understand, and "broad brush," overgeneralizing from one experience, often at play in the development of stereotypes Addresses another cognitive distortion, the belief that one's feelings and thoughts are reality; in this lesson and in Clear Thinking 2
7. Clear Thinking 2	Lesson 7 introduces the concept of "snowball effect"; that is, one thinking trap can lead to more thinking traps or an accumulation of pessimistic thinking. Includes scenarios that address perfectionistic thinking; an example pertains to perfectionistic thoughts about body image Includes discussion about identifying patterns or habits of thought, in addition to intensity, as a way to identify distorted perceptions Includes new, more concrete analogies and images to help students understand the concept of reframing
8. Solving People Problems	Lesson 8 emphasizes respectful and responsible choices about personal behavior based on social norms, realistic evaluation of consequences of various actions, and the well-being of self and others. Includes expanded options to resolving conflicts using a problem-solving model Includes gray areas or less clear-cut examples
9. Letting Go of Stress	Lesson 9 reframes stress, shifting from a perception that the stressor is always harmful to one that stress can pose a healthy challenge. Illustrates how to evaluate expectations as realistic or unrealistic Includes procrastination and avoidance Includes more activities to help students cope with stress (e.g., nature, physical activity, deep breathing, diet)
10. Positive Living	Lesson 10 replaces the previous edition's Positive Thinking lesson. Includes ways to promote a sense of personal control and facilitate the development of healthy habits and activities across school, home, and community settings Provides students with the opportunity to assess their daily routines and whether or not they are helpful Introduces the concepts of balance and evaluating actions that may have short-term and/or long-term benefits

11. Creating Strong and SMART Goals	Lesson 11 introduces setting SMART (specific, measurable, attainable, relevant, and timely) goals (Doran, 1981).
	Promotes self-assessment in areas of physical and emotional health and school, family, and community connections; identification of personal strengths and areas for growth
	Emphasizes effort and a growth mindset (e.g., Dweck, 2006) and perseverance after setbacks
12. Finishing UP!	Lesson 12 provides more integration of critical concepts found across all lessons.
	Promotes awareness of when help may be needed
	Includes a section on accessing community resources and where to go for help
	Emphasizes resilience and persistence

We also address issues that students increasingly experience in global society. We integrate sociocultural issues in discussions of emotional awareness, expression, and empathy. Because *with whom and where* we express our emotions can be just as important as *how* we express our emotions, we discuss emotional expression in terms of not just actions but also the context or setting. Throughout the programs, we use more current and authentic examples and reference problems that students today are likely to experience, such as social networking dilemmas, stereotypes, and other complex social situations. We also have anticipated the developmental changes that students experience with age and peer groups.

Because many of the main concepts of the Positive Thinking lesson (e.g., optimism, resilience) are now infused throughout many of the lessons, we have added a new lesson, Positive Living, to replace the Positive Thinking lesson. This new lesson promotes a sense of personal control over daily behaviors and actions and promotes the development of healthy habits across school, home, and community settings. To build on these concepts, the next lesson incorporates SMART (specific, measurable, attainable, relevant, and timely) goals (Doran, 1981). Setting SMART goals helps to ensure that goals are realistic and achievable.

In the new edition, we have worked to improve issues often experienced in the promotion of SEL, such as sustainability and generalizability. We now offer a diverse menu of activities to promote the integration of content across settings and the maintenance of skills over time. Whereas Lesson 12, Finishing UP!, was primarily a review of the lessons in the original version of the programs, this lesson now better promotes the integration of critical concepts. Last, to reinforce the concepts introduced previously, we draw more explicit connections across the lessons.

In addition to the new content, we also incorporate more methods to promote student engagement and involvement. Many of the lessons include an introductory activity to highlight the relevance of the content, stimulate thought, and/or pique the students' interest in the material. Also, several lessons include a menu of activities so that instructors can select the application activity that best suits his or her students.

SOCIAL AND EMOTIONAL COMPETENCIES

CASEL, the leader in SEL research, policy, and implementation efforts, promotes five person-centered and interrelated competency areas that are essential to cognitive, social, and emotional development: self-awareness, self-management, social awareness, relationship skills, and responsible decision making (CASEL, 2014; Zins et al., 2004). The new versions of *Strong Kids* and *Strong Teens* have stronger, more explicit connections to the five SEL competencies as defined by CASEL. At the beginning of each lesson, the connection to the SEL competencies is explicitly illustrated by a user-friendly graphic. This helps support planning and documentation of the alignment of SEL instruction with these well-established competencies. The connections between the competencies and the corresponding lesson are depicted in Table 4.2.

MINDFULNESS-BASED PRACTICES

In preparation for the second edition of the curriculum, our review of the literature indicated that the use of mindfulness-based practices (MBPs) has grown in its application with youth and in schools (Burke, 2010; Harnett & Dawe, 2012; Meiklejohn et al., 2012; Zenner et al., 2014). MBPs such as breathing exercises, sitting meditation, and yoga have been used for many years. Secularized versions of these practices have been scientifically studied over the past 30 years, most notably through the Mindfulness Based Stress Reduction (MBSR) program (Kabat-Zinn, 2013). MBPs that are used for children and adolescents have been adapted from many of the MBSR practices and rendered developmentally appropriate for use in schools and mental health care settings. Research is in the early stages with youth, yet MBPs show promising evidence for yielding positive benefits in such areas as awareness and acceptance, emotion and behavioral regulation, attention, academic engagement and performance, and social competence (see Burke, 2010; Harnett & Dawe, 2012; Meiklejohn et al., 2012; Zenner et al., 2014, for reviews of this literature).

Table 4.2. Lessons and social and emotional competencies

Strong Kids lesson and topic	Self-awareness	Self-management	Social awareness	Relationship skills	Responsible decision making
1. About *Strong Kids*: Emotional Strength Training	●				●
2. Understanding Your Emotions 1	●		●		
3. Understanding Your Emotions 2	●	●	●		●
4. Understanding Other People's Emotions			●	●	
5. Dealing with Anger	●	●	●	●	●
6. Clear Thinking 1	●	●			
7. Clear Thinking 2	●	●	●		●
8. Solving People Problems	●	●	●	●	●
9. Letting Go of Stress	●	●			●
10. Positive Living	●	●			●
11. Creating Strong and SMART Goals	●	●			●
12. Finishing UP!	●	●	●	●	●

In conceptualizing the infusion of brief MBPs into *Strong Kids—Grades 3–5*, we reviewed literature pertinent to applying MBPs with clinical and nonclinical populations, the use of MBPs in schools and other settings, the hypothesized mechanisms for how MBPs may work to produce their effects (e.g., Teper, Segal, & Inzlicht, 2013), how MBPs may build resilience (e.g., Coholic, Eys, & Lougheed, 2012), and issues relevant to feasibility and acceptability by youth and school personnel. We also drew from the literature describing evidence-based therapies that have cognitive-behavioral roots, which infused principles of mindfulness and practice, such as mindfulness-based cognitive therapy (MBCT), dialectic behavioral therapy, and acceptance and commitment therapy (ACT). Because of the time constraints involved in adding another activity to an existing program, we reviewed examples of practices that were brief (e.g., Flook, Goldberg, Pinger, Bonus, & Davidson, 2014; Schonert-Reichl & Hymel, 2007) and complemented cognitive-behavioral therapy–oriented approaches to teaching students about emotions and self-regulation (e.g., Broderick & Metz, 2009).

Our intention is to preserve the wellness promotion and cognitive-behavioral theoretical orientation that was the basis of the first edition of *Strong Kids—Grades 3–5*. *Strong Kids* is not a mindfulness-centered curriculum. We aimed for a transformative approach whereby an existing program may be enhanced through the use of a variety of brief MBPs and by infusing general concepts of a mindfulness perspective throughout the lessons. Instruction and examples use a tone of acceptance and openness to experience that may range from comfortable to uncomfortable. The use of terms perceived as judgmental (e.g., "good" and "bad," "appropriate" and "inappropriate") were reframed as "helpful" and "unhelpful" whenever the context supported such a change. Furthermore, emotional experience is reframed to include the notion that emotions, and associated thoughts and feelings, also can be experienced and investigated, rather than automatically pushed away or changed.

The MBPs in the 12 lessons are adapted from the foundational elements of MBSR (Kabat-Zinn, 2013) and other evidence-based sources. In designing each exercise, we drew inspiration from resources such as Hooker and Fodor's (2008) overview of activities that have been tested with children, Saltzman's (2014) approach to teaching these concepts to youth, and Semple and Lee's (2011) application of mindfulness within a cognitive therapy orientation with children and internalizing problems.

Each activity is found in the Introduction section and is referred to as a Mindfulness-Based Focusing Activity in the lesson. Students are given an explanation for the activity in Lesson 1, along with some ideas to explain what they can expect in starting the activities. A script is provided for convenience and efficiency and, in keeping with the spirit of *Strong Kids*, to decrease the amount of preparation time for instructors. Please note that these activities are optional. If your institution so chooses, simply omit them and continue with the Introduction to the lesson.

Some instructors may wish to have more background information and additional training in MBPs to better understand and implement these ideas.

For additional information on mindfulness, you may wish to visit our companion web site www.strongkidsresources.com and the following Internet resources:

- Association for Mindfulness in Education (AME): A collaborative association of organizations and individuals working together to provide support for mindfulness training as a component of K–12 education; http://www.mindfuleducation.org/

- Garrison Institute's Initiative on Contemplation and Education: Working to develop the field of contemplative education for K–12 educators and classrooms; https://www.garrisoninstitute.org

- Mindfulness-Based Stress Reduction (MBSR) and the Center for Mindfulness at University of Massachusetts Medical School; http://www.umassmed.edu/cfm/

CHANGES ACROSS THE PROGRAM LEVELS

We were often asked how the programs differ across the developmental levels of the programs. That is, how does *Strong Kids—Grades 3–5* differ from *Strong Kids—Grades 6–8*, and how does *Strong Kids—Grades 6–8* differ from *Strong Teens—Grades 9–12?* The new programs have been revised to better target, differentiate, and address developmental considerations of SEL.

The *Strong Kids* and *Strong Teens* lesson topics were selected to reflect the most critical components of resilience and align to the five competencies of SEL, lending well to the implementation of the program as a universal or schoolwide SEL program. The programs are based on theory and research that indicates that each SEL competency can be taught effectively to children of all ages. Children and adolescents alike can benefit from learning how to identify and manage their emotions, take the perspectives of others, and make responsible decisions. For these reasons, the lesson topics and objectives remain stable across all three levels of the programs. Therefore, although it is beneficial to implement the programs to students each year, *Strong Kids—Grades 3–5* is not a prerequisite to *Strong Kids—Grades 6–8*, and *Strong Kids—Grades 6–8* is not a prerequisite to *Strong Teens—Grades 9–12*. Students can benefit from the programs regardless of the level at which they first receive instruction. However, the SEL topics bring different contexts and different meanings for students as they age. Making a responsible decision can present more complex considerations for an adolescent than for a student in third grade. Thus, although the major objectives remain unchanged across the levels, the ways in which the lessons approach the objectives are adjusted to fit the development of the student. As the levels advance, the instruction and examples become increasingly sophisticated and abstract. Whereas *Strong Kids* focuses on more concrete concepts and issues relevant to elementary and middle school, *Strong Teens* addresses more abstract concepts and uses examples with more complex social situations and issues that are more relevant to teens, such as postsecondary planning.

NEW LESSON COMPONENTS

Although the lessons continue to follow a standardized format, we have added several elements to all the lessons: 1) SEL competencies, 2) suggestions for when instructors are running short on time, 3) instructor reflection, 4) introductory mindfulness-based focusing activity, 5) putting it all together, 6) closing breathing activity, and 7) additional activities. These changes were made in response to the most progressive advancements in research, theory, and science of implementation in the field of SEL.

Running Short on Time?

Time is one of our scarcest resources, particularly in modern, busy schools. This section includes recommended ways instructors can segment lessons when the full amount of time needed to implement a single lesson is not available. Guidance for segmenting lessons is found in Chapter 1 and at the beginning of each lesson. These are only suggested recommendations, and we understand that the implementation will vary for every user or setting.

Instructor Reflection

In keeping with the original intent of the *Strong Kids* programs, we are continuously considering ways in which we might help busy practitioners feel better prepared to teach SEL programs such as *Strong Kids* and *Strong Teens*. This section provides a few helpful suggestions for instructors to get acquainted with the concepts in each lesson and to have the opportunity to practice skills prior to teaching the lesson. Also, this section allows users to reflect on their personal experiences with the skills taught in each lesson to develop a deeper understanding of the content. This deeper understanding can lead to greater self-efficacy, which can facilitate successful implementation of the lesson and result in enhanced student outcomes.

Mindfulness-Based Focusing Activity

A brief, 2- to 3-minute, scripted mindfulness activity is placed at the beginning of each lesson to promote calm, focus, and enhanced awareness of experience in preparation for the lesson content. The mindfulness activities at the start of each lesson begin with a standard activity that promotes nonjudgmental observation of the present moment by instructing students to become aware of their body positioning (hands and feet resting in place) and the sensation of their natural breath. Beginning in the second lesson and onto the last lesson (12), the standard activity is followed by more content-specific practice. For example, in the lesson teaching awareness of thoughts, students are asked to become aware of thoughts as they arrive, to watch them, and to let them pass. In the lesson that focuses on perspective-taking, students participate in an activity that promotes awareness of sounds; in the lesson on managing stress, a loving-kindness exercise toward one's self is applied. In a lesson focusing on awareness of thoughts and attributions, students practice noticing thoughts and labeling them in categories such as "planning," and they practice loving-kindness toward others in a lesson on coping with social conflict. Other activities include noticing the breath and how the body moves during breathing; an exercise modeled after the body scan used in MBSR; a whole-body movement exercise; and imagining success or accomplishment and the thoughts and physical sensations that correspond. A culminating activity for the last lesson incorporates elements of the previous activities. We selected language intentionally to promote a sense of curiosity, kindness, and nonjudgment.

Putting It All Together

This section serves the purpose of the former "integrating key concepts" section and further encourages active application of the key skills within the lesson as a whole concept.

Closing Breathing Activity

At the end of each lesson, a 1-minute diaphragmatic breathing exercise, also scripted, is used to promote relaxation (e.g., Larson, El Ramahi, Conn, Estes, & Ghibellini, 2010), reflection, and assimilation of the lesson content.

Additional Activities and Homework

This section offers additional, innovative ways to teach the content outside of the lesson and may bolster skills maintenance and generalization. For teachers who are unable to make use of homework assignments with their groups, we no longer "require" homework but list it as optional. Extra practice is always best, but whether or not homework is completed should not hinder the next lesson.

SUMMARY

Our efforts to create an effective, user-friendly, and practical mental health promotion program, coupled with the real-world experience and feedback we gained over nearly 20 years of research and development and use, have convinced us that the *Strong Kids* curriculum has much to offer and can be a valuable tool for facilitating SEL and promoting resilience. It is our hope that the changes that have been made to the *Strong Kids* programs are positive and helpful, not only in the lives of the students who will be receiving the program but also in the lives of the adults who will be spending time teaching it.

We hope that users who were acquainted with the first edition of the *Strong Kids* programs find the updated versions familiar, but with new twists and fresh angles, and that new users of the *Strong Kids* programs find the second edition intuitive, cohesive, and timely. As you use the program and its examples to support your students, we encourage you to consider your own experiences. We hope that not only will you make important connections for and with your students, but you may also stumble onto new ways to look at old problems of your own.

REFERENCES

Broderick, P.C., & Metz, S. (2009). Learning to BREATHE: A pilot trial of a mindfulness curriculum for adolescents. *Advances in School Mental Health Promotion, 2*, 35–46.

Burke, C.A. (2010). Mindfulness-based approaches with children and adolescents: A preliminary review of current research in an emergent field. *Journal of Child and Family Studies, 19*(2), 133–144. doi:10.1007/s10826-009-9282-x

Coholic, D., Eys, M., & Lougheed, S. (2012). Investigating the effectiveness of an arts-based and mindfulness-based group program for the improvement of resilience in children in need. *Journal of Child and Family Studies, 21*(5), 833–844. doi:10.1007/s10826-011-9544-2

Collaborative for Academic, Social, and Emotional Learning. (2014). *What is SEL? Skills and competencies.* Retrieved from http://www.casel.org/social-and-emotional-learning/core-competencies

Doran, G.T. (1981). There's a S.M.A.R.T. way to write management's goals and objectives, *Management Review, 11*, 35–36.

Dweck, C.S. (2006). *Mindset: The new psychology of success.* New York, NY: Random House.

Flook, L., Goldberg, S.B., Pinger, L., Bonus, K., & Davidson, R.J. (2013). Mindfulness for teachers: A pilot study to assess effects on stress, burnout, and teaching efficacy. *Mind, Brain, and Education, 7*, 182–195. doi:10.1111/mbe.12026

Harnett, P.H., & Dawe, S. (2012). The contribution of mindfulness-based therapies for children and families and proposed conceptual integration. *Child and Adolescent Mental Health, 17*(4), 195–208. doi:10.1111/j.1475-3588.2011.00643.x

Hooker, K.E., & Fodor, I.E. (2008). Teaching mindfulness to children. *Gestalt Review, 12*, 75–91. Retrieved from http://www.gisc.orgwww.gisc.org/gestaltreview/documents/Teaching MindfulnesstoChildren.pdf

Kabat-Zinn, J. (2013). *Full catastrophe living* (Rev. ed.). New York, NY: Bantam.

Larson, H., El Ramahi, M., Conn, S., Estes, L., & Ghibellini, A. (2010). Reducing test anxiety among third grade students through the implementation of relaxation techniques, *Journal of School Counseling, 8*, 1–19.

Meiklejohn, J., Phillips, C., Freedman, M.L., Griffin, M.L., Biegel, G., Roach, A., . . . Saltzman, A. (2012). Integrating mindfulness training into K–12 education: Fostering the resilience of teachers and students. *Mindfulness, 3*(4), 291–307. doi:10.1007/s12671-012-0094-5

Saltzman, A. (2014). *A still quiet place: A mindfulness program for teaching children and adolescents to ease stress and difficult emotions.* Oakland, CA: New Harbinger Publications.

Schonert-Reichl, K.A., & Hymel. S. (2007). Educating the heart as well as the mind social and emotional learning for school and life success. *Education Canada, 47*, 20–25. Retrieved from http://www.jcsh-cces.ca/upload/Educating_Heart_Spring07-1.pdf

Semple, R., & Lee, J. (2011). *Mindfulness-based cognitive therapy for anxious children. A manual for treating childhood anxiety.* Oakland, CA: New Harbinger Publications.

Teper, R., Segal, Z., & Inzlicht, M. (2013). Inside the mindful mind: How mindfulness enhances emotion regulation through improvements in executive control. *Current Directions in Psychological Science, 22*, 449–454. doi:10.1177/0963721413495869

Zenner, C., Herrnleben-Kurz, S., & Walach, H. (2014). Mindfulness-based interventions in schools—A systematic review and meta-analysis. *Frontiers in Psychology, 5*, 603. Retrieved from http://www.ncbi.nlm.nih.gov/pmc/articles/PMC4075476/

Zins, J.E., Bloodworth, M.R., Weissberg, R.P., & Walberg, H.J. (2004). The scientific base linking social and emotional learning to school success. In J. Zins, M. Wang, & H. Walberg (Eds.), *Building academic success and social-emotional learning: What does the research say?* New York, NY: Teachers College Press.

The *Strong Kids—Grades 3–5* Curriculum

LESSON 1

About *Strong Kids:* Emotional Strength Training

SEL Competencies Addressed in This Lesson

Responsible decision making · Self-awareness · Relationship skills · Self-management · Social awareness

Teacher Notes

Purpose and Objectives

The purpose of this lesson is to orient students to the curriculum and introduce emotional vocabulary. In this lesson students will

- Be introduced to the curriculum and the plan for regular instruction

- Learn the expected behaviors for participation in the curriculum

- Begin to identify emotions

Materials Needed

☐ Supplements 1.1–1.2 (online download)

☐ Supplements 1.3 (online download and preprint)

☐ Supplements 1.4–1.6 (online download)

☐ Supplement 1.7 (homework handout)

☐ Comment box

Running Short on Time?

Suggested stopping points: end of the Optional Pretest Assessments section or the end of the Awareness Statement to Instructor and Students section, and the Closure activity. See Chapter 1 for more information on segmenting lessons.

Instructor Reflection

You and your students are embarking on a 12-lesson journey that explores our social and emotional lives. Research demonstrates that learning about our social and emotional world helps build resilience and can offset the negative effects of the fast-paced and stressful society in which we live. Before you lead your students through each lesson, you may feel more comfortable with the materials if you take some time to reflect on each lesson's content as it relates to you, your understanding of the information, and your own experiences. An Instructor Reflection exercise is provided at the beginning of each lesson to allow you a moment to reflect on the content you are about to present. Also, you may find it helpful to review the introductory material in Chapters 1 through 4 before beginning the lessons. The star icon (see margin), used throughout all lessons, signifies that these chapters offer additional explanation or information pertinent to the lesson content or administrative guidelines, which can help you implement the lesson.

For this lesson, consider how the behavioral expectations for participating in the curriculum align with your classroom behavior expectations. Note that special consideration is given to the fact that students will share personal information that will be treated as confidential within the group. Consider how you might remind students to be respectful to one another when they share. You may also wish to review the list of emotions in Supplement 1.6 and consider how you experience and perceive emotions. Are there some emotions with which you feel more, or less, comfortable? Consider potential roadblocks you may face in presenting this information, or concerns that may arise, and identify colleagues with whom you can collaborate and any resources available to you at your site.

Introduction

 1 MIN.

In this section and the sections that follow, sample scripts are provided. You may use the scripts, or your own words, during instruction. For this first section, talk to students about the fact that they are starting a new program called *Strong Kids*. Give examples on the topics that will be covered, and indicate that the skills they learn will help them be socially and emotionally stronger in their lives. Ask students what they think they might need to be socially and emotionally strong.

Sample Script

Today we will begin a new program called Strong Kids. Strong Kids is about learning ways we can be strong with our minds and bodies and in our relationships with other people. We'll learn how to understand our emotions and other people's emotions. We'll talk about how to solve problems, how to set goals, and how to think in a way that helps us and makes us stronger. We will meet [e.g., once per week] for [e.g., one class period]. This program will help you learn skills that you will practice in order to be socially and emotionally healthy throughout your life. What do you think is needed to be socially and emotionally strong?

Optional Pretest Assessments

10–20 MINS. If you are using assessment measures to evaluate student growth during the *Strong Kids* curriculum, have your students complete the pretests at this time. Administer the same assessment measures again after Lesson 12, Finishing UP! We suggest using the *Strong Kids* Knowledge Test (see Appendix A) to measure students' knowledge of the concepts covered in the lessons. You also may use other assessment tools of your choosing. Visit http://www.strongkidsresources.com to review measures that have been useful. Tell students it is okay if they don't know the answers to the questions on the measurement tools. The tests are used to evaluate what they know now. When all students have a copy of the pretest, provide them with the appropriate instructions. The amount of time it will take to complete these assessments will depend on the number of assessment measures and the length of each. Ten to 20 minutes is an estimate. See Chapter 2 for more information on adjusting the curriculum to fit the needs of your students.

Sample Script

First, I'm going to ask you to answer some questions that will help me understand what you know about emotions. There are no right or wrong answers, and you may not have heard some of the words before, but do your best work and answer all of the questions. Raise your hand if you need help understanding any of the questions. I'll start by reading the directions, then you can begin answering the questions.

Introduce the Mindfulness-Based Focusing Activity

3 MINS. Discuss with students that they will participate in a mindfulness, or focusing, activity at the start of every lesson. Discuss that they may feel awkward or restless at first and they have the option to keep their eyes open. These brief activities are intended to teach students a skill that can help them focus at the beginning of each lesson and concentrate on the lesson. Use Supplement 1.1 to illustrate the limbic system in the brain. For background and implementation information on these activities, please see Chapter 4.

Sample Script

At the start of each lesson, we will begin with an activity to settle our bodies and focus our minds. This focusing, or mindfulness, activity will help to train your brain to pay attention, learn new information, understand how you feel, and make positive choices. In the middle of our brains there is a part that can tell when we feel emotions, like when we feel angry, upset, worried, or sad. We also have a part of our brain, right where our foreheads are, that helps us calm down, think clearly, and make positive choices. We are going to help these parts of our brains work well by trying these focusing activities at the beginning of each lesson.

I will ask you to close your eyes or look at a point on the floor in front of you, breathe, and pay attention to what I'm saying. If you choose to keep your eyes open, please look only at the space in front of you, not at your neighbor. You want to focus on what you feel, not what your neighbor is doing. You may feel a little uncomfortable, awkward, or restless at first, but it gets easier the more we practice.

Mindfulness-Based Focusing Activity

 2 MINS.

Sample Script

Let's begin. Close your eyes, or leave your eyes open and look at a point in front of you on the floor or on your desk. Now, rest your hands comfortably on your desk or in your lap. Feel your feet on the floor or your hands as they rest. Just like scientists are curious, or interested in things around them, we are going to start each lesson by exploring, in a kind and curious way, what it feels like to pay attention to some of the messages our bodies send us and to some of the things around us. Let's start by taking three breaths together and paying attention to our breath. Just breathe as you normally do. [Pause.] Now, pay attention to what it feels like taking a breath in and a breath out. Maybe you feel air going in through your nose or mouth and going out your nose or mouth. [Pause.] Maybe you feel your stomach moving. Let's spend about a minute just noticing what breathing feels like in our bodies. [Allow 1 minute to practice awareness.] Now, let's take two breaths together. [Pause. Model two slow breaths.] When you finish letting out your breath, slowly open your eyes. Now that we've practiced becoming aware of our breathing, we are ready to move on to our lesson.

Defining Behavior Expectations and Participation

 5 MINS.

Use Supplement 1.2 to introduce and review the expectations or rules for being in the group and their definitions. These rules are important to follow so that everyone feels safe in sharing and participating in the discussion. Students will be asked to share personal information but are never obligated to do this, especially if they feel too uncomfortable. See below (after the Sample Script) for an optional idea for a way in which students can communicate if they feel uncomfortable sharing or have questions or concerns. If you choose to include this option, include it as part of your introduction and before reviewing the guidelines in detail.

Sample Script

You are now a part of a group with some important expectations or rules. During the Strong Kids lessons, you may be asked to share stories about when you felt emotions. When someone is sharing a story, we will listen quietly. Sharing this information outside of the group is not allowed. Your classmates are trusting you to keep the information private. If someone outside of our group asks you to share information about something someone in our group shared during these lessons, just say, "I can't tell you that; those discussions are private," or "What's said in the group stays in the group." If you feel uncomfortable sharing, you can stop at any time. If you want to talk about your situation in private, please talk to me personally. It's important to remain respectful toward one another as we are learning these skills. Here are the rules:

Respect others: Listen quietly when someone is speaking. Pay attention.

Come prepared and do your best work: Complete any activities assigned from the last lesson. Participate in activities to the best of your ability.

Personal information stays in the group: What is talked about in the group stays with the group. Do not gossip about what other people have shared. [Consider explaining what gossip is; e.g., saying things about other people that might hurt their feelings.]

Optional: Some students may feel uncomfortable speaking to you about a particular concern. To encourage these students to share or to obtain your assistance privately, you may wish to consider a comment box, with preprinted comment slips, whereby students can write a question or concern and drop it in the box. Download and preprint Supplement 1.3 to show students an example of the comment slip. Please see Chapter 2 for ways in which you can address comments that may be concerning.

Sample Script

You can also fill out the comment slip [show Supplement 1.3] and put it in the Comment Box. On the slip, you will write your name and your concern/question or comments if you are uncomfortable sharing with the group. If I talk about something I read in the Comment Box, I will be careful not to say who wrote it and I will leave out any parts that could give clues about who wrote it. All questions and comments are important.

Activity A: Practicing the Expectations

 3 MINS.

Use Supplement 1.2 to review the expectations and discuss examples and nonexamples of following them. You also can ask the class to share their own examples and nonexamples. Note: An "example" reflects the appropriate or intended use of a term or concept (to do). A "nonexample" illustrates the opposite of the concept (not to do).

Sample Script

Let's discuss some examples of following the rules and some nonexamples of following the rules. Examples mean those choices that you want to or are expected to make. Nonexamples are those choices that you don't want to or shouldn't make. Here are the rules:

Respect others.

- *Examples: You listen quietly while someone is speaking and until that person finishes what he or she is saying.*

- *Nonexamples: You talk to your neighbor while someone is speaking. You "tune out" or begin working on something else.*

Come prepared and do your best work.

- *Example: You complete the work you were asked to do.*
- *Nonexample: You didn't do the worksheet that was assigned. You complete the worksheet in a rushed way right before class or in another class.*

Personal information stays in the group.

- *Example: Someone who's not in the group asks you what someone shared during the class. You tell this person, "What's said in the group, stays in the group!"*
- *Nonexample: You either say what happened or you say, "Wow, I can't tell you what she said, but Marcella was really weird today in class."*

Awareness Statement to Instructor and Students

 2 MINS.

Explain to students that *Strong Kids* will focus on talking about situations and emotions. Discuss that if anyone feels uncomfortable, it is important to seek additional support. Identify people with whom students can talk (e.g., teacher, parent, school counselor, principal) and brainstorm ways that students can communicate their concerns. At the end of the program, students will have another opportunity to identify whether additional support is needed and where they may go to obtain support. As the lessons progress, remain vigilant for students who appear to be experiencing difficulty or having an uncomfortable response to the content. See Chapter 2 for ideas on how to identify and address these issues.

Sample Script

During the next several weeks, we are going to talk about a variety of situations and the emotions you have. If you find that you are feeling worried or upset and aren't sure what to do about it, it's important that you talk to an adult. Let's talk about whom you can talk to if you feel this way. [Invite some discussion on this topic.]

Review the Lesson Topics

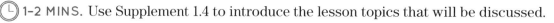

1–2 MINS. Use Supplement 1.4 to introduce the lesson topics that will be discussed.

Sample Script

During this program, we will be discussing these topics that are covered in 12 lessons. As part of each topic, there will be activities that involve partners or small-group discussions, role plays, scenarios, handouts, and video clips that will help you learn the concepts.

Key Terms and Definitions

🕐 2 MINS.   Use Supplement 1.5 as a handout to define the key terms that will be used in this lesson.

Sample Script

Here are some important words or ideas that will help us understand the information we'll talk about in Strong Kids. We'll define the words and discuss examples to understand what they mean.

Introduction to Emotions

🕐 5–10 MINS.   Everyone has emotions. Emotions are like signals that tell us something about our situation.

Sample Script

Stop signs and traffic lights are signals that tell you to slow down, stop, or go. Emotions are like signals, too. Emotions say, "Hey! Pay attention! You're feeling something you like, don't like, or aren't sure about." When we feel worried, sad, excited, or irritated, it's a signal that tells us to pay attention to our situation. It's our body's way of telling us about a situation. Emotions are sometimes called feelings. Everyone has emotions, every day and everywhere! We can also experience more than one emotion at the same time.

Activity B: Identifying Emotions

🕐 4–9 MINS.   Use Supplement 1.6 as a visual aid to show students a variety of emotions they may experience. This activity can be done with a large group or in small groups. Students also can identify and discuss emotions not on this list.

Sample Script

Let's talk about the emotions we are feeling now or have felt at other times and guess how they act like signals. We'll also practice showing the emotions on our faces. Understanding our emotions helps us to persevere and be resilient, or to work hard to meet our goals and bounce back when things are difficult.

Ask students to do the following:

1. Identify an emotion they are feeling in this moment, or another time, such as during a school assignment, an argument with a peer, or a situation at home.

Sample Script

These faces show emotions that we all feel. Taking turns, name an emotion that you are feeling now or that you have felt recently. For example, if I'm going to a birthday party this weekend, I might feel excited.

2. Identify emotions that they experience at the same time (e.g., frustration and anger, worry and irritability).

Sample Script

Did you know we can feel two emotions at the same time? For example, if it's taking you a long time to finish your writing assignment and you'd rather be outside playing, you might feel frustrated and angry. Let's name some emotions you feel at the same time.

3. Guess how the emotion was acting like a signal.

Sample Script

Emotions act like a signal and give us information. For example, if I'm excited about going to the birthday party, it tells me that I like parties. What was your emotion telling you about your situation?

4. Ask students to model what the emotion looks like on their face.

Sample Script

Let's see what the emotion you chose looks like on your face.

Putting It All Together

 2–3 MINS. Use the following activity to practice the concepts discussed in this lesson.

Sample Script

Let's practice what we've learned by putting it all together.

 Using Supplement 1.2, ask students to recall the expectations for being in the group. Then, ask students to name a few emotions they felt during the class period. You can also use this time to discuss students' observations and experiences of the focusing activity at the beginning of the lesson.

Sample Script

What are the expectations or rules for being in the group? What are some emotions you felt during this class? What did you notice during the focusing activity?

Closure

 2 MINS.   Close the lesson using a short breathing activity and a reflection on the lesson content. Students may find it helpful to place their hands on their stomachs, just under their ribs, to feel the expansion and retraction when doing this exercise properly. For background information on this activity, refer to Chapter 4.

Sample Script

Let's take a moment to regroup. At the end of every lesson, we'll do a short breathing exercise. This exercise is just a little different from the one we did in the beginning and will help us end the lesson in a calm place. We'll also take a moment to think about what we learned about today.

Close your eyes, or look at a point in front of you, and rest your hands in your lap. Feel your feet on the floor. Relax the muscles in your body and face. Relax and soften your stomach muscles. Counting to 3, take a deep breath in slowly. Inhale the air down into your lungs. Feel your chest and stomach expand like a balloon. [Pause.] *Now, exhale counting to 4. Feel your chest and stomach collapse as all the air exits your body.* [Pause.] *Again, inhale deep into your lungs so that your stomach expands* [Pause.] *and exhale.* [Pause.] *Take a moment to think about something you learned today that was important to you or that you really liked.* [Pause for a moment to allow time for reflection.] *Counting to 3, take one more deep breath in slowly* [Pause.] *and exhale counting to 4.* [Pause.]

Tips for Transfer Training and Homework

Use the ideas and activities in the following section to practice this lesson's content with your students at other times during the day. Also remember to precorrect, remind, and reinforce concepts from this lesson in activities throughout the school week across settings including home, the bus, and the cafeteria.

Additional Activities

- Using handheld mirrors or other technology whereby students can look at their own faces or the faces of others, ask students to model what their faces look like when they experience an emotion and then look at the face in the mirror or other technology. You can suggest to students that they do this at home also.

- During the school day, prompt students to identify an emotion they are feeling and whether they may be feeling more than one emotion. Ask students to think about how the emotion may be acting like a signal.

- Ask students to keep a journal, and prompt them to write in the journal after each lesson or daily. Students can use the journal for general reflection or for additional skills practice.

Homework Handout

Hand out Supplement 1.7, My Emotions. This homework assignment will ask students to identify and reflect on emotions. Ask students to answer the questions as best as they can.

The Limbic System

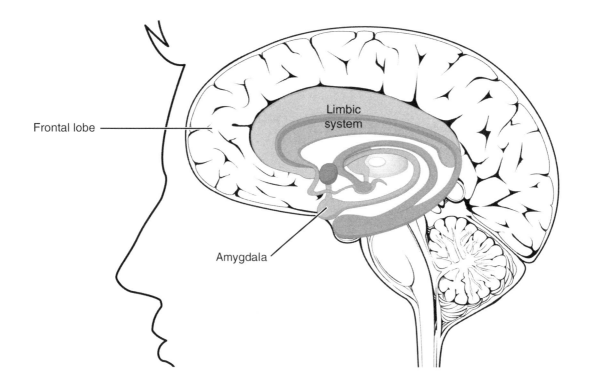

Strong Kids Rules

1. **Respect others:** Listen quietly while someone else is speaking. Pay attention.

2. **Come prepared and do your best work:** Complete any work you were asked to do from the last lesson. Participate to the best of your ability.

3. **Personal information stays in the group:** What is talked about in the group stays with the group. Do not gossip about what other people have shared.

Comment Slip

Name _____   **Date** _____

Question/Comment/Concern _____

_____

_____

_____

_____

_____

_____

_____

_____

Strong Kids Lessons

Lesson 1: We are introduced to the program, learn the rules of the group, and begin to learn about emotions.

Lesson 2: There are physical feelings that go along with our emotions.

Lesson 3: There are thoughts and behaviors or actions that go along with our emotions.

Lesson 4: We can learn about other people's emotions and ways to show empathy.

Lesson 5: We can learn to identify and manage angry emotions.

Lesson 6: We can identify when our thoughts get stuck in thinking traps.

Lesson 7: There are strategies we can use to think about other perspectives in a situation.

Lesson 8: We can learn ways to solve problems and get along with others.

Lesson 9: There are strategies we can use to deal with stress in our lives.

Lesson 10: There are things we can do to live a positive and healthy life.

Lesson 11: We can set goals and do things that will help us lead a healthy life.

Lesson 12: We review the information and skills we've learned.

Key Terms and Definitions

Adversity, troubles, and failure

This is a situation that is difficult, or in which you feel as if you have done poorly.

Examples: Your parents get divorced, your family is having a hard time paying the bills, you're not doing as well in school as you'd like to, you wish you had better friendships, or you made a mistake.

Resilience

Bouncing back from difficulties in your life shows resilience.

Examples: Something is difficult in your life and maybe you feel sad or upset. You use some strategies from *Strong Kids.* You feel better and know you can get through a hard time and bounce back.

Perseverance

This is when you work hard to reach a goal.

Examples: Something in school is a lot of work, but it's important to you to do your best so you keep trying. Or maybe you want to play a sport but you make a lot of mistakes. You keep practicing.

Emotion

A feeling that acts like a signal, an emotion gives us information about our situation and ourselves.

Examples: Some emotions we may feel are happiness, sadness, fear, disgust, surprise, and anger.

List of Emotions

Afraid

Excited

Angry

Bored

Confused

Sad

Frustrated

Disgusted

Embarrassed

Joyful

Happy

Stressed

Jealous

Surprised

Disappointed

Worried

Other emotions: annoyed, ashamed, brave, calm, confident, curious, excited, grieving, guilty, hopeful, hurt, loved, optimistic, relaxed, relieved, scared, shy, upset

My Emotions

Directions: Think of a time when you felt an emotion. Use this memory to answer the next few questions.

1. What is the emotion? Which emotion face did you have?

    _____

    _____

2. Using the circle below, indicate how much of the emotion or emotions you felt.
    An example is provided.

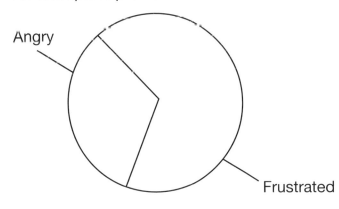
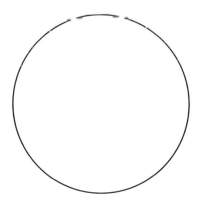

3. Where were you? What was the situation?

    _____

    _____

    _____

    _____

4. How did you know you felt this emotion?

    _____

    _____

    _____

    _____

5. How did this emotion act like a signal? What did it tell you about your situation or yourself?

    _____

    _____

    _____

    _____

LESSON 2

Understanding Your Emotions 1

SEL Competencies Addressed in This Lesson

Purpose and Objectives

This lesson provides students with the knowledge and skills to identify physical feelings that they experience concurrently with emotions. In this lesson, students will

- Develop the ability to identify physical feelings that occur with emotions

- Identify emotions on a continuum from comfortable to uncomfortable

- Measure the intensity of emotions

Materials Needed

- ☐ Supplements 1.6, 2.1 (online download)
- ☐ Supplements 2.2–2.4 (online download and handout)
- ☐ Supplement 2.5 (homework handout)
- ☐ Optional video of a roller coaster

Teacher Notes

_____

_____

_____

_____

_____

_____

_____

_____

Running Short on Time?

Suggested stopping points: end of Activity C and the Closure activity.

Instructor Reflection

Emotions can be experienced in our bodies and may range in feeling from comfortable to uncomfortable. Emotions also vary in intensity and can change according to context (e.g., If you tripped and fell and there was no one around, you might feel startled and perhaps a little concerned. But if there were several people around you, you might feel startled and embarrassed). It is valuable for people to get to know their own personal experience with emotions—there are similarities and differences among us all. To do this, simply notice your emotional experiences throughout the day, however slight or intense, and consider: What is the emotion? Are you experiencing several emotions at once? Are there physical sensations occurring at the same time? Is there comfort, discomfort, or both, and how intense does the emotion feel?

Review

 2–3 MINS. Review the ideas (listed below) that were discussed in Lesson 1: About *Strong Kids:*

- These are the rules of the group: listen, be prepared, do your best work, and maintain confidentiality.

- Identify a person you could talk to if you are having a difficult time.

- We experience a lot of emotions. They act like signals and give us information.

Sample Script

During our last meeting, we started the Strong Kids program. We talked about the rules of the group and what we'll be learning in the program, and we identified a lot of emotions. We also talked about identifying someone you could talk to and how emotions act like signals.

Introduction

 2–3 MINS. Introduce the lesson. Lead students in a focusing activity. Then, show students Supplement 2.1 and share, via discussion, that physical feelings 1) are associated with emotions; 2) can be experienced on a continuum of comfortable to uncomfortable, or both; and 3) can be measured by their intensity. Allow students time to respond to the prompt questions.

Sample Script

Today we're going to learn about how we experience physical feelings when we have an emotion.

Mindfulness-Based Focusing Activity

2 MINS. **Sample Script**

Like last time, let's begin with an activity to settle our bodies and focus our minds. Close your eyes or look at a point in front of you on the floor or on your desk. Now, rest your hands comfortably on your desk or in your lap. Feel your feet on the floor or your hands as they rest. Let's begin by taking three breaths together, just breathing as we normally do. [Pause.] *Now, like last time, focus your attention on how the breath feels going in and going out. You might feel your chest or stomach move. Maybe you feel like your stomach is filling up like a balloon and then the air is going out. Just notice what you are feeling. Whatever you feel is okay. We are simply noticing our breath.* [Pause.] *Describe to yourself what you notice. You might say to yourself, "I feel cool air going into my nose" or "I feel my stomach moving." Continue breathing as you normally do, for about a minute.* [Allow students about a minute to practice.] *You probably notice that you have thoughts that take your attention away from noticing your breath. That's normal. When you notice this, just focus again on your breath.* [Pause for three to five breaths.] *Now, let's take two breaths together.* [Pause.] *When you finish letting out the second breath, slowly open your eyes. Now that we've observed what we feel when we breathe, we are ready to move on to our lesson.*

Introduction (Continued)

1 MIN.   Use Supplement 2.1 as a visual example or show a video of a roller coaster.

Sample Script

Look at this picture [or video] *of a roller coaster. Have you ever been on a roller coaster? Do you remember the emotions you felt? Do you remember the physical feelings you had? Some people feel the emotion "excited" and their bodies feel relaxed or charged up. Other people feel the emotion "scared" and their stomachs feel sick or their bodies feel very tense. Today we're going to talk about how our bodies experience or feel emotions.*

Key Terms and Definitions

5 MINS.   Use Supplement 2.2 as a handout to define the key terms that will be used in this lesson.

Sample Script

Here are some important words or ideas that will help us understand the information we'll talk about today. We'll define the words and discuss examples to understand what they mean.

Physiological Feelings Associated with Emotions

5–10 MINS. When we experience emotions, our bodies can feel them too.

Sample Script

When we experience emotions, our bodies can feel them. Other people may have the same sensations you have, or they might be different. For example,

*if you have a funny feeling in your stomach, like butterflies fluttering, it may be
a signal that you feel worried. Other people might feel their heart beating fast,
feel dizzy or tired, have a headache, shake or tremble, sweat or blush, or have
a strange tingly feeling all over. If you are clenching your jaw or taking short
and shallow breaths, you might be feeling angry. Different people can feel different things. Let's do an activity so you can see how your body experiences
emotions.*

Activity A: Identifying Physical Feelings

🕒 4–9 MINS. Use Supplement 1.6 (List of Emotions, Lesson 1) as a guide. Choose *one* activity
below to give students an opportunity to practice identifying physical sensations associated with emotions. Examples of emotions and corresponding physical sensations are listed below the activities.

Sample Script

*Let's practice noticing the feelings that our bodies have when we have
an emotion.*

1. Play songs or sounds that can evoke emotions (e.g., "Happy" by Pharrell
   Williams, "Don't Worry Be Happy" by Bobby McFerrin). Discuss the emotions students felt and what their bodies were experiencing.

2. Ask students to close their eyes and take three deep breaths. Instruct
   them to recall a situation where they felt an emotion. Instruct them to
   imagine where they were and what they were doing, saying, or thinking.
   Ask them to notice what their body is feeling right now and ask them to
   describe it.

3. Using art supplies, make cue cards with the name of an emotion on one side.
   Students will write down or draw the physical feelings on the other side of
   the card.

Below are example emotions with possible corresponding physical feelings.
Students can also suggest other physical sensations. It can be helpful to prompt
students to use creative or less common language to describe the way their
bodies feel in response to emotions, such as "skin feels prickly" as a reaction
to irritation or impatience or "heart feels fluttery" in response to excitement
or joy.

- Worry: Stomach discomfort, headache, muscles feel stiff, shallow breathing,
  restless, tired

- Fear: Heart beats fast, breath is rapid, tingling

- Stress: Aches and pains, stomachaches/upset, tense muscles

- Sadness: Tired/fatigued, ache in the chest or heart, stomach upset, general pain

- Frustration: Tense muscles, heart beats fast
- Embarrassment: Face feels warm, heart pounding or beating fast

Experiencing Emotions on a Continuum from Comfortable to Uncomfortable

🕑 5–10 MINS. Emotions are felt on a continuum from uncomfortable to neutral to comfortable.

Sample Script

Emotions can feel really comfortable, really uncomfortable, and somewhere in between. Really comfortable might feel like, "I love this feeling and I want to feel this way all the time!" Really uncomfortable might feel like, "Make it stop! I don't want to feel this way anymore!" If it's somewhere in between, we might not even notice the emotion. One way is not better or more normal than the other way to feel. Depending on the situation and the circumstances, it can be totally normal to feel uncomfortable in some situations and comfortable in others. Some situations can even make us feel both uncomfortable and comfortable at the same time. Knowing how we feel gives us more information about ourselves and our experience.

Activity B: Identifying Emotions on the Continuum of Comfortable and Uncomfortable

🕑 4–9 MINS. Use Supplement 2.3 as a handout to practice identifying and exploring emotions in large or small groups.

Sample Script

Now, let's practice not only identifying emotions and the physical feelings we have, but also whether we feel comfortable, uncomfortable, somewhere in between, or both comfortable and uncomfortable.

For each example, ask students the following questions:

- What physical sensations give you clues about how you feel?
- What emotions might you be experiencing? (*Hint:* We can experience more than one emotion at the same time and different people have different experiences.)
- Do you feel comfortable, uncomfortable, or both? (e.g., *comfortable:* I like feeling that way; *uncomfortable:* I don't like feeling that way; *both:* I felt uncomfortable, but noticed that after a while I felt better.)

Physical feelings and possible emotions experienced for each scenario:

Scenario	Physical feelings	Possible emotions
1	Jumpy, feel like screaming or hitting something	Upset, sad, angry
2	Feel like crying, want to be alone	Sad, confused, relieved
3	Energized	Excited, happy, scared
4	Startled, gasped	Surprised, excited, irritated, angry, relieved
5	Restless (getting out of seat), fidgeting, hard to focus	Overwhelmed, irritated, worried
6	Calm, excited	Happy, confident, embarrassed, concerned

It's Normal to Feel Discomfort

 1 MIN. Although we'd like to experience the comfortable emotions all the time, it is not realistic or always helpful.

Sample Script

It feels great to feel comfortable emotions and we often wish we could feel that way all the time. Dealing with uncomfortable emotions can be difficult, but actually, we learn a little bit about ourselves every time we feel and pay attention to an emotion, even if it's uncomfortable. We get stronger by paying attention and learning how to react to our emotions. Emotions change and come and go. If you're on the roller coaster, maybe you feel excited or scared. When it's over, you might feel disappointed or relieved. The way we feel changes moment by moment, every day, and that's okay. We will learn how to identify both ways of feeling and how to manage when we are feeling uncomfortable emotions.

Measure the Intensity of Emotions

 5 MINS. Emotions are experienced in levels of intensity: Some are barely noticeable, whereas others are very apparent. Use Supplement 2.4 to illustrate this idea.

Sample Script

We can think about a thermometer when we want to talk about how much or how intensely we may be feeling an emotion. A thermometer tells us if something is cold, warm, or hot, like how cold or warm it is outside or the temperature of water or food we are cooking. We can think this way about our emotions too. Sometimes we barely feel an emotion and sometimes we feel a whole lot of it! Sometimes, it's in between. It's normal to feel a range of emotion and for that emotion to go up or down over time. Thinking about how much or little of the emotion we feel can give us more information about our situation.

Activity C: Measuring Intensity

4 MINS. Use Supplement 2.4 as a handout for this activity. First, model your own example. Then, use the examples listed after the sample script to begin a discussion on how to rate emotional intensity. Direct students to the supplement, and ask them to point to a location on the thermometer that reflects this measurement. You can also opt to have students use an object, such as a paperclip or pencil, and move it from side to side or make a mark on the paper. Finally, ask several students to volunteer to identify situations where they experienced an emotion.

Sample Script

Let's use the thermometer to describe how much emotion we feel. For example, if you felt a little frustrated, you might point to one of the bottom lines in the "low" area. If you felt extremely frustrated, you might point to one of the top lines in the "high" area. If you think it was in between, you'd point to one of the lines in the middle in the "medium" area. If you felt really, really excited about something, you might point to the top line. Or, maybe you felt just a little excited, so you'd point to the bottom line. I'll go first: I'm thinking of a time when I felt [insert emotion]. I was [insert the situation]. I think my feeling of [insert emotion] was medium on the thermometer, but I noticed that over time, the temperature dropped to low. I noticed in the beginning it felt uncomfortable, but then it gradually went away. Now, let's go through a few examples and use the thermometer to rate how much emotion we feel. Notice how you might feel over time. Then, I'll ask for volunteers to share their own examples.

Here are some example scenarios:
- *Getting a new skateboard*
- *Losing your homework*
- *Trying a new sport or musical instrument*
- *Spending time with friends*
- *Getting a good grade*

Raise your hand if you'd like to share your own examples.

Putting It All Together

5 MINS. Use the following activity to practice the concepts discussed in this lesson.

Sample Script

Let's practice what we've learned by putting it all together.

Use the scenarios from Supplement 2.3 and, in your own words, lead students in a discussion on the talking points listed below.

Sample Script

Let's go back to the practice examples we used a few minutes ago and I'll ask you some questions to practice what we've learned.
- *What is/are the emotion(s) you had?*
- *Does the emotion feel comfortable, uncomfortable, or both?*

- *Thinking about your emotions as if they were on a thermometer, how intense did the emotions feel?*
- *What is the emotion telling you about yourself? (e.g., Some emotions I enjoy, others I don't; I feel it a lot or a little.)*
- *What is the emotion telling you about your situation? (e.g., I like/don't like it; Other people get upset when I feel that way; I feel like I want to flee/fight/freeze.)*
- *Twist: If you were in a different situation, would you feel differently? For example, does it matter if you are alone or with other people? Would you have a different feeling if you were with friends, a teacher, or a parent? Would your feeling be more intense or less intense?*

Closure

🕐 2 MINS. Close the lesson using a short breathing activity and a reflection on the lesson content.

Sample Script

Let's take a moment to regroup. Close your eyes and rest your hands in your lap. Feel your feet on the floor. Relax the muscles in your body and face. Relax and soften your stomach muscles. Counting to 3, take a deep breath in slowly. Inhale the air down into your lungs. Feel your chest and stomach expand like a balloon. [Pause.] *Now, exhale counting to 4. Feel your chest and stomach collapse as all the air exits your body.* [Pause.] *Again, inhale deep into your lungs so that your stomach expands* [Pause.] *and exhale.* [Pause.] *Take a moment to think about something you learned today that was important to you or you really liked.* [Note to instructor: Pause for a moment to allow time for reflection.] *Counting to 3, take one more deep breath in slowly* [Pause.] *and exhale counting to 4.* [Pause.]

Tips for Transfer Training and Homework

Use the ideas and activities in the following section to practice this lesson's content with your students at other times during the day. Also remember to precorrect, remind, and reinforce concepts from this lesson in activities throughout the school week and to encourage students to use the skills taught in this lesson across settings including home, the bus, and the cafeteria.

Additional Activities

- Here are some suggested books:

  The Way I Feel by Janan Cain

  Feelings to Share from A to Z by Todd Snow and Peggy Snow

  Understanding Myself: A Kid's Guide to Intense Emotions and Strong Feelings by Mary C. Lamia

- During class content that includes literature, history, or current events, infuse a discussion regarding the emotions that literary characters, historical figures, or modern-day individuals may have experienced. Ask students to identify whether the author described the emotions as having physical feelings, whether the reader could guess the intensity of the emotion, and whether the emotions were experienced as comfortable, uncomfortable, or both.

- Ask students to participate in a brief journaling activity. Use the Homework activity as a guide.

Homework Handout

 Pass out Supplement 2.5, Identifying and Measuring My Emotions. Students are asked to identify situations in which they feel certain emotions, describe the physical sensations that gave them clues, and estimate the intensity of the emotion.

Picture of a Roller Coaster

Key Terms and Definitions

Emotion

A feeling that acts like a signal, an emotion gives us information about our situation and ourselves.

Examples: Sad, happy, worried, excited, embarrassed, angry

Physical feelings

We can have physical feelings when we have an emotion.

Example: If I feel worried, I might feel shaky or my head or stomach might hurt.

Comfortable

Comfortable feels good or not bad. You might feel like you want to hold on to the feeling.

Example: Sitting in my favorite chair feels comfortable.

Uncomfortable

Uncomfortable feels not good or even bad. You might feel like you want to get rid of the feeling.

Example: Sitting on a bunch of rocks feels uncomfortable.

Emotional intensity

This is how much or how little of an emotion we feel.

Example: Sometimes we feel a little bit of an emotion, sometimes a lot, and sometimes in between.

71

Practice Scenarios

Scenario 1: A classmate said something to you that seemed mean. Your body feels jumpy; you think you might scream or even hit something. You've felt this way before. You wonder if this is a signal to do something about it or stay quiet. You've noticed that this classmate says mean things to other kids, and you watch how these kids react to that classmate.	**Scenario 2:** You just found out someone you know had a bad thing happen to him or her. You think you might cry and you want to be alone. *Twist:* You also notice that other people look sad, too, and you were told that feeling this way is normal.
Scenario 3: You watch a TV show or movie that has some scary parts. You really like the movie, you enjoy being with your friends, and you notice your body feels energized. *Twist:* You also feel your heart beating fast, you feel jumpy inside, and you think about scary things happening in real life.	**Scenario 4:** You are in the cafeteria and someone standing behind you yells really loud. Your body feels startled and you gasp. *Twist:* You turn around and see that another person is doing cartwheels and probably ran into the person who screamed. No one got hurt. Your classmates are laughing.
Scenario 5: You're working on a writing assignment that's due tomorrow. You can't think of what to write, and you don't under-stand the directions. You keep getting up out of your seat or fidgeting. Your thoughts are stuck on how you'd rather be doing some-thing else, and it's hard to focus. You notice some people are writing fast and others are talking to classmates.	**Scenario 6:** Your teacher or coach gives you a compliment such as, "Nice work." Your body feels calm and excited. It's important to you that the teacher/coach noticed how you did. *Twist:* On the other hand, the teacher/coach said this in front of other people and you wonder what they think because they did not get a compliment.

Really comfortable   Really uncomfortable

Merrell's Strong Kids—Grades 3–5: A Social and Emotional Learning Curriculum, Second Edition,
by Dianna Carrizales-Engelmann, Laura L. Feuerborn, Barbara A. Gueldner, and Oanh K. Tran.

Emotions Thermometer

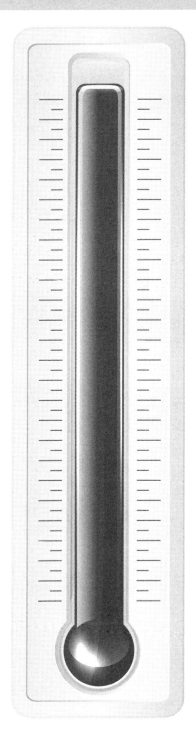

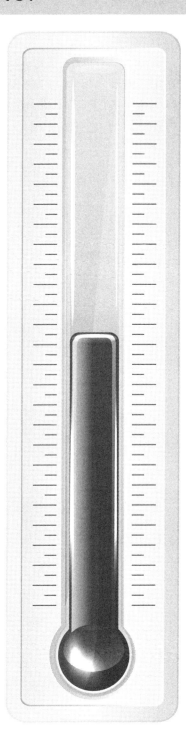

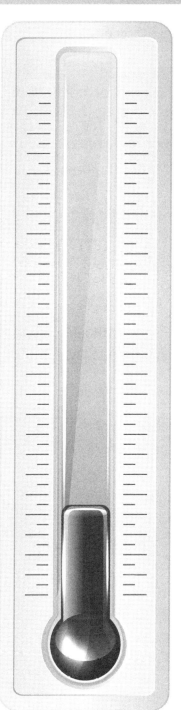

Merrell's Strong Kids—Grades 3–5: A Social and Emotional Learning Curriculum, Second Edition,
by Dianna Carrizales-Engelmann, Laura L. Feuerborn, Barbara A. Gueldner, and Oanh K. Tran.

Identifying and Measuring My Emotions

Name (optional) _____

Directions: Think about situations when you feel emotions. What do you feel in your body? Is the emotion comfortable, uncomfortable, or both? Draw a thermometer on the side of the paper to show how much of the emotion you feel.

I feel afraid when _____.
I can tell because _____.

I feel excited when _____.
I can tell because _____.

I feel frustrated when _____.
I can tell because _____.

I feel sad when _____.
I can tell because _____.

I feel worried when _____.
I can tell because _____.

I feel calm when _____.
I can tell because _____.

I feel really mad when _____.
I can tell because _____.

I feel thankful when _____.
I can tell because _____.

Understanding Your Emotions 2

SEL Competencies Addressed in This Lesson

Responsible decision making

Self-awareness

Relationship skills

Self-management

Social awareness

Teacher Notes

_____

_____

_____

_____

_____

_____

_____

_____

Purpose and Objectives

The purpose of this lesson is to teach students to identify thoughts, emotions, and behaviors; understand the relationships among them; and increase awareness that people have choices in how they think and act, which can promote resilience. In this lesson students will

- Identify thoughts and behaviors that occur with emotions.

- Identify behaviors that communicate emotions in helpful and unhelpful ways and understand that the way we communicate with others may affect our relationships.

- Recognize that the way in which emotions are expressed depends on our backgrounds and the context in which we experience emotions.

Materials Needed

☐ Supplement 3.1 (online download)

☐ Supplements 3.2–3.4 (online download and handout)

☐ Supplement 3.5 (homework handout)

☐ Age-appropriate video clips of different emotions for Activity A

Running Short on Time?

Suggested stopping points: end of Activity B and Closure activity.

Instructor Reflection

Emotions are connected to physical feelings, as discussed in the last lesson, as well as thoughts and behaviors or actions. For example, if you find yourself thinking, "I'll never get everything done" (thought) and rushing to complete tasks or procrastinating (behavior/action), you might suspect that you are feeling "overwhelmed" (emotion). You might also notice that you are experiencing fatigue or a headache (physical feelings). To prepare for this lesson, reflect on particular thoughts and behaviors and how these may be connected to emotions and the physical feelings that may accompany them. What did you feel like doing during these times? What did you do to express the emotion and cope with it? Consider the emotions that feel difficult or particularly uncomfortable. Do you tend to hold your emotions inside or let them out? How do you do this? Under what circumstances would you express the emotions in one way in one situation and in another way in a different situation? Often, this exercise is best done in the moment—write down your experiences so you can relate to these ideas and your students' responses.

Review

⏱ 2–3 MINS. Review the ideas (listed below) that were discussed in Lesson 2: Understanding Your Emotions 1.

- Physiological feelings are associated with emotions.

- Emotions can be experienced as comfortable, uncomfortable, in between, or both.

- It is to be expected that we will feel uncomfortable at times, and that is okay; paying attention to this can help us learn and make us stronger.

- Emotional intensity can be thought of like temperature to help us understand the strength of our feelings.

Sample Script

During our last meeting, we learned that our bodies experience all kinds of feelings when we have emotions. Sometimes we feel comfortable, uncomfortable, in between, or both. We also learned that we can measure how intense emotions feel by using a thermometer to show how much or how little of the emotion we feel.

Introduction

⏱ 2–3 MINS. Using Supplement 3.1, introduce the lesson, which focuses on how our emotions can be linked with our thoughts and behaviors. Then, lead students in a focusing activity.

Sample Script

Today we're going to talk about how we have thoughts and behaviors when we feel emotions. This picture shows how they all go together. We have choices in how we think and act when we feel emotions, especially when we feel them intensely, like when we feel really angry, worried, or upset. Understanding how these go together will help us act respectfully to ourselves and others, no matter what we are feeling.

Mindfulness-Based Focusing Activity

🕐 2 MINS.   **Sample Script**

Let's begin with an activity to settle our bodies and practice focusing our minds. Close your eyes or look at a point in front of you on the floor or on your desk. Rest your hands comfortably on your desk or in your lap. Feel your feet on the floor or your hands as they rest. First, pay attention to your breathing for three breaths. [Pause.] Today we will focus on the emotions we are experiencing this very moment. Maybe you feel excited, worried, sad, awkward, or calm. Any emotion is okay and normal to experience. We can sometimes find clues to emotions in our bodies—maybe in our stomachs, our shoulders, or even our jaws. When you notice an emotion, you can say, "Hello, worry" or "Hello, happiness" and pay attention to what it feels like. You can put your hand over your heart to help you connect with your emotions. Let's take another minute or two to pay attention to the emotions you are feeling. Remember, if you discover your thoughts wandering, simply bring your attention back to noticing your emotions. [Allow students about a minute to practice.] Now, let's take two breaths together. [Pause.] When you finish letting out the second breath, slowly open your eyes. Now that we've observed our emotions, we are ready to move on to our lesson.

Key Terms and Definitions

🕐 5 MINS.   Use Supplement 3.2 as a handout to define the key terms that will be used in this lesson.

Sample Script

Here are some important words or ideas that will help us understand how emotions are linked to our thoughts and behaviors. We'll define the words and discuss examples to understand what they mean.

Thoughts Are Linked with Emotions

🕐 10–15 MINS.   Use Supplement 3.3 as a handout to teach how identifying thoughts can be helpful to understanding emotions. Use the two examples listed below to teach the concepts. For Activity A, use Supplements 3.3 and 3.4. Instead of Supplement 3.4, you may opt to use age appropriate video clips that show people or animated characters showing emotional experiences.

Sample Script

Did you know we often have thoughts that happen at the same time we have emotions, or before or after we have emotions? Identifying our thoughts can be helpful in understanding our emotions. For example, has anyone ever cut in line in front of you? You might have thought to yourself, "Hey! They're not supposed to do that! It's not fair and I'm not sure what to do." Those thoughts might help you figure out that you are feeling irritated, confused, and mad.

Example 1: Use the first cartoon in Supplement 3.3 to illustrate thoughts occurring with emotions.

Sample Script

This cartoon shows a person having thoughts, which are written in the thought bubble overhead. Raise your hand and tell me what the person is thinking. What emotion do you think the person is having based on what he or she is thinking?

Example 2: Use the blank cartoon in Supplement 3.3, write in the "thoughts," ask students to guess at possible emotions the person is experiencing, and draw facial expressions to correspond to the emotion(s).

Sample Script

Let's try another example. Let's pretend that I think I have to do something perfectly and can't make a mistake. I might be thinking, "I'm not sure I can do that." Or, "That looks too hard. If I can't do it right the first time, why even try?" Or, "What if I raise my hand and I have the wrong answer?" Or, "Maybe people are going to laugh at me." You might say these things to yourself or aloud. What emotion or emotions do you think you're feeling? [Possible responses: worried, discouraged, stuck, upset.]

Activity A: Identifying Thoughts and Emotions

 ⏱ 5–10 MINS. Use Supplements 3.3 and 3.4 as handouts. Instead of Supplement 3.4, you can ask students to generate their own example or use age-appropriate video clips that show people or animated characters showing emotional experiences. You might find videos online or in movies/TV shows. Ensure that the content is appropriate for students' ages. Choose *one* activity below to give students an opportunity to practice identifying thoughts associated with emotions.

Sample Script

Let's practice identifying our thoughts and emotions with more examples.

1. Students break into pairs or small groups. Students can use the blank cartoon from Supplement 3.3 or draw their own cartoon. Use Supplement 3.4 as examples or ask students to generate their own examples. Ask students to imagine and generate ideas regarding the thoughts and emotions the person may be experiencing. Instruct students to write words in the bubble that reflect what the person may be thinking.

2. Using brief video clips that show people or characters displaying various emotional behaviors that are appropriate to this age group, instruct students

to imagine and generate ideas regarding the thoughts and emotions the character(s) may be experiencing. Students may also role play the thoughts that they guess the characters are having.

Behaviors and Actions Can Communicate Emotions

⏻ 5-10 MINS. Behaviors or actions can tell us or other people that we are experiencing an emotion.

Sample Script

Sometimes our behaviors or actions tell us or other people that we are experiencing an emotion. For example, if you feel frustrated, you might let out a "Grrr!" or say "I can't do this!" Sometimes, it's obvious what we're feeling by what we say. Other times, our body language shows how we're feeling. For example, if you suddenly get quiet or stay very still, you might be feeling cautious or afraid. If you get out of your seat a lot and sigh really loud [Ugh!], you might be bored. If you're talking a lot and jumping around, you might be feeling really excited about something!

Activity B: Identifying Behaviors and Emotions

⏻ 4-9 MINS. Use Supplement 3.4 as a handout, students' own examples, or the video clips you used in Activity A. For continuity, it is recommended to use the same examples that were used in Activity A. Choose *one* of the following activities to demonstrate the ways in which words and body language communicate emotion.

Sample Script

Now, we'll practice identifying the behaviors or actions that go along with our emotions. You'll use the same examples from the last activity. We're going to use these examples and describe or act out any words, behaviors, or body language that the person in the example used to show his or her emotions. Then, we will talk about or act out the behaviors you might use to show those same emotions if you were in that situation.

1. Have students break into the same groups as in Activity A. Use the Supplement 3.3 handout or other examples the students generated from Activity A. For each scenario, instruct students to 1) describe or act out the words, behaviors, or actions the person may be experiencing and associating with the emotions and thoughts in the scenario, and 2) describe or act out the behaviors the students would personally show to communicate the emotions if they were in that situation.

2. Using the video clips from the last activity, ask students 1) to identify the verbal and nonverbal language that conveys the emotion(s) (e.g., the words the person uses, the person's activity level, facial expressions, tone of voice), and 2) to describe or act out the behaviors they would personally show to communicate that emotion.

Expressing Emotions with Helpful and Unhelpful Behaviors

⏱ **5–10 MINS.** Emotions can be expressed in a variety of ways. Some ways of expressing emotion can be helpful to the situation and everyone involved, whereas others can be hurtful.

Sample Script

Have you ever been in a situation where someone yelled at you, gave you the "silent treatment" by ignoring you, or said something that really hurt your feelings? Or maybe you showed one of these behaviors to someone else. Sometimes, we show emotions by saying or doing something that is hurtful to other people and to ourselves. There are a few times when it may be okay to yell at someone. Maybe your parents or teachers have talked to you about "stranger danger." But in most cases it's important to figure out what to do with an intense emotion. We want to have good relationships with other people and we also want to respect ourselves. Some behaviors can be helpful, or respectful, to others and ourselves. Other behaviors may be unhelpful or disrespectful.

Activity C: Identifying Helpful and Responsible Actions

⏱ **4–9 MINS.** Use Supplement 3.4 as a handout, students' examples, or the video clips you used in Activity A. For continuity, it is recommended to use the same examples that were used in Activity A. Choose *one* of the following activities below to demonstrate the ways in which verbal and nonverbal behaviors communicate emotion. For the activity chosen, ask students to imagine and identify 1) whether the behaviors were helpful or unhelpful and respectful or disrespectful to others and/or themselves and the reasons why, and 2) what could have been done differently to be helpful or respectful and communicate what was wanted or needed.

Sample Script

Now let's practice figuring out whether behaviors and actions are helpful or unhelpful, respectful or disrespectful. We'll also talk about what could have been done differently to be helpful and respectful.

1. Use the scenarios from Supplement 3.3 or students' examples.

2. Use the scenarios from the video clips.

Responding to Emotions to Match the Situation

⏱ **5–10 MINS.** The ways we show emotions can be affected by where we are, who we are with, and what we want or need to get out of a situation. How we show emotions can also be affected by the way we are raised and our cultural norms.

Sample Script

The ways we show how we're feeling often depend on where we are and who we're with. Take, for example, feeling sad. If you're at home with someone you trust and you feel sad about something, you might cry or talk about what's making you feel sad. But if you're in the lunchroom with lots of people, you might try hard to not cry and you might keep your thoughts and feelings to yourself. You may not feel comfortable with other people seeing you cry. Also, different families express emotions differently—some families talk about their feelings a lot, and others don't. How you express your emotions often depends on how your family expresses their emotions. It also can depend on what you want in a situation or what is best for you or other people.

Activity D: Responding to Emotions to Match the Situation

 4–9 MINS. Use Supplement 3.4 as a handout, students' own examples, or the video clips or advertisements you used in Activity A. For continuity, it is recommended to use the same examples that were used in Activity A. Choose *one* of the following activities. Ask students to consider how they might express themselves 1) if they were at home, in the classroom, on the playground, in a restaurant, and/or in other environments that are applicable to the group; and 2) if they were with friends, teachers, or their families. Also ask students for reasons why they would act the way they would, depending on the situation or who they are with. What do they want or need to get in each situation (e.g., to be heard, to be respectful, to hear what others are saying or doing first)? Please note that different cultures have different norms and expectations for expressing emotion. It may be beneficial to discuss these differences with your students. Please refer to Chapter 2 for additional guidance and information on this topic.

Sample Script

Now we'll think about the ways we express ourselves, depending on where we are, who we're with, and what we want in the situation.

1. Use the scenarios from Supplement 3.4 or students' examples.

2. Use the scenarios from the video clips.

Putting It All Together

🕐 5 MINS. Use the following activity to practice the concepts discussed in this lesson.

Sample Script

Let's practice what we've learned by putting it all together.

Choose one or more examples that were discussed with which students might need a little extra practice or review. Ask students to discuss the talking points listed below.

Sample Script

Let's go back to the practice examples we used a few minutes ago and I'll ask you some questions to practice what we've learned.

- Identify the situation, emotion, thoughts, and behaviors.

- Guess the physical feeling the person may have been experiencing.

- Evaluate whether the behaviors were helpful or unhelpful to the individual or in their relationship with another person.

- Discuss how the person may have considered contextual or cultural norms.

Closure

⏱ 2 MINS.   Close the lesson using a short breathing activity and a reflection on the lesson content.

Sample Script

Let's take a moment to regroup. Close your eyes and rest your hands in your lap. Feel your feet on the floor. Relax the muscles in your body and face. Relax and soften your stomach muscles. Counting to 3, take a deep breath in slowly. Inhale the air down into your lungs. Feel your chest and stomach expand like a balloon. [Pause.] *Now, exhale, counting to 4. Feel your chest and stomach collapse as all the air exits your body.* [Pause.] *Again, inhale deep into your lungs so that your stomach expands* [Pause.] *and exhale.* [Pause.] *Take a moment to think about something you learned today that was important to you or you really liked.* [Note to instructor: pause for a moment to allow time for reflection.] *Counting to 3, take one more deep breath in slowly* [Pause.] *and exhale counting to 4.* [Pause.]

Tips for Transfer Training and Homework

Use the ideas and activities in the following section to practice this lesson's content with your students at other times during the day. Also remember to precorrect, remind, and reinforce concepts from this lesson in activities throughout the school week and to encourage students to use the skills taught in this lesson across settings including home, the bus, and the cafeteria.

Additional Activities

- During the day you will notice students responding to their emotions in helpful and unhelpful ways. Provide specific praise when you notice helpful responses. Encourage students to "try again" when their behaviors appear unhelpful. When you notice students engaging in unhelpful behaviors, ask them, "What do you think you are feeling?" "How can you tell?" and "What thoughts are you having?" Then, brainstorm alternative behaviors or actions that are helpful and respectful.

- Encourage students to use their journals to record their thoughts, their feelings, and their behaviors. Students can reflect on whether their behaviors were helpful or unhelpful and consider whether they would have made different choices in their behavior.

- During class content that includes literature, history, or current events, infuse a discussion about the emotional experiences, thoughts, and actions of literary characters, historical figures, or modern-day individuals. Ask students to speculate what the individuals may have been communicating with their behaviors. Would they have acted differently in another environment, at another time, or with other people? Were their behaviors helpful or unhelpful to themselves and others in the short term or the long term?

Homework Handout

 Pass out Supplement 3.5, Ways of Showing Emotions. Instruct students to evaluate the situations and indicate whether the responses were helpful or unhelpful.

Thoughts, Emotions, and Behaviors

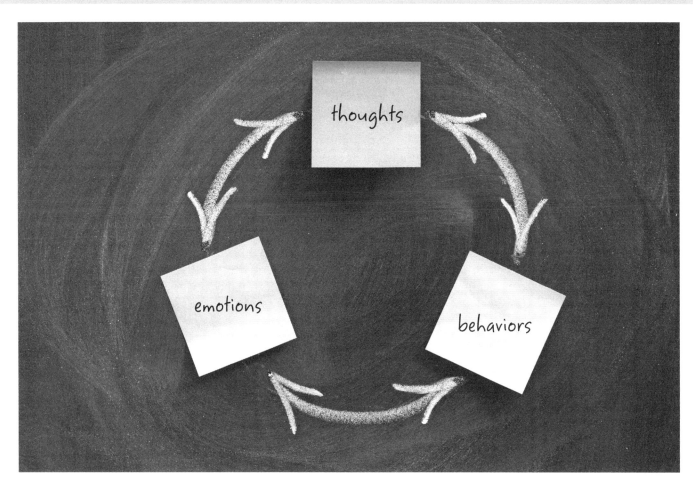

Key Terms and Definitions

Emotion

A feeling that acts like a signal, an emotion gives us information about our situation and ourselves.

Examples: Sad, happy, worried, excited, embarrassed, angry

Thoughts

What we think: We have lots of thoughts during the day. You can have thoughts before, after, or during emotions.

Examples: "I really like ice cream." "I wonder what we're going to learn about next." "I'm feeling frustrated. I can't figure out the math problem!"

Behaviors or actions

What we do or say: We have lots of choices on what we do or say when we feel emotions.

Example: Emma feels annoyed. She can yell, tell someone she feels annoyed, or take deep breaths and let the emotion pass.

Respect/respectful

This is a way of behaving toward yourself or others that shows consideration, thoughtfulness, and courtesy.

Example: Jason's father asks him to take out the trash. He really doesn't want to. Jason decides to finish this chore right away. He knows how busy his dad is with working and taking care of the house, and Jason knows that this small chore will help his family.

Disrespect/disrespectful

This is a way of behaving that shows a lack of courtesy or consideration to others or ourselves.

Example: Lakota makes plans to sit with Maylee at lunch. When she gets her food, she ignores Maylee and sits with Sherrie instead. Maylee is sitting alone and looks confused and sad.

Cartoon Example

Practice Situations

Situation 1: You find out that one of your classmates has been saying things about you that are untrue.

Situation 2: You believe you haven't been invited to a classmate's birthday party.

Situation 3: You are the goalkeeper for your soccer team. During the last 2 minutes of the game, a ball slips by you and the other team scores to win the game.

Situation 4: You lent an electronic gaming device to your friend. When you got it back, you noticed a game wasn't working right.

Situation 5: You don't want your mom or dad to see your report card because of some poor grades you received.

Situation 6: You are looking forward to going to your favorite restaurant on Friday night. When you get home, you find out you're not going.

Ways of Showing Emotions

Name (optional) _____

Read each sentence and decide whether the student's response was helpful or unhelpful.

😊 This is a helpful or respectful way to show emotions.

🙁 This is an unhelpful or hurtful way to show emotions.

_____1.   A student feels frustrated, stops, counts to 10, and then feels calm.

_____2.   A student feels angry and yells at the person next to her.

_____3.   A student feels scared and upset, takes a deep breath, and walks away from the upsetting situation.

_____4.   A student feels annoyed, takes a deep breath, and then bangs his fist on his desk, hurting his hand.

_____5.   A student is aware that she is worried and she refuses to talk to her friends.

_____6.   A student realizes she is feeling worried and talks to the teacher about the situation.

LESSON 4

Understanding Other People's Emotions

SEL Competencies Addressed in This Lesson

Teacher Notes

_____

_____

_____

_____

_____

_____

_____

_____

Purpose and Objectives

This lesson teaches students to cultivate empathy by identifying with and considering others' emotions. In this lesson, students will

- Use context to consider how someone else may be feeling

- Practice taking the perspective of others

- Use scenarios to practice empathy

Materials Needed

☐ Videos of people experiencing an emotion (optional)

☐ Photocopy of volunteer script for the skit in Activity C

☐ Supplements 4.1–4.3 (online download and handout)

☐ Supplement 4.4 (homework handout)

Running Short on Time?

Suggested stopping points: end of Activity B and Closure activity.

Instructor Reflection

Understanding other people's feelings can be difficult. With current technology providing an easy alternative to human interaction, there are lots of ways to avoid interacting with people and lots more mistakes that can be made when you do! Have you ever had an interaction with another person in which you were not certain exactly how to read his or her emotion and/or how to react as a result? How did you find out what he or she was feeling? Once you knew, did you know what to do to support this person in a way that felt right for both of you? What about the other way around? Have you ever found yourself in a situation in which you were in need of support but the person you turned to was unable to provide a supportive voice when you needed one? Think about times you were successful in supporting a friend through a crisis (or when you were supported) and how the interaction played out. Use those experiences as you support your students while keeping in mind that in the 21st century, interactions can occur across a variety of platforms.

Review

🕐 2–3 MINS. Review the ideas (listed below) that were discussed in Lesson 3: Understanding Your Emotions 2.

- Communicating emotions in helpful ways

- Different people show emotions in different ways and in different situations.

- Thoughts and behaviors are linked to emotions, and vice versa.

Sample Script

During our last meeting, we talked about different ways of showing emotions—some helpful and some not so helpful. We talked about how different people can show emotions in different ways and that where you are, or who you are with, might change the way you choose to show your emotions. We also said that thoughts can affect how you feel. Well, today we are going to think more about what emotion looks like so we can notice when other people are feeling certain emotions. This will help us communicate with others in a helpful way.

Introduction

🕐 2–3 MINS. Introduce the lesson. Lead the students in a focusing activity. Introduce the concept of empathy and how it relates to understanding and better identifying other people's emotions in order to support them in some way.

Sample Script

Today, we will learn about a skill called empathy. Empathy is the ability to understand and share in the feelings of another person. We will learn how to notice other people's feelings, how to try to understand other people's feelings better, and how to begin to see a situation from another person's perspective.

Mindfulness-Based Focusing Activity

🕐 2 MINS. **Sample Script**

Before we get started with today's lesson, let's practice settling our bodies and focusing our minds. Like before, close your eyes or look at a point on the floor or on your desk. Rest your hands comfortably on your desk or in your lap. Feel your feet on the floor or your hands as they rest. First, notice the sensations of your breathing as you breathe normally. [Pause for three breaths.] Now just listen. There are all kinds of sounds that we can hear right now. Pay attention to what you hear. Notice what it is and where it's coming from, far and near. Let's listen for a moment. [Allow students about 1 minute.] If your thoughts start to wander, gently bring your attention back to the sounds you hear. Let's practice for another minute. [Allow another minute of practice.] Now, let's take two breaths together. [Pause.] When you finish letting out the second breath, slowly open your eyes. Now that we've listened to the sounds around us, we are ready to move on to our lesson.

Key Terms and Definitions

5 MINS.   Use Supplement 4.1 as a download and handout to define the key terms that will be used in this lesson. Use short video clips or your own examples to illustrate the terms.

Sample Script

Here are some important words or ideas that will help us understand what sort of choices we have when we're attempting to understand other people's emotions. Let's talk about these words a little.

Recognizing Other People's Emotions

18 MINS.   Emphasize to students that making an effort to understand people's feelings in a given situation will help us improve our relationships.

Sample Script

The first part of empathy is thinking about how someone else might be feeling. Asking is the very best way to really know how someone is feeling, because sometimes people can act and feel differently than you might expect. It's not always a good time to ask someone how they are feeling, so sometimes we might have to look for clues that give us a hint about what they might be feeling.

If we notice clues from things people have told us before, from things they do, or from what we know about the situation they're in, we might be able to guess how someone is feeling. Then, we can try to understand what they might be feeling and provide them with support in some good way.

Note: In working through Activities A and B, use as many examples as necessary for students to master identifying visual cues in others. Identify and discuss the behaviors each individual is showing. Ask, "How can you tell?" or "What clues did you see?" to encourage students to focus on the specific cues they are using to make their identification. *Important:* After each example, praise the student's modeling (e.g., Great work showing us "irritated"). Then ask, "Would anyone show the same emotion in a very different way?"

Activity A: Identifying and Modeling Emotions

🕐 8–10 MINS. Use Supplement 4.2 to identify emotions using visual cues. Ask students to share physical emotions and to watch for clues. Allow all students who want to share emotions to do so, even if it involves emotions that have already been discussed.

Sample Script

Let's think about some emotions we might feel during the day.

Read through each emotion listed in Supplement 4.2, including the terms below the pictures. Ask all students who want to show an emotion to put their hand up. In rapid succession, instruct students to display physical actions that illustrate each emotion. Jump in and assist with your own modeling as needed.

Sample Script

[Point to the face that shows happiness.] *Happy—*[Name a student.] *show me happy.* [Name a student.] *show me sad.*

Call on students until all students who had their hands raised have had a chance, even if it involves repeating emotions.

Sample Script

Now it's my turn. See if you can tell what emotion I'm feeling. [Model *embarrassed* or some other emotion that has not yet been modeled.] *What emotion do you think that was? What kind of things could have happened to me to make me feel that way?*

Discuss potential scenarios that may elicit emotions.

Sample Script

Show me what you would look like if you experienced this [Use your own example or one of the suggestions below.]

- You reached out to hug someone who turned away.
- You won a prize that you weren't expecting.
- Your goldfish died.
- You saw yourself on TV.
- Your friend just pointed out that you have something stuck in your teeth and it's been there since breakfast!
- You found ants all over a treat you had left for later.
- A person in your class got a toy that you have really wanted for a long time.

Activity B: Guessing Emotions

🕐 5–7 MINS. Instruct individual students to choose an emotion without telling their class-mates what they have chosen and to model the body language that reflects that emotion. Ask other students to look for clues to help guess the emotion that is being modeled. Remind students that it's not always easy to figure out people's feelings. Reiterate that not everyone experiences or shows emotions the same way.

Sample Script

Now, I need two volunteers to show a couple more emotions. You can show us an emotion from this list or you can show us a completely different emotion. Don't tell us what the emotion is right away. We are going to guess. We may not get it right, but that's okay. That's why we practice thinking about other people's feelings whenever we can. After we've had a few tries, I would like you to tell us the make-believe reason why you are feeling that emotion.

Taking Someone Else's Perspective

🕒 35 MINS. Students identify physical cues of others and understand someone else's perspective through role playing. A student volunteer will be needed for a role-play demonstration. Allow time to prepare with the volunteer student before presenting this activity.

Sample Script

For this next activity, I need one volunteer to pretend to be a teacher. [Allow for a transparent selection process to get a volunteer for the skit. Step aside briefly to chat with your volunteer about his or her role. Consider conducting this selection and discussion process in the minutes prior to class.]

Activity C: How Does He or She Feel?

🕒 15 MINS. Role-play the following situation. You (the teacher) will pretend to be a student called Emma (if female) or Eli (if male). Choose a student to play the part of the teacher. Identify any other roles that might supplement the scenario for your students. Use physical cues such as frowning, irritated voice, disappointed words, or an annoyed look to demonstrate the physical cues that go with emotions.

Sample Script

Watch as [volunteer student] *and I show you a brief skit about a girl called Emma* [boy called Eli]. *I want you to think about Emma's* [Eli's] *emotions during this skit and see if you can guess how she* [he] *is feeling.* [Volunteer student] *is role-playing the teacher and I will be playing the part of Emma* [Eli]. *Afterward, I'm going to ask you some questions about it.*

THE DAIRY FARM: ROLE PLAY

Emma (Eli) is excited for the field trip to the yogurt factory, but on the day of the trip, the teacher [volunteer student] walks into the classroom and announces that the field trip has been cancelled! Instead, students will watch a video about dairy farms and will be assigned homework over the weekend.

Sample Script (Teacher as Emma/Eli)
[Chatting, laughing, and giggling with the person next to him or her. Feel free to ad lib.] *I cannot wait to go to Butterfield! My sister went last year and she said you get as much frozen yogurt as you want! And they have 15 flavors! I want to sit next to you and Alex. I wish I could just be there right now so we don't even need the bus trip!* [etc.]

Sample Script (Volunteer student acting as a teacher)
[Option: Write an alternate version of this script for the volunteer student ahead of class.] *Class, I'm sorry to say that your field trip to Butterfield Dairy Farm has been canceled. Today, instead of getting on the school bus, you will be watching a very cool video about dairy farms that I think you will like. I'm sending you home with some questions about this video, too, so watch carefully.*

Sample Script (Teacher as Emma/Eli)
Using body language only, react to the teacher's news as Emma/Eli might. Allow the students to discuss your reaction. [Possible body language for Emma/Eli: Look around at the other students, mouth open in an "are you kidding me?!" expression, limp body, transition to furrowed eyebrows, looking back at the teacher, slumping across the desk.]

Next, discuss the following questions with the class:

• What do you think Emma/Eli is feeling?

• What did she/he say or do that led you to that conclusion?

• Why is it important to know someone else's perspective?

• What could you do or say if you were Emma's/Eli's friend?

• Have you ever felt like Emma/Eli?

If you felt disappointed watching this skit, then you were taking Emma's/Eli's perspective. You were feeling empathy.

Activity D: Active Listening and Showing Empathy

🕐 20 MINS. Use Supplement 4.3 as a handout to practice active listening skills. Divide students into three groups.

Note: Stay involved with the groups to assist with organization as necessary. Once each group is organized and ready to present its scenario to the whole class, start by reading each situation out loud to the class and then having the designated individual(s) from the group act out the emotion as they choose. In each situation, encourage discussion around how the students would support that friend. Indicate that action is not always necessary and that "active listening" is sometimes all the situation requires.

Consider enhancing this activity by introducing the "twist" to allow additional interpretations to unfold. Or, if time allows, ask if anyone in the rest of the class would have displayed the same emotion in a different way.

Sample Script

There are two kinds of support we can offer when we're helping someone: sympathy or empathy. In both cases, we can show that we are listening to someone by leaning our body slightly forward and toward the person, by looking at the person's face and giving them our full attention while they are talking, and by nodding occasionally to show that we are hearing them. We can also keep a kind expression on our face and repeat to the person what we heard them say when the time is right. For example, you can say, "You're mad you have homework when you'd rather be hanging out." You can also say things like, "I'm so sorry." But empathy takes sympathy a little further by showing how deeply we understand. Usually, this means that something very similar has happened to you and you really do feel what the person feels when you realize the situation they're in. You could say, "That happened to me once, and it made me so mad." Even if we haven't been in a similar situation, we can still feel and show empathy by looking at the situation the way another person sees it.

Let's practice with some examples. Each of your groups is going to get a different story. I'd like you to choose one person from your group to be the main character, and the rest of you will be acting together as the director to help him or her to act out the emotion the person might have in that situation. The rest of the class is going to guess the emotion and offer support.

After each group shows their depiction, ask the students:

- What do you think the main character is feeling?

- What physical cues led you to that conclusion?

- Why is it important to know someone else's perspective?

- What could you do or say if you were a friend of the main character?

Twists

If appropriate, incorporate the following twists into each situation to add dimension.

Situation 1

- *Twist 1:* How might Maylee be feeling if her friend just got a trampoline in her back yard?

- *Twist 2:* How might Maylee be feeling if this was a project that she had known about for a long time and she hadn't even started yet?

- *Twist 3:* How might Maylee be feeling if she knew that her friend also has to do homework this weekend?

Situation 2

- *Twist 1:* How might Tamika feel if her grandmother just came to live at their house and she brought an older dog of her own?

- *Twist 2:* How might Tamika feel if she had been thinking lately that she really wanted a kitten instead?

Situation 3

- *Twist 1:* How might Lakota feel if there is a prize for best poster, and José is an awesome artist?

- *Twist 2:* How might Lakota feel if José once told him that he (José) is kind of shy?

Putting It All Together

🕐 5 MINS.   Use the following discussion to practice the concepts discussed in this lesson.

Sample Script

Let's practice what we've learned by putting it all together.

Use the following talking points to reemphasize the concepts discussed in this lesson.

Sample Script

Let's think about what we've covered during this lesson.

- What is empathy?

- What can you look for to tell what someone is feeling?

- People may have different emotions and perspectives in a similar situation.

- People may show feelings in different ways.

- People can use information about others' feelings to support them.

Closure

🕐 2 MINS.   Close the lesson using a brief breathing activity and a reflection on the lesson content.

Sample Script

Let's take a moment to regroup. Close your eyes. Feel your feet on the floor. Counting to 3, take a breath in slowly. Inhale [Pause.] *and exhale counting to 4.* [Pause.] *One more time, inhale* [Pause.] *and exhale.* [Pause.] *Take a moment to think about something you talked about today that was important to you and you really liked.* [Note to instructor: Pause for a moment to allow time for reflection.] *Counting to 3, take one more deep breath in slowly* [Pause.] *and exhale counting to 4.* [Pause.]

Tips for Transfer Training and Homework

Use the ideas and activities in the following section to practice this lesson's content with your students at other times during the day. Also remember to precorrect, remind, and reinforce concepts from this lesson in activity throughout the school week.

Additional Activities

- During recess, encourage students to look for students who may need support.

- During moments of sharing during class, encourage other students to listen actively and reflectively and to offer empathetic/supportive statements to the person who has shared something personal.

- Prior to receiving a new student in your group or classroom, encourage existing students to reflect on their first day in a new group and decide on positive and welcoming approaches to share with the new student.

Homework Handout

Pass out the homework handout, Supplement 4.4, Empathy Assignment. Students are asked to respond to questions about times when they could tell how someone was feeling, the cues they noticed, and what they did to help that person. They are asked to think of ways they can understand the feelings of someone who they know is having a hard time right now.

Key Terms and Definitions

Empathy

Empathy is understanding another person's feelings or emotions enough to truly know how he or she feels in an experience. Empathy is different from sympathy.

Example: You may have once lost a pet. When you hear that a friend is sad about losing his or her pet, you choose words that show your friend that the news makes you feel sad too and that you have some insight into how he or she is feeling.

Sympathy

Realizing that another person is having an unpleasant experience and being willing to comfort or assist him or her in some way is showing sympathy.

Example: You may never have lost a pet. When you hear that a friend is sad, you choose your words to let him or her know that you are sorry about the loss.

Perspective/point of view

Feelings and opinions each person has about an experience or during an experience make it unique to that person.

Example: Your friend says that he always used to do his homework with his pet on his lap. You imagine what homework feels like now without his pet.

Social cues

What a person may do or say gives us clues about what he or she may be feeling during an experience or as a listener to an experience.

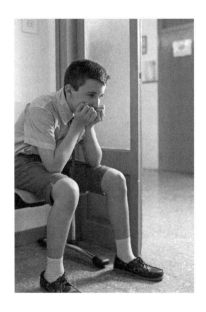

Merrell's Strong Kids—Grades 3–5: A Social and Emotional Learning Curriculum, Second Edition,
by Dianna Carrizales-Engelmann, Laura L. Feuerborn, Barbara A. Gueldner, and Oanh K. Tran.

List of Emotions

Happy

Scared

Bored

Angry

Sad

Surprised

Worried

Excited

Confused

Frustrated

Embarrassed

Joyful

Disgusted

Jealous

Other emotions: apathetic, grieving, dreading, horrified, uneasy, confident, hopeful, shy, annoyed, guilty, proud, inspired, calm, content, awestruck, grateful, relieved, anxious, nervous, vulnerable, ignored, rejected, neglected, ashamed

Small-Group Student Role-Play Scenarios

Situation 1: You are Maylee. Today is Friday. You were supposed to go to your friend's house over the weekend, but instead you have to work on a school project. You would have the whole weekend to play at your friend's house if you didn't have that project due on Monday. You know your parents will make you work on your project and won't let you go to your friend's house. If that project wasn't due on Monday, you could probably go to your friend's house! Act out how you think Maylee might feel.

Situation 2: You are Tamika. At the beginning of the year, your parents told you that if you finished all your homework every week for a whole quarter, you could choose a puppy for your family at break. Today is Friday of your last week and you just got your report to take home that shows that you did finish all of your homework. You know that when you get home you can tell your parents the good news. Act out how you think Tamika might feel.

Situation 3: You are Lakota. You are working with José on a social studies project. The teacher told you to make a poster for your project. You have some great ideas about how to do the poster but noticed that José is already starting on it. You really want your ideas to be included in the poster, but José doesn't say much when you tell him your ideas. Act out how you think Lakota might feel.

Merrell's Strong Kids—Grades 3–5: A Social and Emotional Learning Curriculum, Second Edition,
by Dianna Carrizales-Engelmann, Laura L. Feuerborn, Barbara A. Gueldner, and Oanh K. Tran.

Empathy Assignment

Name (optional) _____

Think of two times when you could tell how someone else was feeling.

1. _____
   _____

2. _____
   _____

How could you tell? (What were the cues that you noticed?)

1. _____
   _____

2. _____
   _____

What did you do, or what could you do to help that person?

1. _____
   _____

2. _____
   _____

Think of someone who you think might be having a hard time now (do not use his or her real name). Think of some ways you can understand this person's feelings using the skills you have learned in this lesson.

1. _____
   _____

2. _____
   _____

LESSON 5

Dealing with Anger

SEL Competencies Addressed in This Lesson

- Responsible decision making
- Self-awareness
- Relationship skills
- Self-management
- Social awareness

Teacher Notes

_____

_____

_____

_____

_____

_____

_____

_____

Purpose and Objectives

This lesson teaches students to understand anger and self-monitor during or before the onset of anger. In this lesson, students will

- List and describe the steps of an anger model

- Develop the ability to name and describe some primary anger management skills

- Apply anger management skills to situations

Materials Needed

☐ Supplement 5.1 (online download and handout)

☐ Supplements 5.2–5.3 (online download)

☐ Supplement 5.4 (online download and handout)

☐ Supplement 5.5 (online download)

☐ Supplement 5.6 (online download and handout)

☐ Supplement 5.7 (homework handout)

☐ Optional: Locate a brief video depicting anger from the point of onset to successful management for the Introduction section

Running Short on Time?

Suggested stopping points: end of Activity D and Closure activity.

Instructor Reflection

Anger takes some management for everyone. Even the calmest of individuals must use strategies to manage his or her encounters with anger, sometimes without even knowing it. In preparation for this lesson, think about your own relationship with anger. Which anger management techniques work well for you, and which don't? Consider how your management techniques vary depending on the situation you are in. Consider the things that made you angry when you were the age your students are now, and how those things have changed with time. As you present today's lesson, keep in mind for yourself and for your students that an important key to managing anger is understanding how anger operates in a general way and for you personally.

Review

🕐 2–3 MINS.   Review the ideas (listed below) that were discussed in Lesson 4: Understanding Other People's Emotions.

- It is important to consider how other people may feel in certain situations.

- One way to consider other people's emotions is by asking them what they are feeling.

- Another way to consider other people's emotions is by looking for clues.

- Not everyone shows emotions in the same way.

Sample Script

Recently, we learned about understanding other people's emotions. We talked about how important it is to consider how other people feel in certain situations. We talked about ways to find out how they feel by asking them or by looking for clues or cues. We also discussed that not everyone shows their emotions in the same way.

Introduction

🕐 2–3 MINS.   Introduce the lesson. Lead students in a focusing activity. If you have any video materials showing the onset and resolution of anger, be ready to show one. *Note:* It is important that any video you show on this topic also does not depict poorly handled anger as overly humorous. *Sesame Street* may have several good examples publicly available online.

Sample Script

Today, we will learn about anger. We will also learn some "anger management" skills so that we have a long list of good choices to choose from the next time we feel ourselves getting angry.

Mindfulness-Based Focusing Activity

⏲ 2 MINS.

Sample Script

Before we get started with today's lesson, let's practice settling our bodies and focusing our minds. Like before, close your eyes or look at a point on the floor or on your desk. Rest your hands comfortably on your desk or in your lap. Today, we will take a few moments to notice what we are feeling in our bodies. First, pay attention to your breath. [Pause.] [Note: The remainder of this script is meant to be read at a slow pace, to allow students time to notice each body part described.] *Now, feel your feet on the floor. Notice how the bottoms of your feet feel. If you can, slowly wiggle your toes three times, noticing what that feels like.*

Key Terms and Definitions

⏲ 5 MINS.   Use Supplement 5.1 as a handout to define the key terms that will be used in this lesson.

Sample Script

Here are some important ideas that we will be discussing. We'll define the words and discuss examples to understand what they mean.

Anger Has a Purpose

⏲ 10 MINS.   Anger is a natural and necessary emotion. Anger signals us to take notice and respond to a situation. Anger can sometimes be a signal to us that there is a problem to solve.

Sample Script

As we've learned so far, our emotions are there for a reason. Just like our eyes and ears, our emotions, like anger, can help us understand more about the situation we're in. Unfortunately, anger is an emotion that can sometimes result in us making choices that don't really help the situation, but anger can sometimes be a signal to us that there is a problem that needs to be solved or a decision that needs to be made. Let's look at some examples of how anger can work to tell us about our experience.

Activity A: Using Anger to Problem-Solve

⏲ 10 MINS.   Use Supplement 5.2 as a handout to discuss the concept of using anger to lead to problem solving. Describe the table and information. Allow students to respond independently or to work in groups to talk about their emotional reaction to each situation. Students should respond to the scenarios provided in the second half of the table by providing their potential reactions, decision-making questions, and possible responses.

Sample Script

Let's look at a couple situations in which some people might get angry. Pretend this really bothers you and try to think about what your very first emotion would be, even before you have decided what to do. Next, tell me what questions you might ask yourself as you try to figure out what to do. Then, let's talk about what you might do. Raise your hand when you have something to say.

Anger Can Be Difficult to Manage

🕐 12 MINS. Convey the idea that anger can sometimes be hard to manage and that for some people unmanaged anger can sometimes lead to aggression or not-so-good choices.

Sample Script

Even though anger is a normal emotion that plays a role in our lives, anger is a very strong emotion and can sometimes be very hard to manage. Sometimes when we are very angry it's hard for our brains to think of good ideas or choices. A lot of those times, if we don't prepare ourselves ahead of time to manage our anger, our angry brain locks out the good ideas that could be helpful to us and only leaves us with a few not-so-good choices to consider. That's why it's important to practice thinking about good choices ahead of time, like we're doing now, so that we have good choices ready when we get really angry. When I say "not-so-good choices," I'm talking about choices that make the situation worse instead of better or that won't solve the problem or make it any better. Can any of you tell me some of the not-so-good choices that we sometimes make, or feel like making, when we're super angry?

Activity B: Analyzing Poor Choices

🕐 10 MINS. Use Supplement 5.3 to discuss some not-so-good choices. For each choice, ask students:

- Why is that choice not so good?

- Can you think of a time when these choices may be appropriate?

Emphasize the notion that students may not be able to realize that it's a not-so-good choice when they're angry.

Note: Consider the possibility that if someone is in real danger, it may be appropriate to make as much noise as possible and to do what is possible to get away. "Imitating, mocking, being rude, and using rude words" may not fit that category, but allow your students the opportunity to come to that conclusion.

Sample Script

Now, we will talk about some examples of not-so-good choices. We will talk about the reasons why the choice is not good and some rare times when the choice might be okay.

Hitting: Can hurt yourself or the other person. Hitting usually gets you into trouble, even if you hadn't been doing anything wrong before.

Screaming: Screaming can disturb other people. Screaming often gets you into trouble, even if you hadn't been doing anything wrong before.

Imitating, mocking, being rude, and using rude words: This hurts other people's feelings and can make things much worse by making other people angry or angrier. Being rude often gets you into trouble, even if you hadn't been doing anything wrong before.

Slamming doors and being rough with things or breaking them: Slamming doors or breaking things can disturb or hurt other people. Slamming doors and breaking things often gets you into trouble, even if you hadn't been doing anything wrong before.

Silent treatment: Sometimes being silent for a while after an angry situation can be helpful because it lets us consider how we could have done things differently. But there are some other times when we get so angry that we are silent because we don't want to talk to someone ever again. This is sometimes called "silent treatment." This is very hard to do if the person you are angry with is a friend, teacher, or family member that you have to talk to eventually.

Understanding Anger

 10 MINS. Engage in a discussion about how anger develops by walking students through a model of anger.

Activity C: Understanding How Anger Develops

 10 MINS. Use Supplement 5.4 as a handout to introduce the concept of how anger develops and Supplement 5.5 to walk through a scenario. As you walk through the scenario in Supplement 5.5, ask students to identify the different parts of the scenario as they relate to the model of how anger develops. Consider dividing your students into groups to think through the consequences of each potential decision/behavior. As an extension to Tamika's second decision or action in the table, ask your students what she should do if her friend admits to telling someone else.

Sample Script

Anger usually has a few steps to it, even though a lot of times the steps get mixed together and you can't see them. [Point to the model in Supplement 5.4.] There's usually a trigger or event, an emotional reaction, a decision about how to behave and an associated action, and then a consequence. We will look at example situations and consider consequences of each behavior. Okay, let's look at the first example of Tamika and how she got angry. [Read through Tamika's scenario. Ask the follow-up questions.]

Developing Anger Management Skills

🕐 15 MINS. Students will think about strategies to manage anger.

Activity D: Making Good Choices

🕐 15 MINS. Use Supplement 5.6 as a handout to introduce skills used to cope with anger and to briefly talk through the strategies that follow with your students.

Sample Script

Now that we've talked a lot about anger—how it works, how it looks, and some of the not-so-good choices—here are several examples of things that you can do to help you deal with your anger. Keep in mind that the way you handle your anger is going to depend a lot on the situation you're in, who you're with, and what you hope to get out of the situation. We handle anger differently when we're in a comfortable or familiar setting than when we're in an uncomfortable or unfamiliar setting. Let's take a look at some strategies here. [Read through the following strategies and allow a discussion of each one.]

Some Good First Choices (anger management strategies) are

- *Ask yourself why you're angry (problem solve): If you ask yourself why you're angry, and really think about your answer, you might figure out a problem you can solve or even uncover some of the sneaky feelings that feel like anger.*

- *Use "if–then" statements to consider the consequences: If–then statements mean that you ask yourself what might happen if you do something. They are best used when you are deciding what to do about a situation or problem. If–then statements help you make better choices by helping you understand the consequences of your actions.*

- *Count up to or down from 10: Sometimes, quietly counting to 10 is something some people do to stop themselves from doing something too quickly. Counting to 10 as soon as you notice you're having an angry reaction can give an angry person just enough think time to make sure their first idea is a good idea. If it's not a good idea, it can be just enough time to change it into a better one (reconsider).*

- *Listen to another person: If you are angry about something or with someone else, talking to someone and listening to their perspective—even the person you're angry with—may help you understand exactly what caused the problem so you can fix it or figure out what you can do in the future to prevent the situation.*

- *Focus on your breathing: Focusing on breathing can help during angry moments in several ways. First, it takes your attention away from the anger for a moment, just like when you count to 10. Second, breathing in a certain way, slowly and deeply (so deeply that your belly moves, too), and in through your nose and out through your mouth, can often help people who are angry to begin to calm down.*

- *Take a walk or step away: Change the environment by taking a walk or stepping away if you can. Just like counting to 10, and thinking about your breathing, walking away from a situation that is making you angry can sometimes help prevent you from reacting to a situation too quickly, or it can give you some time to breathe and think about good choices you can make.*

- *Give yourself some good advice (self-talk): Self-talk means that you say to yourself the things that a good friend would say to calm you down, such as, "Calm down," "Maybe it's not that bad," or "Let it go." It is best used when you first notice that you are angry (emotional reaction stage). Its purpose is to help calm you down. Use self-talk if you notice yourself using any thinking errors (use logic).*

- *Look for the humor—without making fun of someone: Sometimes we get angry for silly reasons that are hard to explain. Maybe you don't even really want to be angry. Sometimes, if there is no danger, you can count to 10 and imagine what it must look like if this whole angry situation was something you were watching in a TV comedy. Sometimes, when you really think about it, some of the things that make us angry can seem really silly. Remember, though, that if you are involved in an angry situation with someone else, they may not think it's funny at the same time you do. It usually works best if you can laugh at yourself.*

Activity E: Applying Anger Management Skills

🕐 10 MINS. Encourage a discussion about *triggers*. Ask your students to volunteer their most frustrating anger triggers and write them down in a list. Then, work together or in groups to develop positive solutions using the anger management strategies they just discussed. Encourage students to use these strategies in real-life situations when the triggers occur.

Sample Script

Can you think of any triggers that make you really angry and have caused you to have an angry outburst in the past? Let's talk about ways we can use the anger management strategies we've learned by talking about a few things that really annoy us. Take a second and then raise your hand if you can tell me about something that serves to trigger your anger. I'll write it on this list and then we can talk about it [in our groups]. [Optional: Some possible triggers to start the discussion could be cutting in line, horseplay that leads to someone dropping something treasured, unfair treatment, unfair serving size.]

Putting It All Together

🕐 5–10 MINS. Use the following activity to practice the concepts discussed in this lesson.

Sample Script

Let's practice what we've learned by putting it all together.

Have students consider the following talking points.

Sample Script

Let's think about some of the things we learned today.

- Is all anger bad?

- Do you think all people experience anger in the same way?

- Once you're very angry, is it easy or difficult to control?

- Why do we sometimes make not-so-good choices when we're angry?

- Do you know anything new about your own anger?

- What are some anger management strategies?

Closure

🕐 2–3 MINS. Close the lesson using a brief breathing activity and a reflection on the lesson content.

Sample Script

Let's take a moment to regroup. Close your eyes. Feel your feet on the floor. Counting to 3, take a breath in slowly. Inhale [Pause.] *and exhale, counting to 4.* [Pause.] *One more time, inhale* [Pause.] *and exhale.* [Pause.] *Take a moment to think about something you learned today that was important to you and you really liked.* [Note to instructor: Pause for a moment to allow time for reflection.] *Counting to 3, take one more deep breath in slowly* [Pause.] *and exhale, counting to 4.* [Pause.]

Tips for Transfer Training and Homework

Use the ideas and activities in the following section to practice this lesson's content with your students at other times during the week. Also remember to precorrect, remind, and reinforce concepts from this lesson whenever possible.

Additional Activities

- Support students who may face some of their triggers (recess, lunch, difficult assignments, physical education) by suggesting anger management strategies whenever possible.

- Post the list of anger management strategies (Supplement 5.6 or another version that you like) in a visible location, and encourage students to think about the consequences associated with their actions.

- Point out positive anger management strategies used by characters in fictional and nonfictional materials during the day.

Homework Handout

Pass out the optional homework handout, Supplement 5.7, Anger Management Worksheet, and explain the instructions. Students are to describe an experience where someone was angry and apply that situation to the anger model. Then, discuss anger management skills that could be used. Students also may find it helpful to use Supplement 5.6 when doing this assignment.

Key Terms and Definitions

Anger

This is a powerful emotion of extreme unhappiness and dislike toward someone or something when you feel threatened or harmed.

Example: I may feel angry when I don't get a chance to play on a certain piece of equipment before it's time to go inside.

Aggression

This is using hurtful words or inappropriate physical behaviors toward people or things.

Examples: Hitting, screaming, breaking things, kicking, slamming doors

Anger management

Having a good set of tools ready before you get angry will help you manage anger.

Example: You choose appropriate behaviors even though you're very angry.

(Emotional) reaction

This is an action or a feeling that comes about as an immediate response to some event. When we talk about feelings, reactions are often the things we do before we've had a chance to think about it. Even if when we think about it we might choose to do the same thing, the emotional reaction is the most immediate response.

Example: When my dad came home from his trip early and came to my school, my first emotion was shock and confusion, but then I was only happy.

What Problem Does
My Anger Want Me to Solve?

Situation where you feel angry	Examples of emotional reactions	Decision-making questions	Possible responses
A friend always seems to interrupt you when you are telling a funny story just at the funniest parts. This has happened several times before.	You want to shout at him using angry words like "Shut up!"	Does he know he does it?	Ask him afterward.
	You want to stop telling the story.	What can I do to try to prevent these interruptions?	Should you shout at him?
	You want to stop telling funny stories while he's around.	What can I do to prevent myself from feeling frustrated when he does?	
	You want to cry.		
Someone peeled your gold star off the good behavior chart.	You want to cry.	How can I make sure the teacher knows?	Let the teacher know.
	You want to accuse someone.		Should you peel off someone else's star?

Here are some more scenarios to think through:

1.   Some people were roughhousing in line and caused you to drop your pudding.

2.   Someone else finished a picture you had started coloring.

3.   Your team came in last because some of your teammates were goofing around.

Merrell's Strong Kids—Grades 3–5: A Social and Emotional Learning Curriculum, Second Edition,
by Dianna Carrizales-Engelmann, Laura L. Feuerborn, Barbara A. Gueldner, and Oanh K. Tran.
113

Not-So-Good First Choices

Hitting

Screaming

Imitating, mocking, being rude, and using rude words

Slamming doors and being rough with things or breaking them

Giving the silent treatment

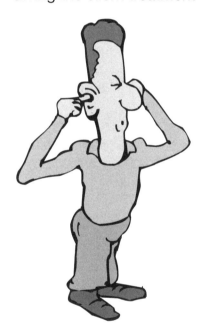

Anger Model

Trigger	Emotional reaction	Decision/action	Consequence
The event or situation that can cause a person to feel a particular emotion like anger	The emotion you have because of the situation; sometimes the emotion you have right away may be different from the emotion you have after you've thought about it.	What you decide to do or say when you realize that a particular situation is making you angry	What happens as a result of what you decided or did

Tamika's Problem

Scenario	Part of anger model?
 Yesterday, Tamika was struggling with a problem that she felt she couldn't talk to anybody about, but her best friend convinced her to tell him and promised he would keep it secret. Tamika just overheard two people talking about it!	
Tamika immediately feels hot in the face. She knows that the only person who could have told them is her best friend. She feels betrayed, embarrassed, and worried about how people will act around her now that they know her problem.	

Decision/action	Consequence
At first, Tamika considers finding her friend and shouting at him to make sure he knows how angry she is.	
After a while, she decides to just find him and ask him if he did tell anyone and why.	

Anger Management Skills and Strategies

Strategy	Description
Notice and acknowledge that you feel anger.	Simply notice what anger feels like in your body. You are a human being and it's normal and expected to feel anger. Tell yourself, "Oh, I'm feeling angry. Okay."
Ask yourself why you're angry (problem solve).	See if you can determine a problem to be solved. See if there are any of the sneaky emotions making you feel angry.
Use if–then statements to consider the consequences.	As you are deciding what to do, ask yourself, "If I do _____, then what will happen?"
Count up to or down from 10.	Quietly count up to or backward from 10 in your mind. This could give you just enough think time to make sure your first idea is a good idea.
Listen to another person.	Listen to someone—either a friend or the person that you're upset with.
Focus on your breathing	Concentrate on breathing in through your nose and out through your mouth so that your tummy moves. Breathing this way can often help people who are angry begin to calm down.
Take a walk or step away.	If it is possible to walk away from a situation that is making you angry, it can sometimes prevent you from reacting too quickly and can give you some time to think clearly about good choices you can make.
Give yourself good advice (self-talk).	Give yourself good advice like "Calm down," "Ignore it," or "Let it go." Use self-talk if you notice yourself using any thinking errors.
Look for the humor.	If there is no danger, picture the situation as a scene in a comedy and see if you can laugh at yourself. Be sure not to make fun of someone else.

Anger Management Worksheet

Name (optional)_____

Directions: Describe a time when you saw someone get angry. Change the names of people if they are people that you know. This could have been from a TV show. Be sure to include each step of the anger model in your description.

Trigger: _____
_____

Emotional reaction: _____
_____

Decision and action: _____
_____

Consequence: _____
_____

Directions: Now that you know more about anger management, tell us what skills this person used to manage his or her anger. If the person didn't handle anger well, what are some skills that could have been used when that person got angry? (You can use Supplement 5.4 as a guide for identifying anger management skills.)

_____

_____

_____

Merrell's Strong Kids—Grades 3–5: A Social and Emotional Learning Curriculum, Second Edition,
by Dianna Carrizales-Engelmann, Laura L. Feuerborn, Barbara A. Gueldner, and Oanh K. Tran.

LESSON 6

Clear Thinking 1

SEL Competencies Addressed in This Lesson

Teacher Notes

_____

_____

_____

_____

_____

_____

_____

_____

Purpose and Objectives

To teach students an awareness and understanding of common thinking traps. In this lesson students will

- Understand the influence of thoughts on emotions and behaviors

- Develop an awareness of their own thoughts

- Identify common thinking traps that affect behavior, thoughts, and emotions

Materials Needed

☐ Supplements 6.1–6.2 (online download)

☐ Supplement 6.3 (online download and handout)

☐ Supplement 6.4–6.5 (online download)

☐ Supplement 6.6–6.7 (online download and handout)

☐ Supplement 6.8 (homework handout)

☐ Optional props (dark glasses, binoculars, and fortune cookie)

☐ Activity C sheet (thermometer image from Lesson 2)

Running Short on Time?

Suggested stopping points: end of Activity B and Closure activity.

Instructor Reflection

This lesson identifies thought patterns that can lead to overly pessimistic thinking and hinder well-being. In this program, these thoughts are called "thinking traps." We all fall victim to thinking traps sometimes. At times, thinking traps help us deal with our situation in the moment or help us feel better about the situation in the short term, without really dealing with the problem or helping us see the reality of it. To help you prepare for this lesson, see if you can identify with some of the thinking traps in this lesson. Have you noticed these thinking traps in your own life? If so, what were the consequences? Did they affect your emotional state, your behaviors, and your interactions with others?

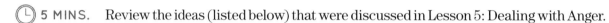

Review

⏱ 5 MINS. Review the ideas (listed below) that were discussed in Lesson 5: Dealing with Anger.

- Anger is a necessary and natural reaction.

- There are some good ways and some not-so-good ways to deal with anger.

- Refer to the steps of the Anger Model.

- There are healthy strategies for expressing anger.

Sample Script

During our last meeting, we talked about ways to deal with your anger—what it looks like, what we do or say when we feel angry, and healthy ways of dealing with anger. We have a lot of choices for how we respond when we feel angry. Not-so-good choices might be unhelpful to ourselves and others, but positive choices can help us feel better. We learned that, a lot of times, it helps to take a moment to think about our angry feelings before we do anything about them.

Introduction

⏱ 5 MINS. Introduce the lesson. Lead students in a focusing activity. Then, show students Supplements 6.1 and 6.2 and discuss how people have emotions, thoughts, and sometimes thinking traps.

Sample Script

Today we're going to learn about the thoughts we have when we experience emotions.

Mindfulness-Based Focusing Activity

⏱ 2–3 MINS. **Sample Script**

Before we get started with today's lesson, let's begin with an activity to settle our bodies and practice focusing our minds. Close your eyes or look at a point

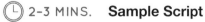

in front of you on the floor or on your desk. Rest your hands comfortably on your desk or in your lap. Feel your feet on the floor or your hands as they rest. First, pay attention to your breathing for three breaths. [Pause.] *During these exercises, you may notice that your mind wanders when you are trying to pay attention to one thing. It's okay and normal that your thoughts wander. For the next minute or two, focus on your breath. When you notice your attention wandering to your thoughts, you can say to yourself, "Oh, I'm thinking," and then bring your attention back to your breath.* [Allow students 1–2 minutes to practice.] *Now, let's take two breaths together.* [Pause.] *When you finish letting out the second breath, slowly open your eyes. Now that we've observed our breathing and thoughts, we are ready to move on to our lesson.*

Show Supplement 6.1 first, followed by Supplement 6.2. This activity illustrates that how we think about a situation affects our emotions and behaviors.

Sample Script

[Show Supplement 6.1.] *How does this make you feel? Does it make you feel scared? Disgusted?* [Then, show Supplement 6.2.] *This woman studies frogs. How might she feel about this picture? So, how I think about frogs affects how I feel and how I act when around them. If I think frogs are cool, I feel excited to see the frog! But, if I think they will hurt me, I feel scared. This is like everything in life! How we think about something affects how we feel about it. Today, we will continue to discuss emotions. We will learn how our thoughts can affect our emotions and how we behave. In this lesson, we'll learn ways to be more aware of our thoughts and identify thoughts that might not be very helpful or healthy for us.*

Key Terms and Definitions

⏱ 5 MINS. Use Supplement 6.3 as a handout to define the key terms that will be used in this lesson.

Sample Script

Here are some important words or ideas that will help us understand how our thoughts are connected to our emotions and behaviors. We'll define the words and discuss examples to understand what they mean.

Thoughts Associated with Emotions

⏱ 10 MINS. Use Supplement 6.4 as a visual aid. Recognizing our thoughts helps us understand our emotions.

Sample Script

When we feel emotions, we have thoughts that go with those emotions. Sometimes, we don't even notice what we are thinking and feeling because it happens so quickly or we get used to certain feelings and thoughts. It's important to pay attention to both our feelings and our thoughts. With practice, we can get really good at noticing our thoughts and feelings. Then we can better understand how they can affect the way we behave. This understanding can help us feel better, make better friendships, and enjoy school more!

Activity A: Thoughts Associated with Emotions

 5–10 MINS. Using Supplement 6.4 as a visual aid, ask for volunteers to share three to five thoughts and emotions. An example is provided in the sample script. To help your students understand this connection, you might share one of the examples from your own life. Using Supplement 6.4, model your thoughts, your self-talk, and your feelings. You can use the board to write down student responses, drawing connections between the thought and the emotion.

Sample Script

Let's take a closer look at this. Think of a time when you were frustrated [or another emotion of your choice]. What kinds of thoughts and self-talk did you have when you realized you were frustrated? I wonder if your thoughts led you to feel more frustrated? Or, maybe your thoughts helped calm you down. Who would like to share another example?

Identifying Thinking Traps

 20 MINS. Use Supplement 6.5 as a visual aid. Sometimes, the way in which we think about a situation is not always accurate and can lead to a thinking trap.

Sample Script

Thinking traps are thoughts that are inaccurate or unrealistic interpretations of events. For example, what if you accidentally tripped on a rock while carrying something important that broke, and then you decided you were clumsy because of that one thing? That would be the thinking trap. Many times, thinking traps can happen when we experience strong emotions, like those toward the top of our emotional thermometer. Thinking traps can make us feel even worse or make the situation worse. They can lead us to feel like this person you see here, stuck in a trap! But if we better understand these thinking traps, we can affect the way we feel about something. We can also change the way we react to something. Today, we will discuss common thinking traps.

Activity B: Identifying Thinking Traps Part 1

 10 MINS. Use Supplement 6.6 as a handout to guide students in a thorough explanation of the common thinking traps. Consider using one of the examples from Activity A to begin the discussion. Provide students with the opportunity to ask questions for each thinking trap.

Sample Script

Sometimes, these thinking traps feel like they happen without us even noticing them—until we're right in the middle, or stuck. But if we practice noticing these traps, we can get better at spotting them early, before we get too stuck. Let's look at the different thinking traps we might fall into from time to time.

Activity C: Identifying Thinking Traps Part 2

 10 MINS.

Use Supplement 6.7 as a handout and the optional props (e.g., dark glasses) to discuss the eight situations. Ask students to identify which thinking trap is being demonstrated by referring to the Common Thinking Traps handout (Supplement 6.6). Read each situation aloud, and encourage students to follow along on the projector. After reading each situation, ask, "Which of the thinking traps is occurring in this story?" If students identify more than one thinking trap, lead them to the best answer, but also explain that we can get stuck in more than one trap at a time. Provide feedback as needed.

Note: If your students are struggling, provide other examples that are directly relevant to them. Or, ask them to come up with examples of their own.

Sample Script

Let's talk more about thinking traps. In your handout, there are example situations and we will identify the thinking trap in each situation. For example, Emma. She made a little mistake in math class. She thought this little mistake was a HUGE deal. Class, what thinking trap is it if I feel like a small mistake is a big problem? [Binocular vision—you may choose to use binoculars.] *But Emma didn't recognize it was a trap, so she was stuck! At the end of the class, she felt like the WHOLE class went HORRIBLY. She ignored the good things that happened. She ignored what she did well! Class, what thinking trap is it if I see only the bad things about something?* [Dark glasses—you may choose to put on dark glasses.] *Yes, Emma got stuck in dark glasses ALL day. As she was getting ready for bed, she thought, "Tomorrow's math class will be horrible, too." Class, what thinking trap is it if I predict something without enough evidence?* [Fortune telling—you may choose to bring out a fortune cookie.]

So you see? If I didn't realize my thoughts were a trap, and I believed them, they could cause me to feel grumpy for days! How do you think the thinking traps of binocular vision, dark glasses, and fortune telling [show props] affected how Emma acted with her friends that day? Her family? How do you think she acted in math class the next day? Ok, let's continue with the other examples.

Putting It All Together

10–15 MINS. Use the following activity to practice the concepts discussed in this lesson.

Sample Script

Let's practice what we've learned by putting it all together.

This activity uses the Supplement 6.8 handout and can be completed in small groups. If using small groups, have each group identify a note taker and a leader; the rest of the members are helpers. The members in the group can take turns being leaders and note takers until everyone has had a chance being a leader and a note taker. The leader identifies a situation in which he or she got stuck in a thinking trap. Leaders can also use situations they saw on television of someone stuck in a thinking trap. For each thinking trap, the helpers ask the leaders the following six questions. The note taker records the answers. You can also use this time to discuss students' observations and experiences of the focusing activity at the beginning of the lesson.

1. What was the situation? What happened?
2. What were your emotions and physical feelings?
3. Was the emotion comfortable, uncomfortable, or both?
4. Where was the emotion on the thermometer?
5. What were your thoughts?
6. What thinking trap were you stuck in?

Closure

🕐 2 MINS.

Sample Script

Close the lesson using a brief breathing activity and a reflection on the lesson content.

Let's take a moment to regroup. Close your eyes and rest your hands in your lap. Feel your feet on the floor. Relax the muscles in your body and face. Relax and soften your stomach muscles. Counting to 3, take a deep breath in slowly. Inhale the air down into your lungs. Feel your chest and stomach expand like a balloon. [Pause.]. Now, exhale counting to 4. Feel your chest and stomach collapse as all the air exits your body. [Pause.] Again, inhale deep into your lungs so that your stomach expands [Pause.] and exhale. [Pause.] Take a moment to think about something you learned today that was important to you or you really liked. [Note to instructor: Pause for a moment to allow time for reflection.] Counting to 3, take one more deep breath in slowly [Pause.] and exhale counting to 4. [Pause.]

Tips for Transfer Training and Homework

Use the ideas and activities in the following section to practice this lesson's content with your students at other times during the day. Also remember to precorrect, remind, and reinforce concepts from this lesson in activities throughout the school week and to encourage students to use the skills taught in this lesson across settings including home, the bus, and the cafeteria.

Additional Activities

- Have students make flash cards with the thinking traps and images on one side and example scenarios on the other side.

- Ask students to be on the lookout for thinking traps in television shows or books they may be interested in.

- Ask students to journal and record their thoughts and self-talk for a day or several days. Ask them to identify patterns and traps. Use the supplements in this lesson as guides.

Homework Handout

Pass out the homework handout, Supplement 6.8, Practice Situations Worksheet, and explain the instructions. Students will list situations where they got caught up in a thinking trap or saw someone on TV get caught in a thought trap. They will identify the thinking trap.

Picture of a Frog

Picture of a Scientist

Key Terms and Definitions

Thoughts

These are ideas or opinions in the mind.

Example: The thoughts we have about something can affect how we feel about it. If I think something will be fun, I am likely to feel more comfortable about it. If I think something will be boring, I may feel uncomfortable about it and avoid it.

Self-talk

The things we say to ourselves, self-talk can be negative, positive, or neutral.

Example: Self-talk can be helpful or encouraging (e.g., "I can do this!") or discouraging (e.g., "I can't do this. I'm going to fail").

Thinking traps

These are thoughts that are an inaccurate or unrealistic interpretations of events.

Example: If you tend to focus on negative things, you might be stuck in the dark glasses thinking trap.

Picture of a Thought Bubble

Picture of a Man Trapped in a Hole

Merrell's Strong Kids—Grades 3–5: A Social and Emotional Learning Curriculum, Second Edition,
by Dianna Carrizales-Engelmann, Laura L. Feuerborn, Barbara A. Gueldner, and Oanh K. Tran.

Common Thinking Traps

Binocular vision

Looking at things in a way that makes them seem bigger or smaller than they really are

Example: I made small a mistake in class, and I think it is a much larger mistake than it actually is.

Black-and-white thinking

Looking at things in only extreme or opposite ways (e.g., thinking of things as being good or bad, never or always, all or none, friend or enemy)

Example: You had one fight with your good friend. Now you think, "We always fight. She hates me."

Dark glasses

Thinking about only the negative parts of things

Example: Your parents met with your teacher. Your teacher said many good things about you. She also said your writing needs improvement. Now, you think all the comments were bad.

Fortune telling

Making predictions about what will happen in the future without enough evidence

Example: You don't want to try out for the basketball team because you predict you will not make the team.

(continued)

Common Thinking Traps *(continued)*

Making it personal

Blaming yourself for things that are not your fault or thinking things are about you when they are not

Example: Your friend was quiet at lunch because she had had a fight with her mother that morning. You think it's because she is mad at you.

Blame game

Blaming others for things that are your responsibility

Example: You didn't follow the rules, and your teacher would not allow you to continue playing the game. You think it's your teacher's fault because she doesn't like you.

All alone

Thinking you have problems that no one else understands

Example: You give a report in front of the class, and you are so nervous you shake. You feel like you are weird. You think no one else gets nervous in front of people like that.

Broad brush

Judging something based on one experience with it

Example: You have eaten one green food and did not like it. Now, you think ALL green foods are terrible.

Example Situations

1. Jason's parents are getting a divorce. He thinks that this is all his fault because he has been getting into trouble lately.

2. Maylee's teacher suggested that she run for class president. She decided not to run because she knew that no one would vote for her.

3. Tamika got a bad grade on her spelling test. Now she thinks that she is the worst student in the class.

4. Lakota's soccer coach gave him a lot of praise and encouragement in soccer practice. As Lakota was leaving practice, the coach mentioned that he should practice his dribbling skills at home. Lakota was upset about how poorly he played at practice.

5. Maylee was grounded for not doing her chores. She thought to herself, "I am always the bad kid. My sister Sherrie is always the good kid."

6. Tamika got in trouble with her parents for taking juice into the living room. Her brother bumped into her and the juice spilled all over the floor and stained the carpet. Her parents told her she had to clean it up because they had told her not to take the juice out of the kitchen. Tamika felt that her brother should be the one to clean it up.

7. Emma lost her favorite pet. She feels like no one else knows what it's like to lose something they care about.

8. Jason met someone from Alabama [or insert neighboring state or province] and he thought the person was rude. Now he thinks everyone from Alabama is rude.

Practice Situations Worksheet

Name (optional) _____

Directions: List four situations where you got stuck in a thinking trap. For each trap, write down the emotion you experienced; if the emotion was comfortable, uncomfortable, or both; where on the thermometer your emotion was; what the thought was; and the name of the thinking trap. You can also use situations you saw on television of someone stuck in a thinking trap.

Situation	What was your (or the person's) emotion?	What did it (might it) feel like? Comfortable, uncomfortable, or both?	Where on the thermometer was your (or the person's) emotion?	What was your (or the person's) thinking?	What type of thinking trap did you (or the person) get stuck in?
1.					
2.					
3.					
4.					

Emotions Thermometer

LESSON 7

Clear Thinking 2

SEL Competencies Addressed in This Lesson

Teacher Notes

_____

_____

_____

_____

_____

_____

_____

Purpose and Objectives

This lesson provides students with the skills to evaluate thought patterns, consider alternative views, and reframe thinking traps. In this lesson, students will

- Develop the ability to notice or observe thoughts

- Discriminate healthy thought patterns that promote resilience from thought patterns that may be less helpful and hinder social and emotional growth

- Learn and apply techniques to reframe thinking traps

Materials Needed

☐ (Optional) Props for thinking traps: Binoculars, dark glasses, and fortune cookies

☐ Ruler or object for measuring purposes

☐ Feelings Thermometer from Lesson 2

☐ Homework assignment or the Putting It All Together activity from Lesson 6

☐ Supplements 7.1–7.2 (online download)

☐ Supplement 7.3 (online download and handout)

☐ Supplement 7.4 (online download)

☐ Supplements 7.5–7.8 (online download and handout)

☐ Supplement 7.9 (homework handout)

Running Short on Time?

Suggested stopping points: end of Activity B and the Closure activity.

Instructor Reflection

The Clear Thinking 2 lesson teaches students to evaluate their thought patterns and reframe thinking traps. Consider the unhealthy or less-than-helpful thought patterns you may have identified from your own life in the previous reflection section. How did they affect your emotional state? Did they gain momentum and get worse? Did you act on them? At the time, did you recognize that the thought pattern was a trap? If so, did you avoid getting ensnared in the thoughts by objectively reframing the thoughts and allowing them to pass by? If not, how might you reframe similar traps in the future?

Review

🕒 5 MINS.   Review the ideas (listed below) that were discussed in Lesson 6: Clear Thinking 1.

- Thinking about our thoughts

- Different thinking traps: binocular vision, dark glasses, black-and-white thinking, fortune telling, making it personal, the blame game, all alone, broad brush. Use Supplement 7.1 to review the thinking traps.

- The connection between our thoughts, our emotions, and our behaviors

Sample Script

During our last meeting, we talked about different thinking traps. By identifying thinking traps, we can keep them from becoming bigger problems that could affect the way we feel and the way we act. Also, avoiding getting caught up in traps can help us think clearly, get out of a bad situation, or make a situation better.

Introduction

🕒 5 MINS.   Introduce the lesson. Lead students in a focusing activity. Using Supplement 7.2, lead students through the introductory script. Consider using or showing the props—binoculars, fortune cookie, and dark glasses—to enhance the introductory discussion.

Sample Script

Today, we are going to continue talking about thinking traps and why it's important to get out of them. Today, we will also talk about how we can figure out when we are in one and how to get out.

Mindfulness-Based Focusing Activity

🕐 2-3 MINS. **Sample Script**

Let's begin with an activity to settle our bodies and practice focusing our minds. Close your eyes or look at a point in front of you on the floor or on your desk. Rest your hands comfortably on your desk or in your lap. Feel your feet on the floor or your hands as they rest. First, pay attention to your breathing for three breaths. [Pause.] Now, turn your attention to your thoughts. Do you notice that you can have a lot of thoughts in a very short time and they can jump all over the place? Thoughts are like clouds in the sky. They change shape all the time. Let's pay attention to our thoughts for a minute or two. Like a scientist watching clouds, notice the thoughts and when they change. Notice if there is a type of thought that keeps coming back. [Allow students 1–2 minutes to practice.] Now, let's take two breaths together. [Pause.] When you finish letting out the second breath, slowly open your eyes. Now that we've paid attention to our thoughts, we are ready to move on to our lesson.

Introduction (Continued)

Sample Script

If we don't realize we've made an error in the way we are thinking about something, our thoughts can keep getting worse and worse as time goes on. One wrong thought can lead us to another wrong thought. This is kind of like a snowball rolling down a hill and collecting more and more snow along the way and getting bigger and bigger as it goes. When this happens, [Show Supplement 7.1.] things can feel worse than they actually are. Remember Emma, who made a mistake in math class and got stuck in the binocular vision thinking trap? [Show binoculars.] She thought this little mistake was a HUGE deal. She didn't recognize she was stuck in this trap, and it made her gloomy all day. She was wearing dark glasses. [Show dark glasses.] At the end of the day, she was stuck in the fortune-telling trap. [Show fortune cookie.] She was so upset that she predicted that the next day would be horrible, too.

One thought can lead to another and another and pretty soon we are REALLY stuck. In today's lesson, we will learn how to avoid getting stuck in thinking traps, how to spot when we are getting caught in a thinking trap, and what to do if we do get caught in a thinking trap. Today, we will learn about different ways of thinking about things. Also, we will learn that just because we think something doesn't mean it's true or that we need to act on it. We could simply identify the thinking trap for what it is—a trap!

Key Terms and Definitions

🕐 5 MINS.   Use Supplement 7.3 to define the key terms that will be used in this lesson.

Sample Script

Here are some important words and ideas that will help us understand ways to see traps and to consider other ways of thinking. We'll define the words and discuss examples to understand what they mean.

Recognizing Thinking Traps

10 MINS. We can recognize thinking traps by evaluating our thoughts and by looking for the evidence that supports or does not support them. Use Supplement 7.4 and the Emotional Thermometer from Lesson 2 to help discuss emotional intensity and evidence.

Sample Script

How do we know when we're stuck in a thinking trap? When we think about our thoughts like we do with our emotional thermometer [Show the emotional thermometer.] *and realize that we are having strong, uncomfortable emotions about a thing or things that haven't happened yet except in our heads, we could be in a trap. Remember how we figured out how to tell how other people might be thinking and feeling by looking for clues? Well, we can be our own thought detectives, too,* [Show Supplement 7.4.] *like the detective in this picture. When we are feeling down, we can use evidence to find out if we are in a thinking trap. Evidence is a clue that helps us find out if something is true or realistic or not. When you look closely for evidence about certain thoughts, you will find that some thoughts are true because they are based on something realistic. For example, you may have worried or anxious thoughts about failing a test.* [Show the emotional thermometer to identify an intense feeling.] *Is it realistic to think you might fail a test if you did not study?* [Yes.] *So, even though you feel uncomfortable, that's not really a trap because your emotions are telling you to study next time, right? But, what about if you have studied everything the teacher told you, for a long time, and prepared thoroughly but still are having thoughts like, "I'm going to fail this test!" Is that a realistic thought?* [Probably not.] *You might be caught in a thinking trap. Can anyone tell me what the trap might be called if we are predicting the future without first looking for good evidence?* [Fortune telling.]

Activity A: Looking for Evidence to Find Thinking Traps

5 MINS. Use Supplement 7.5 as a handout to discuss using evidence to examine our thoughts. Help students understand the process of identifying a thinking trap using evidence to determine if the thought is realistic. Review each situation, asking the following questions:

- What is the thought?
- What is the evidence?
- How do I know that it's true or right?

We think our thoughts are the truth, but sometimes they're just thoughts that we made up from other thoughts.

Sample Script

Let's practice evaluating our thoughts by looking for evidence. Sometimes evidence supports our thoughts, and sometimes it doesn't. That's how we can figure out if we're in a thinking trap.

Using Evidence to Find and Reframe Thinking Traps

🕐 20 MINS. We can use evidence to begin to change how we think about a situation or our emotions. Let your students know that once they find evidence that indicates they may be in a thinking trap, they can begin working to reframe the thoughts. Students will need to find a ruler or an object for measuring purposes.

Sample Script

Did you know we can change the way we think about a situation by using the evidence we found? Remember, just because we have a thought, that doesn't mean it is true! Sometimes, strong emotions like anger can keep us from thinking clearly. Sometimes, we just don't have all the facts.

Activity B: Finding Evidence

🕐 5 MINS. In a large group, use Supplement 7.6 to demonstrate that there may be different ways of looking at the same situation.

Sample Script

Our minds can play tricks on us in lots of different ways and convince us that something is true, even when it's not. For example, look at line (a) and line (b). Which line do you think is longer? [Allow some guesses.] When we first look at these lines, we may think line (a) is longer. But let's examine some evidence. [Use a ruler or small object to measure the lines.] What did you find? Right, they are the same size even though they look different! Sometimes, our thoughts can lead us to believe things that aren't true. If we know this about our thoughts, we can avoid getting too caught up in them when things start to feel uncomfortable. Instead, we can look for evidence to consider different ways of thinking about things.

Remember from our last lesson that Maylee was grounded for not doing her chores? She thought to herself, "I am always the bad kid. My sister Sherrie is always the good kid." How does she know she might be in a trap? [Elicit responses that suggest that the use of words like always or never often lead us into traps like black-and-white thinking.] What can she do? She can look for evidence that shows that she does many things well too. She could also look for evidence that her sister, Sherrie, makes mistakes sometimes, too. "Well, I guess Sherrie makes mistakes just like me." After she sees that she was stuck in a trap, she now sees the trap for what it is and thinks, "No one is always good or bad. In fact, Sherrie and I do a lot of things well, but we both make mistakes, too. I was thinking in black and white." After examining the evidence, and seeing things more clearly, Maylee feels better and can climb out of that trap!

Activity C: Reframing Using Evidence

🕐 5 MINS. Use Supplement 7.7 to guide students through the process of using evidence to consider different perspectives or ways of thinking or reframing. Reframing means looking at things differently or from another perspective. As a result of reframing, you may feel differently about a situation and often can get out of a thinking trap. Read the examples aloud.

Sample Script

Sometimes, when find we are in a trap, the evidence can help us to look at something from a different angle and consider different ways of thinking about things. This is called reframing. Reframing is a way of looking at something differently. Think about the lines we just looked at. The one line just seems bigger because of how it is positioned among the other lines. We can frame things differently in life, too. For example, we could look at a situation that isn't going well as if it is a problem. Or, we could use reframing and see it as a challenge. For example, if I'm told I didn't make the basketball team, I might think about that as a sign that I'm no good and I should give up. Or, I could think about that as a challenge to get better. In fact, some famous basketball players got really good doing just that! It's exciting to think how reframing can give us more power over our own lives. We can choose how to think about things and then how we react to them! Here is how it would look if we wrote it down. In your handout, there are some example situations. Let's take a look. [Show and discuss Supplement 7.7.]

Activity D: Reframing Thinking Traps

10 MINS. Use Supplement 7.8 and the following list of questions to discuss how to use methods of reframing. Encourage students to think about times they were caught in a thinking trap to be used for discussion. If your students are having difficulty providing examples, start the discussion by providing some examples from your own life or examples that are relevant to your students. Once a list of scenarios is generated, facilitate a discussion. Ask the following questions:

1. What was the thought?

2. What clues or evidence did you have that tell you it might be a thinking trap?

3. Was it a thinking trap?

4. What was the thinking trap?

5. What is a different way of thinking about it? How could it be reframed?

Sample Script

Let's practice finding thinking traps by using evidence and reframing our thoughts. Let's use our own examples.

Putting It All Together

15 MINS. Use the following activity to practice the concepts discussed in this lesson. Ask students to take out their homework assignment or the Putting It All Together activity from Lesson 6, and use Supplement 7.8 as a handout. In small groups, students will work to see how identifying thinking traps and reframing can be useful in everyday situations. If there is time, ask for volunteers from the class to role-play some of the examples. Have the students model situations in which thinking traps could be reframed.

Sample Script

Let's practice what we've learned by putting it all together. When should we use evidence to examine our thoughts? We can think about our emotions by using a make-believe thermometer to figure out if we might be in a trap. If our emotions are medium and getting higher, and we feel uncomfortable, it's time to check and see if perhaps we're just caught in a thinking trap. Or, if we are thinking similar thoughts over and over again that make us feel uncomfortable, it could be a trap. Then, we can use clues to start looking at the facts or evidence behind our thoughts. Then, we use our evidence to spot a thinking trap. If we think it is a trap, we can reframe the thought by seeing if there is a different way to think about it or a different explanation for it. We are going to use the activity [or homework] *you did last week when we talked about how to identify thinking traps, This way, we can use our own examples to practice reframing.*

In your small groups, identify a note taker and a lead detective like we did last time. The rest of the members in the group are helpers. Go around your group and take turns being lead detectives and note-takers. The lead detective identifies a situation when he or she got stuck in a thinking trap. The helpers suggest ways to reframe thinking traps. The note-taker records the answers to the questions.

Closure

🕐 2 MINS.   Close the lesson using a brief breathing activity and a reflection on the lesson content.

Sample Script

Let's take a moment to regroup. Close your eyes and rest your hands in your lap. Feel your feet on the floor. Relax the muscles in your body and face. Relax and soften your stomach muscles. Counting to 3, take a deep breath in slowly. Inhale the air down into your lungs Feel your chest and stomach expand like a balloon. [Pause.] *Now, exhale counting to 4. Feel your chest and stomach collapse as all the air exits your body.* [Pause.] *Again, inhale deep into your lungs so that your stomach expands* [Pause.] *and exhale.* [Pause.] *Take a moment to think about something you learned today that was important to you and you really liked.* [Note to instructor: pause for a moment to allow time for reflection.] *Counting to 3, take one more deep breath in slowly* [Pause.] *and exhale counting to 4.* [Pause.]

Tips for Transfer Training and Homework

Use the ideas and activities in the following section to practice this lesson's content with your students at other times during the day. Also remember to precorrect, remind, and reinforce concepts from this lesson in activities throughout the school week and to encourage students to use the skills taught in this lesson across settings including home, the bus, and the cafeteria.

Additional Activities

- Create a class poster (e.g., Mr. Juan's class doesn't get stuck in traps!) with the thinking trap icons and sample scenarios from students' lives.

- Flip that thought! Provide scenarios that students can reframe, such as a difficult situation that is reframed as a challenge. Make a "before" and "after" reframing list. In the discussion, talk about ways our thoughts, feelings, and behaviors might be different in the before and after scenarios.

- Create or modify an existing board game to include using evidence to identify thinking traps, reframing, and avoiding thinking traps (extra moves) and getting caught in thinking traps and allowing them to snowball (losing a turn or moving backward).

Homework Handout

Pass out the homework handout, Supplement 7.9, Reframing Thinking Traps Worksheet. Explain how to fill in the columns. Encourage students to identify at least two events for the chart. Remind the students not to identify to whom they are referring in the homework.

Thinking Traps

Binocular vision

Looking at things in a way that makes them seem bigger or smaller than they really are

Example: You're invited to a beach party. It will be lots of fun but you don't want to have to wear a bathing suit, and that is *all* you can think of.

Black-and-white thinking

Looking at things in only extreme or opposite ways (e.g., thinking of things as being good or bad, never or always, all or none, friend or enemy)

Example: You feel irritated because you think your friend never makes mistakes. You feel like you are always the one who messes up.

Dark glasses

Thinking about only the negative parts of things

Example: You don't like school. When you think about it, all you can think of is the mistakes you make and the problems you have with your teacher.

Fortune telling

Making predictions about what will happen in the future without enough evidence

Example: You failed your writing test. Now you think you will not do well in writing next year.

Making it personal

Blaming yourself for things that are not your fault or making things about you when they are not

Example: If I had stopped the dog and played with it, he wouldn't have been hit by the bicycle.

Blame game

Blaming others for things that are your responsibility

Example: You waited until the night before it was due to tell your parents about a big science project. They couldn't help you get the materials you needed, and you got a bad grade. You're angry with your parents.

All alone

Thinking you have problems that no one else understands

Example: Your parents fight over money sometimes. You think your family is the only one in your class to have arguments over money.

Broad brush

Judging something based on one experience with it

Example: You tried soccer and found it to be difficult. Now you think that you are bad at all sports.

Picture of a Snowball

Key Terms and Definitions

Evidence

Clues that help you find out if something is true or realistic are called evidence.

Example: Evidence can give you information to help you solve a problem. A detective uses evidence to solve a mystery. We can use evidence to help us figure out if our thoughts and self-talk are realistic or true.

Reframing

This is looking at things differently and seeing things from another perspective.

Example: By using reframing, we can change the way we think and feel about things. We can use reframing to see a difficult situation as a challenge rather than a problem.

Picture of Looking for Evidence

Evidence for or Against

Thought	What is the evidence?		Is it realistic?
A	**For?**	**Against?**	
My friend never chooses me when it's time to choose sides for dodge ball. He hates me.	Over the past week, whenever we've played dodge ball, José has not chosen me for his team.	He plays with me at my house. We eat lunch together. He laughs at my jokes. He is really serious about dodge ball. I'm not.	If he hated me, he probably would not want to spend any time with me or even talk to me.
B	**For?**	**Against?**	
I am such an awful dancer. I will never make the dance team. I'm never good at anything.	All of the other students are catching on to the dance steps. I keep falling. I have failed both tryouts.	I cannot predict the future. I can't be good at everything, and there are other things that I am better at.	The team leader has some very specific requirements for someone who makes the team, and, so far, I have not been able to do them. It is reasonable to expect that I might not make the dance team this time around. There are other activities I can join instead.

Looking for Evidence to Reframe

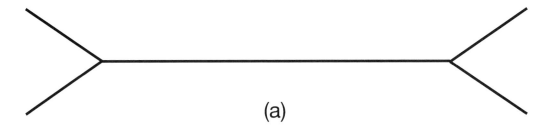

(a)

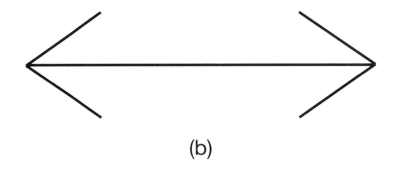

(b)

Reframing Thinking Traps Examples

What was my thought?	What thinking trap did I get stuck in?	What is a more realistic way of thinking about it? (Reframe)
My friend never chooses me when it's time to choose sides for dodge ball. He hates me.	Black-and-white thinking	José probably knows that I don't really like to play dodge ball, so he picks other people who like to play.
I am such an awful dancer. I will never make the dance team.	Fortune telling	If I don't make the dance team, I still have other things I can do.
Everything at home is bad.	Dark glasses	Some things at home seem bad right now, but there are some good things, too.
That fight with my mom was so horrible!	Binocular vision	The fight wasn't really that bad. She just raised her voice.

Reframing Thinking Traps Using Evidence

What was the thought?	What is the evidence (for or against)?	Was there a thinking trap (yes or no)?	What was the thinking trap?	What is a more realistic way of thinking about it? (Reframing)

Reframing Thinking Traps Worksheet

Name (optional) _____

Directions: Identify two situations in your life right now where you might be doing some unhealthy thinking that you would like to change. Use the questions at the top of the chart to
help you identify the thoughts and reframe these thoughts.

What was the thought?	Was there a thinking trap (yes or no)? What is the evidence?	What was the thinking trap?	What is a more realistic way of thinking about it?	How could I approach things differently next time?

LESSON 8

Solving People Problems

SEL Competencies Addressed in This Lesson

Teacher Notes

_____

_____

_____

_____

_____

_____

_____

_____

_____

Purpose and Objectives

This lesson provides students with ways to have healthy, positive relationships with others by making responsible, respectful, and realistic decisions when confronted with a social conflict. In this lesson, students will

- Learn ways to be aware of one's actions and maintain a healthy attitude

- Distinguish between helpful and unhelpful decision-making strategies to resolve conflict

- Identify and apply the steps of a problem-solving model to resolve conflicts

Materials Needed

☐ Supplement 8.1 (online download)

☐ Supplements 8.2–8.4 (online download and handout)

☐ Supplement 8.5 (homework handout)

Running Short on Time?

Suggested stopping points: end of Activity B and the Closure activity. When continuing the lesson, begin with the Mindfulness-Based Focusing Activity found in the Introduction section and the introduction to the four-step problem-solving model.

Instructor Reflection

Disagreements are a natural part of life, so it is important to consider how we handle them. Take a few minutes to reflect on the conflicts you've had with others in the past and the actions you took to try to solve the problem. It may be helpful to write down a few notes to help you process this information. Thinking about your past conflicts, did you act quickly or take your time? Did you listen? Did you use effective communication skills? Did you look for information to better understand the situation? Did you consider a variety of solutions or look at potential results outcomes to various actions? Did you notice an urge to act or retreat from the conflict? How did you feel about your behavior toward the other person? What roadblocks did you have in solving the conflict? Did your actions improve the situation?

Review

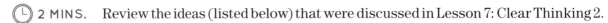

🕒 2 MINS.   Review the ideas (listed below) that were discussed in Lesson 7: Clear Thinking 2.

- Recognizing thought patterns

- Distinguishing healthy thought patterns that promote resilience and thought patterns that may hinder social and emotional growth

- Eight thinking traps (binocular vision, black-and-white thinking, dark glasses, fortune telling, making it personal, blame game, all alone, broad brush)

- Using evidence to reframe thinking traps

Sample Script

During our last meeting, we discussed ways to be more aware of our thought patterns, identify thinking traps, and use evidence to help us consider other ways of looking at our situations.

Introduction

🕒 5–8 MINS. Introduce the lesson. Lead students in a focusing activity. Show students
 Supplement 8.1 as an introductory activity, and discuss what is happening in the picture and how it is important to reflect on how both parties may feel as well as potential solutions.

Sample Script

Today, we will learn about ways to make responsible, respectful, and realistic decisions when confronted with conflict. A conflict is when you and someone else don't agree on something that is important to one or both of you.

Mindfulness-Based Focusing Activity

 2 MINS.

Sample Script

Let's practice settling our bodies and focusing our minds. Close your eyes or look at a point on the floor or on your desk. Rest your hands comfortably. Feel your feet on the floor or your hands as they rest. Notice your breathing for three breaths. [Pause for three breaths.] Now, think about a person who has been nice to you or who you know cares about you. Can you picture this person in your mind? Think about what this person has done for you or said to you that was kind. [Pause.] Notice how you feel when you think of this person. You might feel grateful or thankful that you have him or her in your life. You might feel like smiling. [Pause.] You can think kind thoughts toward this person by saying to yourself, "I am wishing you happiness" or "I am wishing you good health." Use your own words and say them to yourself while you think about the kindness this person showed you. We'll do this for about a minute. [Pause.] Now, let's take two breaths together. [Pause.] When you finish letting out the second breath, slowly open your eyes. We are ready to move on to our lesson.

Introduction (Continued)

 1 MIN.   Show Supplement 8.1 (a picture of two students arguing).

Sample Script

What do you see happening in this picture? Are the kids getting along or finding ways to share? What do you think will be the end result? When we are in a situation in which we are not getting along with another person or can't agree, it's important to stop and think how we're feeling and what we will do to solve the problem. We'll come back to this picture again later. Today, we will learn a skill called problem solving or conflict resolution. This is an important skill to have so that we make respectful and responsible decisions when things aren't going the way we want. It's important that our problem gets resolved in a way that is agreeable and respectful for everyone involved. In this picture, would it be okay if one student grabs the laptop away and gets to use it all by him- or herself?

Key Terms and Definitions

 5 MINS.   Use Supplement 8.2 as a handout to define the key terms that will be used in this lesson.

 Sample Script

Here are some important words or ideas that will help us understand problem solving or conflict resolution. We'll define the words and also discuss examples to understand what they mean.

Maintaining a Responsible and Respectful Attitude During Conflict

🕐 10–12 MINS. Convey that everyone approaches conflict and views situations differently, but it's important that we make responsible decisions and show respect for our self and others in our behaviors.

- Everyone is different. Everyone will not always think, act, or feel the same way as you do in a situation. (Refer back to the lesson on understanding other people's feelings to help deepen understanding.)

- Your attitude can affect how you respond in a disagreement and your ability to be responsible and respectful toward others.

- You can have multiple thoughts and feelings and emotions at varying levels of intensity in a conflict (refer to the volume slider).

Sample Script

Our thoughts, emotions, and attitude are different depending on the conflict we have. This is okay. There isn't just one feeling, thought, or attitude that you have in doing something. However, it is important to be respectful and responsible in how we treat others. Let's think about the picture we saw earlier with the two kids fighting over a laptop. The boy may be thinking something like, "I'm so angry with this girl and I don't want to share the laptop with her. She laughed at me earlier when I tripped while running in PE class. If I push her down, then she will let go of the laptop." The girl may be thinking something like, "I got this laptop first. If he would let go of this laptop, I would suggest that we take turns." Now let's consider if the boy was in a similar situation with another peer who hadn't laughed at him earlier—would he have those same feelings? What if the girl was in a similar situation— would she have ideas on how to solve the problem? Are both kids being respectful or responsible? Do they have a positive attitude that will help in this conflict?

Activity A: Being Respectful, Responsible, and Aware of Our Attitudes in Communication and Listening

🕐 5 MINS. Students will engage in a discussion about activities they enjoy with a partner or small group, while practicing listening skills and asking questions. Model to students ways to listen intently and give praise for sharing, such as, "Thank you for sharing that! It sounds like you really enjoy [activity]." Or "I liked how you showed interest and respect by listening and looking at that person and asking good questions." Encourage students to show respect by offering compliments to those who have shared. Be aware of students' attitudes and physical demonstrations of listening. (*Note:* Consider cultural norms for attentive and active listening.)

Sample Script

Let's explore how we can use communication skills through listening and asking questions. Let's be respectful and responsible while being aware of our attitude in a situation. I'd like us to discuss a topic that we might all have different perspectives on [e.g., what we each like to do in our free time]. Sometimes, when a person really enjoys something, he or she will use words like, "It's the best!" It doesn't mean that he or she is intending to disagree with what you think is the best, but it's just a way of talking or that's the person's perspective on something. Let's see if we can have a conversation about things that we enjoy that are different among us, and practice listening and asking questions like, "What do you like about that activity?" Please get with a partner/small group to share activities and hobbies that you like to do.

A Closer Look at Key Terms and Definitions: Conflict

5 MINS. Use Supplement 8.1 and review the key points listed below. Then, ask students to discuss ways in which they would resolve that conflict.

- Not all conflicts are bad. They can be neutral or good. Conflicts can help us understand how we feel about a situation and that not everyone may feel the same way, which is normal.

- Conflicts are inherent with the human experience, and we can learn from conflicts.

- Conflict does not have to end with a "winner" and a "loser." The aim is to end the conflict with all people feeling respected and reasonably satisfied with the outcome.

- Conflict can range from intensity level depending on the situation, setting, and individuals involved. For example, a student saying something mean can look very different from a conflict with your parents for not doing homework.

Sample Script

Problems are sometimes called conflicts or disagreements. Raise your hand and tell me about a conflict you had recently. Conflicts or disagreements are not necessarily bad. In fact, they can be opportunities to learn about a person's viewpoint or perspective. Disagreements do not have to end with one person winning and one person losing. They can be solved by respecting both people's views, agreeing to disagree, or compromising. Conflict resolution is a way to solve our problems or disagreements one step at a time. For example, think about the picture I showed you earlier about the two kids fighting over a laptop. [Refer to Supplement 8.1.] Let's think about what you would do to resolve this situation if you were that boy or girl.

Twist: Would they have the same conflict or react in the same way if they were in class or if someone got physically hurt in that situation?

Options to Conflict Resolution: What Can I Do?

🕐 5–10 MINS. There are many options to solving conflicts.

Sample Script

There are many ways to resolve conflicts that are respectful, responsible, and realistic in a situation. We've talked about maintaining respect toward another person. It's also important to be realistic and choose a goal or option that is achievable for those involved. We're going to talk about problem-solving strategies in the next activity.

Activity B: Conflict Resolution

🕐 5 MINS.

Use Supplement 8.3 as a handout to discuss different options for conflict resolution. Have students review the list of options in Supplement 8.3 and share and discuss in small groups when these options might be used. You can post the list in your classroom for a visual reminder.

Sample Script

When you are in a social situation that is difficult, you could ask yourself "What are my options?" or "What can I do to resolve this conflict?" Here are some options to keep in mind that can help you. Can anyone share if you've used any of these?

Introduction to the Four-Step Problem-Solving Model

🕐 1 MIN. A problem-solving model is a way to solve disagreements one step at a time. Conflicts are challenging, and using problem-solving strategies requires patience and creativity! Sometimes, thinking traps or not being able to take others' perspectives can be a roadblock to effective problem solving and, as a result, it is more difficult to achieve a workable compromise.

Sample Script

Sometimes, conflicts can seem confusing and impossible to resolve. It's even hard to figure out what the conflict is exactly, and it may make you want to just not deal with it at all or to resort to giving the other person the silent treatment. Ignoring conflicts may seem to work in the moment, but in the long run, the problem is not being dealt with in a healthy way. We will learn how to look at a problem in small steps to help us see the conflict more clearly in order to problem solve in a situation.

Four-Step Problem-Solving Model

🕐 20 MINS. Use Supplement 8.4 as a handout to discuss the steps to problem solving. Remind students that they can reference this table to help them remember the steps.

Sample Script

Did you know there are four steps we can use to solve a problem? We're going to practice using these with different situations. Using the steps will help us come to a good solution. You will also learn about showing empathy and how to compromise when it is appropriate to in social interactions. In situations where you try and nothing is working in the moment, you may sometimes have to smile, be patient, and politely say, "I hear what you are saying. Maybe we can talk about this another time and try again to solve the problem?" Or sometimes, if everyone doesn't know about the four steps to problem solving, it can turn into a bigger argument. Be patient and open minded to different perspectives and strategies. Here are the four steps in the problem-solving model and a visual picture to help you remember.

Activity C: Problem-Solving Application

10 MINS. Use Supplement 8.4 again to apply the four-step problem-solving model to example situations. There are three situations listed below the Sample Script:

Sample Script

Now that we've talked about the steps, let's apply some example situations to these steps. I will read the first situation and we will discuss the steps together as a class. We will write our thoughts in the middle column under Situation 1. For Situation 2, you will partner with the person next to you [or get into small groups], go through the problem-solving model, and write down your ideas in the Situation 2 column.

Situation 1

- Problem: Your classmate wants to use the only class computer at the same time you do.

Twist: You know that your classmate does not have a computer at home, but you do.

Situation 2

- Problem: Your classmate has broken your trust by telling a secret of yours.

Twist: Now would it make a difference if you had already shared it with a few other people?

Situation 3

- Problem: You overheard that your friend said something mean about you that isn't true and your feelings are hurt.

Twist: Your friend will be attending your birthday party this weekend and you know that she has something special planned for you.

Activity D: Discuss Examples and Nonexamples of Problem Solving

10 MINS. Begin with the example problem below to discuss the ways in which a conflict might be solved. Review the six problem-solving scenarios, listed below, to facilitate this discussion, and ask students to evaluate whether the scenario is an example or nonexample of a helpful way to solve a problem. You also may use other current and realistic conflicts that may be particularly

relevant to your students. Remember, the problem-solving skills students just discussed may be inappropriate in some situations (e.g., in a life-threatening situation, a discussion with a potentially dangerous individual may not be appropriate).

Sample Script

Let's discuss examples of problem-solving strategies—what to do and what not to do. First, let's go back to the situation earlier about the two kids fighting over the laptop. [See Supplement 8.1.] I will read aloud some strategies and you tell me if they are examples (healthy) or nonexamples (unhealthy). Examples are the strategies we want to do. Nonexamples are what we don't want to do. Then, I'd like for you to share in small groups your own situations and strategies that you have used in conflicts. Think about situations at school, at home, or in your community.

Example problem: Begin with this situation to illustrate (show Supplement 8.1). Two students want the same laptop. Choose some of the problem-solving strategies listed below (listed as Problem-Solving Scenarios 1–6), and prompt students with this question: "Is this an example of problem solving or a non-example of problem solving?" For the items that are nonexamples of problem solving, ask students how they would use problem-solving skills to resolve the conflict.

Problem-solving scenario 1 (example): The students identify the problem, say what they each want to happen with the laptop, and each list and discuss a few potential solutions. One of the solutions is to equally split the time each uses the laptop. They agree on this solution and shake hands.

Problem-solving scenario 2 (nonexample): The students argue, interrupt each other, and grab the laptop back and forth from each other, and then one student tells the teacher.

Problem-solving scenario 3 (nonexample): The students identify the problem, say what they each want to happen with the laptop, and each list and discuss a few potential solutions. They can't agree on any of the solutions and so they continue to argue with each other. Eventually, they bring other students into the situation.

Problem-solving scenario 4 (nonexample): The students identify the problem, but each student is so interested in describing what they each want to happen with the laptop that they don't really listen to what the other person wants.

Problem-solving scenario 5 (example): The students identify the problem, say what they each want to happen with the laptop, and each list and discuss a few potential solutions. One of the solutions is to agree to use the laptop on different days, and give one another their "word." The students ask each other the next day if this plan still works for them.

Problem-solving scenario 6 (nonexample): The teacher takes the laptop away from both students; the students give each other a dirty look, and both are angry because now they don't get to use the laptop.

Putting It All Together

⏲ **5 MINS.** Use the following activity to practice the concepts discussed in this lesson.

Sample Script

Let's practice what we've learned by putting it all together.

In small groups or as a class, use the following questions to ask students to share the lesson's talking points. You can also use this time to discuss students' observations and experiences of the focusing activity at the beginning of the lesson.

- Provide examples for responsible, respectful, attitude, conflict/problem, communication, resolution, resolve, and problem solving/conflict resolution.

- What are some strategies for dealing with conflict?

- Describe the four-step problem-solving model.

- Why is being responsible, respectful, realistic, taking perspectives, using communication skills, and thinking about choices important to conflict resolution?

Closure

⏲ **2 MINS.** Close the lesson using a brief breathing activity and a reflection on the lesson content.

Sample Script

Let's take a moment to regroup. Close your eyes and rest your hands in your lap. Feel your feet on the floor. Relax the muscles in your body and face. Relax and soften your stomach muscles. Counting to 3, take a deep breath in slowly. Inhale the air down into your lungs. Feel your chest and stomach expand like a balloon. [Pause.] *Now, exhale, counting to 4. Feel your chest and stomach collapse as all the air exits your body.* [Pause.] *Again, inhale deep into your lungs so that your stomach expands* [Pause.] *and exhale.* [Pause.] *Take a moment to think about something you learned today that was important to you and you really liked.* [Note to instructor: Pause for a moment to allow time for reflection.] *Counting to 3, take one more deep breath in slowly* [Pause.] *and exhale, counting to 4.* [Pause.]

Tips for Transfer Training and Homework

Use the ideas and activities in the following section to practice this lesson's content with your students throughout the week to help reinforce the skills. Also remember to precorrect, remind, and reinforce concepts from the lesson in activities throughout the school week and to encourage students to use the skills taught in this lesson across settings including home, the bus, and the cafeteria.

Additional Activities

- Here are some suggested books:

  Emma Gets Along: A Conflict Resolution Story by Deborah Alexander

  Talk and Work it Out by Cheri J. Meiners

  Making Choices and Making Friends: The Social Competencies Assets by Pamela Espeland

- Have students make a list of things they said or did to keep cool during a conflict this week.

- Have students ask family members or neighbors to describe conflicts they've experienced. Discuss how the steps to conflict resolution could have helped.

Homework Handout

Pass out the homework handout, Supplement 8.5, Using a Problem-Solving Model to Resolve Conflicts. Explain to students that they will use the problem-solving model to work through a problem in the past or a current situation and that they will provide a new resolution to the problem.

Picture of Two Students
Fighting Over a Laptop

Merrell's Strong Kids—Grades 3–5: A Social and Emotional Learning Curriculum, Second Edition,
by Dianna Carrizales-Engelmann, Laura L. Feuerborn, Barbara A. Gueldner, and Oanh K. Tran.
Copyright © 2016 by Paul H. Brookes Publishing Co., Inc. All rights reserved.

Key Terms and Definitions

Responsible

This is making good choices, being able to choose right from wrong, and caring for others; and following through with your word or promise.

Example: The students found a wallet with some cash in it. Instead of taking the money or keeping the wallet, they decide to turn it in to the office.

Attitude

This is the way you choose to think about things and how those thoughts are reflected in your behaviors.

Example: Kenji knew he would have to change his attitude working on a group project with a student he does not always get along with.

Conflict

This is a disagreement or something that doesn't match or work well together.

Example: The students had a conflict when they could not agree on how to start the project.

Problem solving/conflict resolution

This is a way of dealing with a problem in a helpful/constructive manner and finding some way to reach an agreement.

Example: The students used conflict resolution to decide who would go first in the game.

Resolution

This is when we (try to) settle the conflict or find a solution.

Example: The students' resolution was to take turns playing the game.

Resolve

This means to reach a decision or find a solution.

Example: The students were able to resolve their disagreement by finding a solution and deciding to try it.

Conflict Resolution: What Can I Do?

Compromise

One or both people agree to give up a little of what they originally wanted but are okay with it in order to resolve the conflict.

Agreement

One person decides that the other person's point of view is relevant and both people can agree to share the same point of view.

Agree to disagree

Both people decide this is something they will likely not agree on and they will accept this fact. Having differing perspectives is okay!

Friendly rivalry/leave it to chance

People decide play a game to resolve the conflict, or they decide to just not do anything and see how things turn out (e.g., game of Connect Four winner gets the toy/object/time on preferred playground equipment or electronic device; flipping a coin).

Seeking guidance from an adult

Adults help to make a decision.

Making a deal

Both people agree to do one thing in exchange for something else (e.g., "If I do this, will you do that?").

A Four-Step Problem-Solving Model for Conflict Resolution

Four-step problem-solving model	Situation 1 example	Situation 2 example
1. **Identify the problem:** What are you arguing about? • Have the other person state his or her wants and feelings. • Describe how you feel. • Read the other person's body language. • Summarize both people's wants and feelings and what they suggest. Is there a disagreement?		
2. **Develop a plan (solutions):** List some of the ways you can solve this problem. Each person should generate at least two solutions. • Is someone willing to compromise? • It is important to be open minded and respectful instead of being spiteful or sarcastic during the brainstorming of ideas step. • Which way seems the most reasonable, responsible, and respectful for those involved?		
3. **Evaluate the plan:** Determine if the plan will work. • What would happen if. . .? • Would it be safe and fair? • How would everyone feel? • Does it work for all involved? • Is it a win–win situation? • Is the plan realistic and will it help make the situation better?		
4. **Implement the plan:** Everyone agrees to try the plan.		

Using a Problem-Solving Model to Resolve Conflicts

Name (optional) _____

Directions: Think of a problem or conflict that you had with a person in the past for which you would have done something differently. How did you handle it? How could you have handled it better? Use the problem-solving steps you learned today and provide a *new ending* to this problem or conflict. Refer to Supplement 8.3 for ideas on alternatives to conflict.

Four-step problem-solving model	Situation
1. **Identify the problem:** What are you arguing about?	
2. **Develop a plan (solutions):** List some of the ways you can solve this problem. Each person should generate at least two solutions.	
3. **Evaluate the plan:** Determine if the plan will work.	
4. **Implement the plan:** Everyone agrees to try the plan.	

Merrell's Strong Kids—Grades 3–5: A Social and Emotional Learning Curriculum, Second Edition,
by Dianna Carrizales-Engelmann, Laura L. Feuerborn, Barbara A. Gueldner, and Oanh K. Tran.
167

LESSON 9

Letting Go of Stress

SEL Competencies Addressed in This Lesson

Purpose and Objectives

This lesson provides students with the skills to understand the different kinds of stress and its effects and ways to proactively cope with stress. In this lesson, students will

- Identify helpful and unhelpful stress and stress triggers

- Understand the effects stress can have on our emotional and physical well-being

- Learn the difference between realistic (achievable) and unrealistic (unachievable) expectations on ourselves that may produce stress

- Learn relaxation and coping techniques to reduce stress

- Learn how to choose helpful ways to manage and release stress

Teacher Notes

_____

_____

_____

_____

_____

_____

_____

_____

Materials Needed

☐ Supplement 9.1 (online download)

☐ Supplements 9.2–9.5 (online download and handout)

☐ Supplement 9.6: Letting Go of Stress (homework handout)

Running Short on Time?

Suggested stopping points: end of Activity B and Closure activity. When continuing the lesson, begin with the Mindfulness-Based Focusing Activity found in the Introduction section and Activity C.

Instructor Reflection

Stress is a normal part of life. It can occur when there are difficulties in our lives; it can also occur when there are good things happening, like a job promotion, a wedding, and travel. How we perceive it and deal with it, the intensity of the stress we experience, and the kinds of expectations that we place on ourselves can all affect stress level. There can be helpful stress that helps and encourages us to work harder or smarter at tasks or there can be unhelpful stress that slows us down and acts as a barrier to accomplishing tasks. When stress occurs, there are positive ways to manage it. What types of stress have you experienced that affected you in a positive way? What types of stress did you find difficult to manage or affected you negatively? Were your expectations for yourself or the situation realistic or unrealistic? Think about what you did to manage your stress. Was it a temporary fix or did it work for you in the long term?

Review

🕐 2–3 MINS. Review the ideas (listed below) that were discussed in Lesson 8: Solving People Problems.

- Importance of being responsible, respectful, realistic, taking perspectives, using communication and listening skills, and thinking about choices in conflict management

- Options for resolving conflict

- The four-step problem-solving model to conflict resolution

- Examples and nonexamples of conflict resolution

Sample Script

During our last meeting, we discussed ways to solve problems during conflicts. We talked about being responsible, respectful, and realistic; taking others' perspectives; and using communication and listening skills during conflict with others. We also talked about ways we can solve problems and make healthy choices in times of conflict. We also discussed the Four-Step Problem-Solving model and examples and nonexamples of conflict resolution.

Introduction

🕐 10 MINS. Using Supplement 9.1, introduce the lesson, which focuses on how emotions and thoughts may be different in each picture and how different situations may evoke different feelings. Then, lead students in a focusing activity.

Sample Script

Today, we will learn about stress and how it differs for everyone. Stress can affect our physical and emotional health, so we will learn to distinguish the kind of stress that can help us from the kind of stress that doesn't help us and can even slow us down. We need to know ways to cope with stress so we can stay healthy and be able to do the things we need to do every day.

Mindfulness-Based Focusing Activity

🕐 2 MINS.

Sample Script

Let's practice settling our bodies and focusing our minds. Close your eyes or look at a point on the floor or on your desk. Rest your hands comfortably. Feel your feet on the floor or your hands as they rest. Pay attention to your breathing for three breaths. [Pause for 3 breaths.] Today's lesson will talk about ways we can take good care of ourselves. One thing we can do is be kind to ourselves. Sometimes we focus on the mistakes we make or we feel like we're not good enough. Just like we thought of kind thoughts to send to a person the last time we met, we can send kind thoughts to ourselves. You might say to yourself, "I am wishing myself happiness." Take a moment to think of something kind to say to yourself and say it silently and with a little smile. We'll do this for about a minute. [Pause for 1 minute.] Now, let's take two breaths together. [Pause.] When you finish letting out the second breath, slowly open your eyes. We are ready to move on to our lesson.

Introduction (Continued)

🕐 8 MINS.

Sample Script

Let's take a look at these pictures. What is happening in each picture? What do you think these students are feeling? Now, look closely. Do you notice anything in common in these pictures? Despite the fact that the students may have different feelings and thoughts, all of the students might be feeling stress. Stress is the way your body gets you ready to face challenges with attention, energy, and strength. When you feel you can cope, stress gives you the motivation to get things done. This is considered healthy or helpful. Stress can be caused by feeling worried or anxious, like when you're studying for a test. It can be caused by feeling excited, but uncomfortable, like going to a friend's party and not knowing anyone else there. But there can be problems when your stress feels overwhelming and you have a hard time dealing with it. Have you ever felt sick to your stomach or been so worried about something that you ended up getting a headache? You may even feel a combination of things like anger, frustration, fear, or anxiety, which can make your stomach hurt or cause your body to tighten up. When you're feeling stressed, you may not sleep or eat well or even think or remember things very well. Stress is part of being human. It can be a positive challenge in our life and make us work harder to get what we want, or sometimes stress can get in the way of achieving our goals. We will learn about how to manage our stress before things become too overwhelming and it affects our everyday activities.

Key Terms and Definitions

Use Supplement 9.2 as a handout to define the key terms that will be used in this lesson. Then, discuss the concepts in the table (at the bottom of the handout) regarding commons signs of stress that affect different areas of daily functioning.

Sample Script

Here are some important words or ideas that will help us understand stress and what it may look like. We'll define the words and discuss examples to understand what they mean. [After going through the definitions, review the concepts in the table. Then ask about which signs of stress students have experienced.] Here are some signs of stress in four different areas. Can you think of any other signs that can go in this table? Write your responses on your handout so that you can remember all the signs.

Effects of Stress on Body, Emotions, and Behavior

10 MINS.   Stress affects your body, emotions, mind, and behavior. Too much stress or feeling stressed for a long period of time can cause health problems.

Sample Script

Stress not only affects your thoughts, emotions, and behavior, but it also affects your health. Sometimes, you may think you are sick because of a headache or because you can't sleep or eat, but stress could be part of the problem. Being able to recognize common stress symptoms may be the first step in managing them. Stress that's left unchecked can contribute to a lot of health problems in adults like high blood pressure, heart disease, obesity, and diabetes. It can also affect people your age in certain ways, too, and even interfere with your ability to focus in school.

Activity A: Stress Symptoms and Sample Situations

15 MINS.   Use the Supplement 9.3 handout to facilitate a discussion (in large or small groups) about the ways in which your body, emotions, thoughts, mind, and behaviors may show stress symptoms. Read the situations aloud, or students can read them in small groups. Discuss the scenarios depicting how stress may be exhibited in different people and situations. Ask students to discuss/write their reactions under each column to explain how they might feel. Students should be able to relate to some of the signs of stress and see that other students may feel differently in stressful situations. Consider modifying the situations to make them even more relevant to your students' current situations.

Sample Script

There are some situations that would make almost anyone feel relaxed and there are other situations that would make almost anyone feel stressed. For example, going to a favorite place to eat to celebrate getting a good report card would make anyone feel good and relaxed; however, being on a plane with a lot of turbulence would make most people feel stressed. Sometimes people can feel more stress about a particular situation because of their attitude or the way they are thinking about the situation. They may be caught in thinking traps, they might be having a bad day, or they might not feel confident in what they are doing. There are helpful and unhelpful ways to react to stress. An unhelpful way would be choosing to do something that can make the stress or the person feel worse in the long term. A healthy way is choosing to do something that can help the situation or make a person feel better in the long term. Let's talk about some example situations and think about how you might feel, what's affected, and helpful and unhelpful ways of dealing with stress.

Stress Triggers and Healthy and Unhealthy Coping Strategies

🕐 20–30 MINS. Identifying healthy ways of coping and the triggers that make us stressed will lead to better awareness and more effective coping strategies.

Sample Script

We can find ways to cope with our stress that are helpful and healthy. We can also figure out the specific triggers that may make us feel stressed. First, we'll start by talking about coping strategies.

Activity B: Healthy and Unhealthy Coping Strategies

🕐 10–15 MINS. Generate specific ways students can relax or find positive solutions when they are stressed or are about to encounter a stressful situation. Encourage them to share what they have used in the past or might try. Write ideas suggested by the students on the board, even those you may consider unhelpful. Be prepared to refer students to appropriate school resources if students need help with these issues for themselves or their friends and family. If students do not mention any solutions, refer to the examples in the table below. The next step will be to evaluate them as helpful/healthy or unhelpful/unhealthy ways to deal with stress and discuss whether the outcomes would be desirable in the long term.

Sample Script

Let's talk about some of the ways we manage our stress. What are some things you could do when you're feeling stress or when you know you're about to get into a stressful situation? Think of things that you've done when you felt stressed or overwhelmed about a situation. I'll write them up on the board, and we'll discuss them. After we make our list, I would like volunteers to come and put a plus sign next to the examples that are helpful or healthy and a minus sign next to the ones that are unhelpful or unhealthy ways. We will discuss these choices and talk about their outcomes. Keep in mind that some examples can be both helpful and unhelpful. I want you to also keep in mind that whatever strategies you use, ask yourself these questions: "Will this cause me more stress in the long run?" and "Will this help me feel better or work harder?"

Here are examples of helpful/healthy (+) and unhelpful/unhealthy (-) ways of dealing with stress:

(+) Helpful/healthy ways	(-) Unhelpful/unhealthy ways	Both helpful and unhelpful ways
(+) Talk about the problem with friends or family.	(-) Use alcohol or other drugs	(+/-) Cry.
(+) Take a walk or hike outside.	(-) Eat a whole cake by yourself.	(+/-) Scream in the bathroom.
(+) Do physical activity (yoga, martial arts, skateboarding, dancing, swimming).	(-) Sleep all day.	(+/-) Remove yourself from the situation for an extended period of time.
(+) Count to 10 to give yourself time to think.	(-) Get angry at your family or friends.	
(+) See a medical provider to see if there is some way he or she can help you.	(-) Tell yourself that you are the worst person in the world.	
(+) Face the source of your fears (e.g., if you have to make a speech, practice beforehand to build comfort).	(-) Procrastinate by playing video games.	
(+) Choose healthy foods.	(-) Distract yourself by going on the computer and surfing the Internet or chatting with your friends for an amount of time that gets in the way of doing household or school responsibilities.	
(+)Talk to a friend, a family member, or a clergy member.	(-) Stop exercising.	
(+) Practice deep breathing and meditation.	(-) Chew on pencils, paper, or other objects.	
(+) Create a drawing or other artwork.	(-) Smoke cigarettes.	
(+) Imagine a calm place or rest in a peaceful place in nature.		
(+) Refer to your *Strong Kids* training and think about strategies you learned.		
(+) Engage in a hobby such as reading, drawing, or riding your bike.		

(+) Write in a journal.		
(+) Get a massage or take a soothing bath.		

Activity C: Personal Triggers and Stress Identification

 🕐 **10–15 MINS.** Use Supplement 9.4 as a handout and have students discuss, role play, and respond to the following questions about their personal stress in small groups: 1) What was your body feeling? 2) What thoughts, emotions, and behaviors did you have? 3) What was the level of your emotions on the intensity scale? 4) How did you reframe thinking traps? 5) Did you have realistic expectations and strive for excellence, or did you expect perfection? 6) How did you cope? and 7) How did it work? Allow time for students to complete the handout, then come together for a class discussion. Facilitate a discussion on the pressure that one may put on oneself or expecting to be perfect at something. Emphasize that it is okay if they do not feel stress or do not know how stress affects their body.

Sample Script

We've talked about stress and how it may affect your body, thoughts, emotions, and behavior in the example situations and healthy and unhealthy ways to deal with stress. Now, I would like you to get with a partner and discuss stress in your lives. First, make a list of the things that cause you stress. These are triggers. Remember, different things can make people feel more or less stressed. Sometimes thinking traps can create more stress, like black-and-white thinking, when we expect too much from ourselves or we expect to be perfect at something. There's no right or wrong thing to put on your list. Then, choose the one thing that stresses you the most. Role play that situation in your group. Then, talk about how you felt and what you did in that situation. Talk about your physical feelings, your thoughts, and your emotions. How did you know you were stressed? How did you cope with your stress in that situation and was it helpful or unhelpful in the long term? Then, in the body diagram, identify and put an X if you know what part of you hurts, feels tension, or feels uncomfortable in some way when you are stressed. Some people may feel their stress in their neck, their back, their jaw, their stomach, or multiple places in their body. Some people may not even feel stress or know where their stress affects their body. That's okay; everyone is different. After you have finished the diagram, answer the questions on your handout. Afterward, we will come together and talk about our similarities and differences.

Relaxation Techniques to Manage Stress

🕐 **10 MINS.** Relaxation techniques can be used to manage stress and help our bodies relax. These techniques can be done anywhere to help relieve stress.

Sample Script

Now that we've talked about stress, let's figure out ways to help our bodies relax and decrease the tension so that we can let go of stress and feel better. We will try a relaxation exercise together. In the future when you start to see yourself get stressed by noticing small symptoms or if you identify a trigger, you can think back to this exercise. You can do this on your own in a quiet place or even when you are doing other things. At the end of the relaxation activity, I would like for you to quietly say something positive about yourself.

Activity D: Relaxation Exercise

 5–10 MINS. Use Supplement 9.5 as a handout to describe a brief relaxation exercise. Relaxation exercises with deep breathing have benefits of improved health, decreased stress, and improved overall emotional well-being. Two options are provided: abdominal breathing (Option 1) or muscle relaxation (Option 2). Choose the one that is most appropriate for your students and you can use the other option for another time. Optional: dim the lights and play relaxing music during either exercise.

Sample Script

We are going to do some relaxation exercises to include deep breathing or diaphragmatic breathing. This type of breathing helps with improving health by boosting the immune system and reducing negative stress hormones. It improves mood, mental focus, and concentration and overall emotional well-being. The first relaxation exercise is called diaphragmatic breathing [Option 1]/muscle relaxation [Option 2]. We will try to [Option 1] focus on the movement of our stomachs for abdominal breathing OR [Option 2] tighten and loosen our muscles for muscle relaxation. Let's get started.

Putting It All Together

 5 MINS. Use the following activity to practice the concepts discussed in this lesson.

Sample Script

Let's practice what we've learned by putting it all together.

Review the concepts from this lesson that are listed below. You can also use this time to discuss students' observations and experiences of the focusing activity at the beginning of the lesson.

- Stress is a normal part of being human, and it can be different for everyone.
- Identify common signs of stress.
- Identify how you feel when stressed.
- Identify your stress triggers.
- Identify realistic and unrealistic expectations for yourself.

- Identify helpful and unhelpful ways of reacting to stress.
- Identify the benefits of relaxation exercises.

Sample Script

Today, we learned about stress and relaxation. Everyone feels stress differently and it varies from situation to situation. A little stress is normal; it can make you work harder. If you are super relaxed and don't care about how things turn out, you may not be motivated to accomplish your goals or do things that are challenging. Remember that there are healthy and unhealthy ways to deal with stress, which can help you or make things worse in the long run. It can be helpful to make decisions about how you spend your time. Working too much and worrying too much can cause stress, just like playing too much can cause stress. If you're only dealing with school and have no time to play, you can get stressed. On the other hand, doing too many activities that are fun can also cause stress if it causes you to fall behind in your schoolwork. If you take care of yourself and get enough sleep and food, and if you exercise and leave time for fun stuff, you'll probably be less stressed out! You can also use one of the relaxation exercises we used today. Remember all the things we learned today and try them at home or anywhere you're feeling stress.

Closure

🕒 2 MINS.   Close the lesson using a brief breathing activity and a reflection on the lesson content.

Sample Script

Let's take a moment to regroup. Close your eyes and rest your hands in your lap. Feel your feet on the floor. Relax the muscles in your body and face. Relax and soften your stomach muscles. Counting to 3, take a deep breath in slowly. Inhale the air down into your lungs. Feel your chest and stomach expand like a balloon. [Pause.] *Now, exhale, counting to 4. Feel your chest and stomach collapse as all the air exits your body.* [Pause.] *Again, inhale deep into your lungs so that your stomach expands* [Pause.] *and exhale.* [Pause.] *Take a moment to think about something you learned today that was important to you and you really liked.* [Note to instructor: Pause for a moment to allow time for reflection.] *Counting to 3, take one more deep breath in slowly* [Pause.] *and exhale counting to 4.* [Pause.]

Tips for Transfer Training and Homework

Use the ideas and activities in the following section to practice this lesson's content with your students throughout the week to help reinforce the skills. Also remember to precorrect, remind, and reinforce concepts from this lesson in activities throughout the school week and to encourage students to use the skills taught in this lesson across settings including home, the bus, and the cafeteria.

Additional Activities

- Here are some suggested books:

  Stress Can Really Get on Your Nerves! by Trevor Romain and Elizabeth Verdick

  Dealing With the Stuff That Makes Life Tough: The 10 Things That Stress Girls Out and How to Cope with Them by Jill Zimmerman Rutledge

  Be the Boss of Your Stress by Timothy Culbert and Rebecca Kajander

- Writing Activities

  For older students, share this instruction: "For the next four days, if you feel stress, take 15–20 minutes to write down your deepest feelings about an emotional challenge in life (past or current). See what happens if you take a few minutes to write down what is making you stressed and then walk away. Think about these questions at the end: 1) What are your thoughts and how did you feel? 2) How did you manage your stress? 3) Did it work?"

  For students who enjoy drawing, encourage them to keep a sketch pad in their backpack. For one week, instruct them to draw their thoughts and how they feel. At the end of the week, students should think about these questions: "Did I feel stress? How did I cope with my stress?"

Homework Handout

Give out the homework handout, Supplement 9.6, Letting Go of Stress. Explain that students will write about situations in which they felt stressed; they will choose strategies that work for them, plan for an anticipated stressor, and choose a relaxation technique.

Pictures of Stressful Situations

Studying for a test

Bullying

Trying out for the basketball team

Giving a speech in class

Moving

Graduating

Key Terms and Definitions

Stress

A feeling of physical and/or emotional tension or pressure that is often related to being challenged to perform or react outside of your typical range of behaviors (outside of your "comfort zone"), this feeling can happen before, during, or after a difficult or exciting situation.

Example: You can feel stressed, worried, uncomfortable, or overwhelmed when you have too much to do or when you are trying to concentrate on something important and you feel distracted and nervous inside. Stress can also occur when there is uncertainty or if the outcomes are unknown.

Excellence

Work diligently to reach goals that are ambitious yet realistic. You learn from disappointments and setbacks and keep trying.

Example: You have a goal in mind and know it will take work to accomplish it. You understand mistakes are part of the process of learning and growing, and you feel good about your effort.

Perfectionism

This is striving for flawlessness or exceptionally high performance standards.

Example: You feel as if you have do everything right and you are not allowed to make a mistake. You often are concerned about what other people think of you. It may take you a very long time to finish a project because you re-do much of the work since you aren't quite satisfied, even after knowing the product you will hand in will likely get a good grade.

Helpful or healthy stress

This kind of stress helps us work harder to get what we want; it usually doesn't lead to feeling overwhelmed or exhausted.

Example: You may do a better job on your research project if the stress inspires you to prepare well before you have to present it to the class (e.g., healthy competition, positive anticipation of an event, and personal goals can be sources of good stress).

Unhelpful or unhealthy stress

This kind of stress can interfere with accomplishing our goals and make us feel upset more often than not.

Example: You continue thinking about the research project so much, you become exceedingly worried to the point you feel sick and take time off, and don't finish the project (e.g., deadlines that may be very difficult to meet, feeling unprepared, not knowing the outcome of something that may be life changing).

Situational triggers

This is something that can lead to stress.

Example: A particular activity (e.g., giving a speech), place (e.g., being at a family member's house where there is a lot of conflict), person/people (e.g., being with people you don't know or don't like), or a personal expectation (e.g., having to do well on a test or you may get a

(continued)

Merrell's Strong Kids—Grades 3–5: A Social and Emotional Learning Curriculum, Second Edition,
by Dianna Carrizales-Engelmann, Laura L. Feuerborn, Barbara A. Gueldner, and Oanh K. Tran.

lower grade at the semester) can be a trigger for stress. Triggers can vary from person to person and situation to situation. The situation is a source of tension that may heighten/increase your emotions and trigger stress.

Relaxation

This is a feeling of letting go of stress. You can do this by physically loosening tense muscles or finding other healthy ways to deal with the things that are bothering or overwhelming you. Deep breathing and taking a walk in nature are examples of healthy ways to relax.

Example: The test was so hard that doing some relaxation breathing was the only way to begin to relieve the tension.

Realistic/unrealistic expectations

These are expectations you have for yourself that can affect stress. Expectations can be too high (e.g., you expect too much from yourself) or too low (e.g., you expect too little from yourself). Realistic expectations are challenging yet achievable.

Example: Are the expectations you have achievable for that situation (realistic), or are the expectations you have too far to reach or obtain (unrealistic), at least in the moment? Unrealistic expectations can add stress if they make you more overwhelmed.

Common signs of stress

Stress can affect how your body feels (physical), how you think (thoughts), how you feel (emotions), and how you behave (behavior). There are different signs or cues that let you know that you are experiencing unhealthy stress.

Example: Signs of stress

Thoughts	Emotions	Physical	Behavior
Worrying	Irritability or short temper	Aches and pains	Sleeping too much or too little
Anxious or racing thoughts	Feeling overwhelmed	Rapid heartbeat	Eating too much or too little
Thinking traps	Moodiness	Nausea, fatigue	Nervous habits (nail biting, pacing)
Difficulty concentrating	Unhappiness	Sensitivity to sounds and noises	Procrastination

Stress Symptoms and Example Situations

Example situations	Physical (How might your body feel?)	Emotions, thoughts, behaviors (What thoughts, emotions, and behaviors may occur?)	Realistic or unrealistic expectations (Were expectations realistic or unrealistic?)	How stressful might this be for you? (What level of stress would you have?) How might you deal with this stress?
Situation 1. (Mark)				
Situation 2. (Sonia)				
Situation 3. (Jen)				
Situation 4. (Antonio)				

Situation 1 (school example)

Mark forgot that he had a vocabulary test today and didn't study for it. The teacher passes out the test, and Mark sits and stares at his test. [Refer to the questions in the table.]

Situation 2 (social example)

During lunch time, Sonia goes and sits next to her best friend. Her friend then moves and sits next to a group of other friends and gives Sonia a bad look. [Refer to the questions in the table.]

Situation 3 (community example)

Jen was out shopping with her mom and stopped by the video game section. When she finished looking at the video games, she turned to leave, and she didn't see her mom anywhere in the store. [Refer to the questions in the table.]

Situation 4 (home example)

At home, Antonio sees his parents arguing with each other about work and taking care of the house. Sometimes he even hears them arguing at night when he is in bed. [Refer to the questions in the table.]

Personal Triggers and Stress Identification

1. Write down the things that cause you stress (triggers). Then rank order your list. Now, circle the thing that causes you the most stress.

    _____

    _____

2. Using the diagram below, put an *X* on the areas of your body where you feel stress.

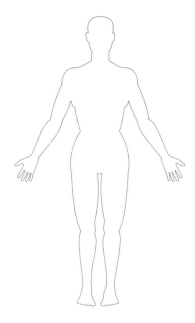

3. What emotions, thoughts, and behaviors did you have in that situation?

    _____

    _____

4. Where was the stress on the intensity scale?

    _____

    _____

5. Were your expectations realistic? Were you striving for excellence or getting caught in perfectionism?

    _____

    _____

6. How did you cope with your stress? Did you reframe thinking traps? Did it work in making your situation better?

    _____

    _____

7. What might you do to plan for the next time you encounter this trigger? What are some ways you could proactively manage your stress or manage it before it gets too intense?

    _____

    _____

Relaxation Techniques

Option 1: Abdominal breathing (optional: play relaxing music)

Sitting comfortably, notice how your body feels at rest. [Pause for 10 seconds.] *We will begin to do a breathing exercise. You have the option to put your hand on your stomach to feel how your body works to move air in and out in a way that can be relaxing. Like this.* [Instructor models putting hand on own stomach.] *Now, while you focus on taking a breath in, let your stomach expand as you inhale. You may imagine filling up a balloon. Watch me.* [Instructor models inhaling with stomach expanding.] *Now, as you let the air out and exhale, let your stomach fall back toward your spine, like this.* [Instructor models exhale with stomach moving back toward spine.] *You don't need to push the air out with a lot of force. Think of it as a nice, easy, natural cycle of relaxed and comfortable breathing. Try it a couple more times.* [Pause to allow practice.] *To keep a nice easy rhythm, you may want to count to 3 while you inhale, and to 4 while you exhale. Keep your mind on gently breathing with your counting. Now, let yourself take about six relaxed breaths. Remember: Breathe in by letting your stomach expand out. Then naturally breathe out by letting your stomach come back in. Notice how you begin to relax and calm yourself with this gentle breathing. Enjoy the feeling.*

Option 2: Progressive muscle relaxation

- *Close your eyes. Take a few minutes to breathe in and out in slow, deep breaths.* [Pause for a few breaths.]

- *When you're ready, shift your attention to your right foot. Take a moment to focus on the way it feels.*

- *Slowly tense the muscles in your right foot, squeezing as tight as you can. Hold for a count of 10.* [Pause for 10, brisk counts. You may count aloud or instruct the class to count silently.]

- *Relax your right foot. Focus on the tension flowing away and the way your foot feels as it becomes limp and loose.*

- *Now, shift your attention to your left foot. Tense these muscles, squeezing tightly, and hold for 10 counts.* [Pause for 10 brisk counts.] *Then, relax your left foot.*

- *We will focus on contracting and relaxing other muscles in your body. It may take some practice at first, but try not to tense muscles other than those I'm mentioning.*

- *Now focus on* [insert the next body part, following the sequence below, and use the language above]:

  1. Right foot
  2. Left foot
  3. Right calf
  4. Left calf
  5. Right thigh
  6. Left thigh
  7. Hips and buttocks

(continued)

8.   Stomach

9.   Chest

10.   Back

11.   Right arm and hand

12.   Left arm and hand

13.   Neck and shoulders

14.   Face

Now feel the weight of your whole, relaxed body, from the tips of your toes to the top of your head. You are ready to return to your day refreshed and relaxed.

Letting Go of Stress

Name (optional) _____

1. Write down times or situations in which you felt stress.

    _____

    _____

    _____

2. We talked about strategies that can help you deal with stress. Some are listed below. Check off one or two relaxation strategies that you think you can try to use, or write in one that has worked for you.

    ☐   Talk to a trusted friend or adult.

    ☐   Exercise or take a walk in nature.

    ☐   Think positively about yourself and the situation; have healthy expectations.

    ☐   Address the situation using the problem-solving model, one step at a time.

    ☐   Focus on your breathing and relaxing your muscles.

    ☐   Identify and reframe thinking traps.

    ☐   _____

3. This week when I _____

    (write in stressful situation), I will _____

    (write in relaxation technique).

4. After you have tried using one of the techniques you checked off above, write about how it worked for you. Did it work? What will you do next time in the same situation?

    ☐   It helped!

    _____

    _____

    ☐   I'll try something different next time.

    _____

    _____

LESSON 10

Positive Living

SEL Competencies Addressed in This Lesson

Responsible decision making

Self-awareness

Self-management

Social awareness

Relationship skills

Teacher Notes

_____

_____

_____

_____

_____

_____

_____

_____

Purpose and Objectives

This lesson teaches students how to incorporate positive habits into their day-to-day lives. In this lesson, students will

- Understand the value associated with positive daily choices

- List some typical actions or behaviors that contribute to a healthy and positive lifestyle

- Distinguish between examples and nonexamples of positive life choices

Materials Needed

☐ Supplements 10.1–10.6 (online download and handout)

☐ Supplement 10.7 (homework handout)

Running Short on Time?

Suggested stopping points: end of Activity B and Closure activity.

Instructor Reflection

There is a fundamental relationship between our actions and our emotions. You have probably read that exercise can boost your mood and that stress can make you sick. There also is research that suggests other behaviors and acts such as gratitude, interacting with nature, and volunteering have powerful and positive impacts on mood and health. Before teaching this lesson, take a few minutes to reflect on experiences in which your behaviors positively influenced your mood, your health, or how you felt. Think about your own immediate highs associated with behaviors like achieving (or exceeding!) goals, with exercising, or with doing something good for someone else. Also, think about the longer-lasting or delayed effects you've found from eating healthily and/or getting a good amount of sleep. During this lesson, you will be encouraging your students to strive for general well-being by cultivating positive living habits through daily choices.

Review

🕐 2–3 MINS. Review the ideas (listed below) that were discussed in Lesson 9: Letting Go of Stress.

- Stress triggers
- Common stressors
- Healthy coping strategies and setting realistic expectations

Sample Script

During our last meeting, we discussed what stress triggers are and how to recognize some of the signs of stress. We talked about how to set realistic expectations for ourselves so we don't make ourselves so stressed out. We also practiced setting realistic expectations for ourselves.

Introduction

🕐 3–5 MINS. Introduce the topic of positive living. Lead the students in a focusing activity, then discuss the concept of positive living as a way of developing the habit of looking for the healthy and positive choices in all the things we do.

Sample Script

Today we're going to learn about how we can develop positive habits by making positive choices in the things we do every day. One of the easiest ways to keep a positive attitude is to be on the lookout for choices we can make that make us feel positive in lots of different ways.

Mindfulness-Based Focusing Activity

🕐 2 MINS.   **Sample Script**

Before we begin, let's practice settling our bodies and focusing our minds. Close your eyes or look at a point on the floor or on your desk. Rest your hands comfortably. Feel your feet on the floor or your hands as they rest. Pay attention to your breathing for three breaths. [Pause for 3 breaths.] Now, picture in your mind a small tree or a flower waving in the breeze. Allow your upper body to slowly sway back and forth like the tree or the flower in the wind. If you want, you can put your arms at your side. Relax your body and notice what your body feels like when it's moving. Move as slowly and as little as you can. If you feel uncomfortable, you can stop swaying and focus on your breath. [Pause.] *You may notice that you have thoughts while you are swaying. That's okay. When you notice yourself thinking about something else, just bring your attention back to the feelings in your body as you sway. I'll tell you when to stop in about a minute. You can also stop when you are ready.* [Pause to allow about a minute of practice.] *Let's stop swaying and take two breaths together.* [Pause.] *When you finish letting out the second breath, slowly open your eyes. We are ready to move on to our lesson.*

Key Terms and Definitions

 5 MINS. Use Supplement 10.1 as a handout to define the key terms that will be used in the lesson.

Sample Script

Here are some important terms that will help us understand the role of positive living. We'll define the words and discuss examples to understand what they mean.

What We Do Influences How We Feel

12 MINS. Things we do physically in our daily lives can influence our emotions and our attitudes. Convey the following ideas:

- It helps to develop healthy habits related to things that have a positive impact on our lives.

- Healthy habits are things we do regularly that are good for us. This means we do them with enough frequency, effort, and attention to have a positive influence on our lives without the activity feeling like a burden or a stress to us. Even good things can be overdone.

- A positive lifestyle includes cultivating a positive attitude in all of life's daily activities: thinking, eating, playing, working, and interacting with other people.

Sample Script

Did you know that the things we do can influence the way we feel? We can make all kinds of choices in what we do, like eating, playing, working, and being with other people, that can support a positive lifestyle and a positive attitude. In Lesson 8, when we learned about Solving People Problems, we talked about how our attitudes can affect our interactions with other people. Well, it works the other way around, too, which means that sometimes the things we do every day (with or without other people) can affect our attitudes. Today, we're going to talk about developing healthy habits, which means doing certain things just enough for them to help us—not too much or too little.

Activity A: Activities that Make Me Feel Good, Good About Myself, or Happy

10 MINS. Use Supplement 10.2 as a handout to facilitate a discussion for this activity. This supplement lists example activities. Encourage your students to provide additional examples. Use a white board or some other means of documentation to record students' responses so that everyone can see them. As you write, see if you can organize the students' suggestions into the four categories noted in Supplement 10.3: physical health, emotional and mental health, community connections, and family and social connections.

Sample Script

Let's take a look at some examples of activities we can do that can help us live a healthy life. We'll also make a list of our own examples. Can anyone think of examples of doing things that make you feel positive while you're doing them and even after you've done them?

How Often Is Too Often?

10 MINS. Continue to use Supplement 10.2 to discuss how some activities and actions can improve emotion and well-being in the short term, whereas other activities are great as positive and healthy habits for frequent, long-term use. Use the list of suggestions that the students provided to compare activities. Emphasize that even though certain activities may feel good in the short term (eating ice cream/treats, playing video games, using social media, talking on the phone, watching TV/movies, reading comic books), they should probably be sought out less often than activities that have longer-lasting positive boosts, when those choices exist.

Sample Script

Let's think about some of these activities and actions that we've listed here. I decided to put them into different groups. For now, I want to make sure that we focus on the activities and actions that can develop into habits that make us healthier, stronger, kinder, or smarter in some way every time we do them. Now, we are going to identify activities in two ways: 1) things we enjoy because they make us feel good right away but not necessarily for a long time; and 2) things that help us to become better and better every time we do them.

Activity B: How Often Should I Do This?

10 MINS. Divide the students into groups and use the activities that were generated by the students and recorded (or other activities of your own selection) for this activity. Ask students to decide whether the activity has more long-term or short-term impact. Ask students to decide if the activity should be a frequent activity (a habit) or an occasional activity. Ask questions such as, "What could happen if we do this too much or not enough?" and "Is this something that should become a frequent habit or is it an 'only sometimes' thing?"

Sample Script

I'm going to give each of your groups the name of an activity and I'd like you to work in your group to decide whether you think that activity should be a frequent habit, meaning something we do very regularly, or just an occasional activity, and why.

Areas of Life that We Can Focus On

⏱ 30 MINS. Sometimes small adjustments in only one or two important areas of life can influence other parts of our lives.

Sample Script

Often it only takes making small changes to make a big difference in our lives. Let's talk about some things we can do that can have a powerful impact.

Activity C: Healthy Habits

⏱ 10 MINS. Use Supplement 10.3 as a handout, along with the list your students created and/or the list provided below, and walk through the examples and suggestions provided in the different life areas that can influence general well-being.

- Eating healthy foods in the right amounts at the right times and for the right reasons

- Exercising regularly, but not too much

- Spending time in the outdoors either doing activities or appreciating nature/meditating

- Helping others who are in need

- Being polite to others

- Helping around the house

- Engaging in quiet time/down time/meditation

- Getting enough sleep at night

- Taking responsibility for things that you should (stepping up)

Sample Script

Let's look at our list again and see if there is anything we've forgotten. [Use the list above to augment your list if necessary.] *Remember how I broke it into four categories?* [If you haven't already, conduct an activity to label the items on your list into the four categories: physical health, emotional and mental health, community connections, family and social connections.] *Let's talk about what kinds of healthy habits we expect to see in each of these areas.*

Activity D: Seeing Healthy Choices Every Day

10 MINS. Use Supplements 10.4 and 10.5 as handouts (weekday and weekend routines) and encourage students to think about what they *routinely* do in any given day. Encourage students to look for opportunities to develop and support healthy choices in their day-to-day activities by incorporating healthy habits.
Choose one of the following options to conduct the next activity:

- Option 1: Divide your class into discussion groups in which individual students interview each other on different areas of their day using the questions provided or others that they improvise.

- Option 2: Lead the whole class through steps asking the questions provided and/or by supplementing with additional questions to eliminate yes/no type answers. For example, "Do you have a choice about this?" How would you change this?" "What specifically do you do in this area?"

- Option 3: Extract a subset of questions from across the day and collect "data" on the general habits of your class.

Sample Script

Now, let's look at the activities we do during the week and on the weekends.
We'll use these examples to help us think of things we can do in our own lives.

Activity E: Helping Tamika Improve Her Day

10 MINS. Use Supplement 10.6 as a handout to work on the scenario as a class or by breaking the class into groups. Read the Scenario Script to introduce the scene. Students will examine the character's daily routine and make suggestions on changes that can be made to have healthy habits.

Sample Script

Let's practice looking at another student's daily routine to see if we have any ideas for how Tamika Oliver can have healthy habits.

Scenario Script

Tamika noticed that she didn't always feel great. She wasn't sick but some days it took a lot of work for her to find reasons to be happy. She wasn't sure exactly what to do, so she decided to look for small things to change in her life every day. Can you help identify some of the things Tamika can change that might have a long-term positive effect on her life and that could help her feel more energized and motivated? Here's a hint: It may be best to skip some stages and return to them when you know more information about her day.

Putting It All Together

5–10 MINS. Use the following activity to practice the concepts discussed in this lesson.

Sample Script

Let's practice what we've learned by putting it all together.

Use Supplement 10.3 as a handout again. Using the questions in the following Sample Script, call on students to discuss the main ideas that were reviewed in this lesson.

Sample Script

We are going to review some of the main ideas discussed in today's lesson. Raise your hand if you know some of these ideas.

- *What is healthy or positive living about?*
- *What are some parts of healthy living?*
- *How can we feel better about ourselves?*

Closure

 2 MINS. Close the lesson using a brief breathing activity and a reflection on the lesson content. At the end, prompt students to bring a photo of themselves at a younger age.

Sample Script

Let's take a moment to regroup. Close your eyes. Feel your feet on the floor. Counting to 3, take a breath in slowly. Inhale [Pause.] *and exhale counting to 4.* [Pause.] *One more time inhale* [Pause.] *and exhale.* [Pause.] *Take a moment to think about something you learned today that was important to you and you really liked.* [Note to instructor: Pause for a moment to allow time for reflection.] *Counting to 3, take one more deep breath in slowly* [Pause.] *and exhale counting to 4.* [Pause.]

For next week's lesson (Lesson 11: Creating Strong and SMART Goals), you will need to bring a picture of yourself at a younger age for one of our activities. It can be any age, but at least 2 years ago. If you don't have a picture of yourself, you can draw a picture of yourself at a younger age. Bring the picture to class for our next lesson.

Tips for Transfer Training and Homework

Use the ideas and activities in the following section to practice this lesson's content with your students at other times during the day. Also remember to precorrect, remind, and reinforce concepts from this lesson in activities throughout the school week.

Additional Activities

- Encourage students to think about healthy choices every day by engaging in an activity called "Healthy Idea for the Day." Draw one of the healthy ideas from this lesson from a bag or box where you've placed all the good ideas.

Make whatever you pick into the Healthy Idea for that day. For example, if on Monday you select "being polite to others," your students should look for opportunities to be polite that day, and so forth. Keep a visible log that tracks the activity for each day so that it can serve as a prompt during the day's other events.

- When students experience a moment of success after significant effort or difficult choices, point out the connection between the choices they made previously and the successes they are enjoying currently.

- When students demonstrate positive living behaviors like biking to school, exercising, or eating healthy snacks, take a quiet moment to connect the dots for the student to this lesson.

Homework Handout

Pass out the homework handout, Supplement 10.7, and review the instructions. Explain that students will keep a journal for a week and look for situations in which they have a choice. Encourage students to keep a record of when they deliberately make a choice because they believe it is the best choice for a positive lifestyle and attitude.

Key Terms and Definitions

Habit

A usual way of behaving, this is something that a person does often in a regular and repeated way.

Example: Tamika wants to get into the habit of making her bed every morning before she leaves the house.

Moderation

Choosing to avoid too much or too little of any one thing, behavior, or activity is moderation.

Example: Even though José really likes to use his computer to stay in touch with his friends at his old school, he knows that it's healthy to leave enough time to make connections with new friends, too.

Attitude

This is the way you choose to think about things and how those thoughts are reflected in your behaviors.

Example: Tamika doesn't enjoy every green vegetable that her mom prepares, but she eats them anyway and doesn't complain because she knows they're good for her.

Choice

This is the act of making a decision when there is more than one option from which to select.

Example: José has an hour between dinnertime and bedtime, and he wants a good night's sleep. He decides to read a book instead of eating sweets or playing video games.

Feeling Good Activities

Physical activity

Swimming, running, riding a bike, hiking, skiing, skateboarding;
playing football, soccer, baseball, hockey, volleyball; doing yoga

(continued)

Developing skills you enjoy

Cooking, sewing, drawing, playing an instrument

(continued)

Spending time outdoors

Gardening, hiking, going to the beach, vacationing in summer, enjoying spring break

(continued)

New or rare things

Traveling, going to see live theater

(continued)

Friends and family time

Helping parent/guardian around the house, playing with a pet, visiting grandparent(s), volunteering, hanging out with friends, hanging out with one special friend

(continued)

Recreation

Watching a good movie, reading a good book, singing, listening to music, playing with friends, watching a comedy, playing video games

(continued)

Certain tastes and smells

Smelling flowers, tasting foods you enjoy

(continued)

Quiet time/time to rest your brain

Going to your place of worship, spending time alone, meditating
or resting your brain, resting

Healthy Habits

Physical health 	Make healthy meal choices every day and eat treats responsibly. Eat lots of fruits and vegetables and avoid sugary, fatty, and processed foods. Eat when you're actually hungry, and stop when your body tells you to. Engage in activities that get you moving every day to make sure you are using your muscles to get them strong and keep them that way. Get the right amount of sleep to allow your muscles to rest; 7- to 12-year-olds should be getting 10–11 hours of sleep each night. For example go to bed at 8:00 p.m. and wake up at 6:00 a.m.
Emotional and mental health 	Spend some time outdoors. Make sure you get fresh air and an opportunity to step away from screens (computer and TV) and books (this could be combined with exercise). Find time to enjoy silence and reframe thinking traps (this could be combined with your time outdoors). Make goals: Learn how to do new things or get better at other activities. Be optimistic: Expect good outcomes, and look for ways to ensure good outcomes when you can. Refrain from comparing yourself to other people. Find reasons to be grateful for what you have.
Community connections 	Help other people when you can. Volunteer and do your part to play a role in something larger than yourself.
Family and social connections 	Maintain healthy relationships. Interact positively and pleasantly with friends and family and people in your community (this can be combined with helping other people when you can). Do not say mean things about other people—either in person, on the phone, in texts, or online. Think about what other people need out of a situation as well as what you need out of a situation.

Weekday Habits and Routines

Time/activity	Habits and routines (PH, Physical Health; FC, Family Connections; CC, Community Connections; SC, School Connections; MH, Mental Health)
Waking up and breakfast	Do you have enough time to eat a healthy meal and brush your teeth? (PH) Do you wake up easily, or is waking up a big struggle for you? (FC)
Getting to school	If you travel with others to school, are you kind and attentive? (CC) Do you get to school and your classes on time? (SC)
Morning at school	Are you polite to your teachers and friends? (SC) Do you follow the rules? (SC) Are you able to pay attention? (SC)
Lunchtime	Do you make healthy meal choices? (PH) Do you eat only as much as you need? (PH) Do you pay attention to what you eat and eat at a thoughtful pace? (PH/CC) Do you chew with your mouth closed/finish chewing before you talk? (CC)
Afternoon at school	Do you pay attention to what the teacher says and follow directions? (SC) Do you ask questions if you don't understand? (SC) Do you complete your assignments? (SC) Do you help others when helping others is allowed? (CC/SC)
Afternoon/after school	Do you make it to your ride-on time? (CC) Do you engage in any after-school activities that are healthy for your body and mind? (PH/MH) Do you make time for your homework/ask for help when you need it? (SC)
Evening/dinner	Do you help with dinner preparations and cleanup? (FC) Do you eat moderate portions and make healthy choices? (PH)
Bedtime	Do you do all the things you need to do to get ready for bed without resisting or waiting to be told? (FC) Do you get to bed at the right time? (FC)

Weekend Habits and Routines

Time/activity	Habits and routines (PH, Physical Health; FC, Family Connections; CC, Community Connections; SC, School Connections; MH, Mental Health)
Waking up and breakfast	Do you wake up at a good time so that you're not in bed for more than 2 hours longer than you are in school during a school day? (FC)
	Do you eat a healthy breakfast and clean up after yourself? (PH)
Morning activities and events	Do you do things around your house without being told to? (FC)
	Do you do things in your community when you can? (CC)
Lunchtime	Do you eat a healthy lunch and clean up after yourself? (PH)
Afternoon activities and events	Do you find ways to get outdoors that can be helpful to your family or community? (PH/CC)
	Do you look for school assignments that may require you to make a trip to a store with your parents or to your local library? (SC)
Events before dinner and evening activities	Do you get clean and calm before dinner? (FC)
	Do you offer to help or offer healthy suggestions for meals that you will eat? (FC/PH)
	Do you avoid playing video games and doing other online activities right before bedtime so you can sleep better?

Example Situation:
Helping Tamika Make Healthy Choices

Hint: It may help to skip some stages and return to them when you know more information about Tamika's day.

Typical routine	What would you change and why?
Wake-up time: Tamika typically wakes up at 6:45 a.m.	
Getting dressed in the morning: Tamika typically takes a long time—sometimes more than 20 minutes—to find something to wear.	
Eating breakfast: Tamika usually eats a toaster pastry while watching a cartoon.	
Leaving the house: Tamika always leaves the house in a hurry and feels like she's forgetting something.	
On the way to school: Tamika takes the 7:30 a.m. bus and is usually sleepy. She doesn't talk to anyone and doesn't pay much attention to the other kids.	
At school: Tamika tries really hard to listen to the teachers.	
At lunchtime: Tamika is very hungry by lunch, so she chooses many different foods from the cafeteria and eats a lot.	
After lunch: Tamika plays with her friends before class.	
At home: Tamika goes straight to the fridge, finds a snack, and watches TV until someone tells her to stop.	
Before bed: Tamika is usually doing homework until bedtime and feels very stressed out as she tries to get to sleep.	

What Did You Do
Toward Positive Living This Week?

Name (optional) _____

	Monday	Tuesday	Wednesday	Thursday	Friday	Saturday	Sunday
Morning at home							
Morning before lunch							
Lunchtime							
Afternoon activity							
Evening before dinner							
Dinnertime							
Bedtime							

LESSON

11

Creating Strong and SMART Goals

SEL Competencies Addressed in This Lesson

Teacher Notes

_____

_____

_____

_____

_____

_____

_____

_____

Purpose and Objectives

This lesson teaches students the skill of goal setting and increasing positive activity as a means to a healthy life. In this lesson, students will

- Understand the importance of increasing and maintaining positive activities

- Increase an awareness of their own strengths and limitations

- Set SMART goals

- Monitor progress toward goals

- Develop resilience in the goal attainment process

Materials Needed

☐ Supplement 11.1 (photographs or drawn pictures of each student at a younger age [2+ years ago])

☐ Supplement 11.2 (online download and handout)

☐ Supplement 11.3 (online download and worksheet)

☐ Supplements 11.4–11.6 (online download)

☐ Supplement 11.7 (homework handout)

☐ Green, red, and yellow colored pencils or crayons for the Healthy Living Domains activity

Running Short on Time?

Suggested stopping points: end of Activity C and the Closure activity.

Instructor Reflection

This lesson teaches students to set goals to achieve a healthier, more resilient life. To prepare for this lesson, reflect on the times in your life that you have made personal goals (e.g., New Year's resolutions) or professional goals (e.g., getting a specialized license). Reflect on why you created the goals, and reflect on your progress toward these goals. If you have achieved your goals, what do you think contributed to your success? Or if you haven't achieved your goals yet, have you achieved part of the goal and what have been your obstacles so far? Now, consider an area in your life for which you could create a new goal or modify an existing goal. Do you see a way the strategies within this lesson can assist you in creating that goal and a plan for monitoring your progress?

Review

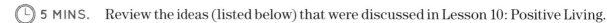

5 MINS.   Review the ideas (listed below) that were discussed in Lesson 10: Positive Living.

- Ways to make healthy choices to improve positive living

- Making healthy choices with regard to eating, playing, working, and being with other people to support a positive lifestyle and a positive attitude

- Doing things to help us feel better about ourselves

Sample Script

During our last meeting, we talked about how the things we do can influence or change the way we feel. We talked about how making healthy choices in all the things we do, like eating, playing, working, and being with other people, can support a positive lifestyle and a positive attitude. We also talked about developing good habits in our everyday activities.

Introduction

10 MINS.   Introduce the lesson. Lead students in a focusing activity. Use Supplement 11.1 as a handout and have students take out a pencil. Introduce the concept of goal setting and creating an action plan to meet goals. Students will engage in a brief startup activity of writing about who they are.

Sample Script

Today, we will learn how to set goals and accomplish them! Setting and accomplishing goals is something that all of us can do to grow and to change things in our lives for the better. Together, we will set goals for ourselves and create a plan to make them happen.

Mindfulness-Based Focusing Activity

 2 MINS.

Sample Script

Let's begin with an activity to settle our bodies and practice focusing our minds. Close your eyes or look at a point in front of you on the floor or on your desk. Rest your hands comfortably on your desk or in your lap. Feel your feet on the floor or your hands as they rest. First, pay attention to your breathing for three breaths. [Pause.] *Today, we will imagine the feelings we have when we're successful or good at something. Think of something you've done that made you feel good about yourself.* [Pause.] *Did you feel happy, proud, or excited?* [Pause.] *What does this emotion feel like right now?* [Pause.] *What are the thoughts that go with your feeling of success? Do you think, "I did it!"? Whatever emotion you experience, and however your body feels, is okay. Just notice those feelings.* [Pause for about 30 seconds to allow practice.] *Now, imagine yourself being successful at doing something new or reaching a goal. Notice how your body feels, the emotions you have, and your thoughts.* [Pause for about 30 seconds to allow practice.] *Now, let's take two breaths together.* [Pause.] *When you finish letting out the second breath, slowly open your eyes. Now that we've pictured or imagined success, we are ready to move on to our lesson.*

Introductory Optional Activity

 5 MINS. Use Supplement 11.1: Your Younger Self for this activity. This activity requires students to have obtained a picture of themselves at a younger age. Some students might forget and others might not have a copy to bring in to class. If this is the case, students can close their eyes and imagine themselves or draw a picture.

Sample Script

Now, take out your picture of yourself at a younger age and look at it. What were you like then? What were your thoughts like? How did you behave? How did you feel? How are you different today from the time when the picture was taken? Share your picture with someone sitting next to you. Each of you, take 1 minute to talk about how you were then and how you are different now. [Pause.] *Some changes are physical and are caused by growing up, our bodies growing older and getting bigger. But other changes are caused by things we learn and things we choose to do from day to day. Sometimes, we can't see these changes. Today, you might be a better skater or a better artist than you were last year. You might be better at math. How did that happen? Probably not by chance! We change because of what we learn, feel, think, and do—every day. When you think about yourself in the _____ grade* [Name a grade or two above the students], *you probably don't see yourself exactly the same way as you are today. Are there things about yourself that you are able to change—that will help you grow and be stronger? What can you do today to be the person you want to be tomorrow? Next week? Next year? That's what we're going to talk about today.*

Key Terms and Definitions

 5 MINS. Use Supplement 11.2 as a handout to define the key terms that will be used in this lesson.

Sample Script

Here are some important words or ideas that will help us understand healthy living and goal setting. We'll define the words and discuss examples to understand what they mean.

Healthy Living Domains

 15 MINS. Use Supplement 11.3 as a handout to show students that there are areas in our lives in which we can develop healthy habits. Students will need red, green, and yellow colored pencils or crayons.

Sample Script

These circles represent the areas of our lives in which we can be healthy. We are going to talk in more detail about what we're doing in these areas.

Activity A: Healthy Living Domains

 Continue with the Supplement 11.3 handout. Ask students to think about each domain and the activities they do for each, and record them on their worksheets. Examples may include getting enough sleep each night (physical health), eating healthy foods (physical health), getting outside in nature (emotional health), reframing thinking traps (emotional health), volunteering (family and community), helping out a brother or sister (family and community), being present or attentive in class (school), and completing homework (school).

Sample Script

We all have things we do well, and we all have things we wish we could do better. Do you know your own strengths? Do you know the areas in your life that could use some improvement? Here's an activity that will help us figure that out. Take out your Healthy Living Domains worksheet and fill in the blanks with what you do now to keep healthy in each domain. For example, in the physical health area, if you eat well and get enough sleep, you can put those in that area. If you help your brother or sister, you can put those activities in the family and community area. If you come to class prepared, you can put that in the school area. If you are keeping a journal, you can put that in the emotional health area, and if you volunteer, you can put that in the family and community area. Then, use green to color the area you have the most activities in or that are the easiest for you to do. Use yellow to color two areas you do some things in, but you would like to do more. Last, use red to color the area you don't have any activities in or things you'd like to start working on.

Relationships Among Healthy Living Domains

🕐 5 MINS.   Each healthy living domain has a relationship with the others. What we do in one domain affects the other domains.

Activity B: Interactions Among Healthy Living Domains

Use the example in the Sample Script below, or another example to illustrate how making an improvement in one area of your life can affect other areas. Ask students to generate other examples from their own lives.

Sample Script

Did you know that if we make healthy choices in one area, they can affect other areas of your life too? Most times, what we do to improve one area of our life affects other areas of our life. That's a bonus! Suppose José wants to improve his physical strength. He decides he wants to try out for the basketball team at school. If he achieved his goal by trying out, doing his best, and making it on the team, how would his other circles be changed? [Allow students to offer some suggestions.] Can you think of another example of a positive living activity in one area that positively affects other areas?

Goal Setting: Introduction

🕐 10 MINS.   Goal setting is important to achieve what we want in life. There are ways to set goals that work well for us and other ways that do not work well.

Sample Script

Setting goals is important to achieve what we want in our lives, and the way we set our goals can affect whether or not we achieve them. We're going to talk about some examples where goal setting went well and other times where it did not go so well.

Activity C: Examples and Nonexamples of Goal Setting

🕐 10 MINS.   Use Supplement 11.4 and the example from Activity B (José) to discuss examples and nonexamples of goal setting and attainment.

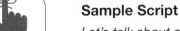

Sample Script

Let's talk about examples of goal setting—how the goal was set and how it went. Remember José? He wanted to improve his physical strength and tried out for the basketball team. How would he set his goal to do his best and try out for the team? Let's talk about some actions he might take and decide whether they are examples or nonexamples of goal setting. Remember, examples are the ways that setting a goal might work well. Nonexamples are ways of setting a goal that may not work so well.

Setting Specific, Measurable, Attainable, Relevant, and Timely (SMART) Goals

 10 MINS. Use Supplement 11.5 to introduce students to SMART goals. Setting SMART goals is a descriptive approach designed to help people set more attainable goals.

Sample Script

Many people struggle to achieve their goals because they do not set SMART goals. People can make the mistake of setting goals that are too big, unrealistic, or unattainable. Not us! Today, we will learn to create SMART goals. SMART goals are specific, measurable, attainable, relevant, and timely. They help us achieve what we want. Let's talk more about what these words mean.

Activity D: Steps to Setting and Attaining Goals

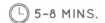
 5–8 MINS. Use Supplement 11.6 as a handout to review the four steps to setting and attaining goals. Use the examples provided below, modify them to fit the needs and interests of your students, or ask students to generate their own examples to individualize the content. As part of the discussion, introduce and dissect goals that do not meet the SMART criteria, such as being taller by next week, having prettier eyes, or making someone like them.

Sample Script

1. *Identify your goal area. Refer to your Healthy Living Domains worksheet [Supplement 11.3], and review the area you colored red. Identify a specific action in that area for which you would like to create a SMART goal. For example, if my physical circle or area is colored red, and I am tired often, I may choose to create a goal to get better sleep. By using our circles to identify a goal area, we will make sure our goals are relevant to healthy living! That's the "R" in SMART!*

2. *Create your SMART goal. Now that we have a relevant goal, let's create a goal that is specific, measurable, attainable, and timely. Using my example from before, I might create this goal: By the end of this month, I will get at least 8–9 hours of sleep each night, at least 5 days a week. This is specific and measurable because it explains how much sleep I aim to get and how often. It is attainable or realistic because I know I am capable of sleeping this much; I just might need to turn out the lights and turn off the TV or my computer earlier. The goal is timely because I have a date set by which I hope to achieve or attain my goal. This is at the end of this month.*

3. *Implement your plan. Now we need to make sure we have a plan for attaining our goals. They won't happen on their own, so we'll need to work toward them. We'll need to plan. This includes thinking about things that could help us attain our goals and thinking about things that might get in the way of attaining our goals. To help you attain your goal, you might write out a calen-*

dar or tell someone you trust about your plans. Perhaps a friend has a similar goal and you can be goal buddies and support each another. Perhaps your family can help you attain your goal. Also, think about what could get in the way of your goal. Using my example, if I have a neighbor friend who stays over late playing video games, I might need to ask him or her to start leaving earlier so I could get to sleep earlier.

4. *Check your progress. We will need to check our progress toward our goal. Using my example, I might record my hours of sleep on my calendar each night and check my progress each Sunday morning. I need to know if I'm on track to attaining my goal. I need to know if I need to make changes. If I've already attained my goal, how can I keep from going back to how things were before? Maybe I feel so much better that I decide to try to get 8–9 hours of sleep every night. With enough practice, our goals can become healthy life habits or routines; we may not need to think about them quite so much.*

If you find you're not making progress toward your goal, the important thing is not to give up! We all make mistakes. Sometimes we see mistakes as frustrating and we feel like quitting, but we can use reframing instead. We can reframe a mistake and see it as a chance to learn more. If we do this, mistakes can be good for us; they can help us learn. By not giving up after we mess up, we can become stronger and show more resilience.

So, when you see you aren't making progress toward your goal, you can be a detective or a scientist and look for evidence or clues that will help you figure out what went wrong: Was my goal a true SMART goal or was it too broad or unrealistic? Did something get in the way? What can I do to avoid this next time? Are there things I can do or people I can talk to who can help me? How can I change my plan and try it again?

Putting It All Together

🕐 **10 MINS.** Use the following activity to practice the concepts discussed in this lesson.

Sample Script

Let's practice what we've learned by putting it all together.

In small groups or individually, ask students to generate their own SMART goals and action plans toward goal attainment. After a few minutes, ask if students want to share their goals. If students do not want to share, that is okay. Continue sharing examples of steps and the overall process. Provide positive feedback for students who shared examples. Emphasize that goal setting and increasing positive activity are important as a means to a healthy life.

- Define SMART goals, goal setting, and goal attainment.

- List the steps to goal attainment.

Sample Script

Today, we learned more about the activities we do and about how we might want to change them to live happier, healthier lives. We learned to create SMART goals and learned a skill called goal attainment. I want you all to practice goal attainment at home, at school, and with your friends.

Closure

 2 MINS.   Close the lesson using a brief breathing activity and a reflection on the lesson content.

Sample Script

Let's take a moment to regroup. Close your eyes and rest your hands in your lap. Feel your feet on the floor. Relax the muscles in your body and face. Relax and soften your stomach muscles. Counting to three, take a deep breath in slowly. Inhale the air down into your lungs. Feel your chest and stomach expand like a balloon. [Pause.] *Now, exhale counting to 4. Feel your chest and stomach collapse as all the air exits your body.* [Pause.] *Again, inhale deep into your lungs so that your stomach expands* [Pause.] *and exhale.* [Pause.] *Take a moment to think about something you learned today that was important to you or you really liked.* [Note to instructor: Pause for a moment to allow time for reflection.] *Counting to 3, take one more deep breath in slowly* [Pause.] *and exhale counting to 4.* [Pause.]

Tips for Transfer Training and Homework

Use the ideas and activities in the following section to practice this lesson's content with your students at other times during the day. Also remember to precorrect, remind, and reinforce concepts from this lesson in activities throughout the school week and to encourage students to use the skills taught in this lesson across settings including home, the bus, and the cafeteria.

Additional Activities

- Letter: Ask students to write a letter to themselves or draw a picture of themselves achieving their goal. In this letter, have them include their SMART goals and the reasons why they made this goal. Have students hand them in. Then, at the end of the *Strong Kids* program (or at some later date as appropriate), return the letters to students and have them reevaluate their plans.

- Strength inventories: Hand out a sheet of paper with all students' names on it to each child, so that each child has a list of all the students in the class. Ask students to write down a strength that they sincerely associate with each student in the class. We recommend that students record their names at the top of their lists to help instructors monitor for sarcastic or spiteful statements. When students are finished with their lists, collect and review the statements, inventory the strengths, and share them so that students can see themselves and their strengths in a new way.

- Resilience: Have students read books or watch videos that highlight perseverance, resilience, or grit. Include famous people who showed determination in the face of failure (e.g., Malala Yousafzai).

Homework Handout

Pass out the homework handout, Supplement 11.7, Personal Goal Organizer. Explain to students that they are to complete a personal goal organizer for home, school, and free time. Students will evaluate their goals.

Your Younger Self

Key Terms and Definitions

Healthy living

This is living in a way that helps you be stronger and happier.

Example: There are things that we can do in our daily lives to help us be healthier, like reframing thinking traps, helping friends, and getting enough exercise.

Goals

These are specific objectives that you want to achieve.

Example: Goals can be short term, like completing an assignment, and they can be long term, like creating a new healthy living routine or activity.

Goal setting

This is defining a goal and creating a plan of action to achieve that goal.

Goal attainment

This is completing your action plan and achieving your goal. Goal attainment helps us feel more confident in our skills and abilities and helps us get what we want out of our lives.

Healthy Living Domains

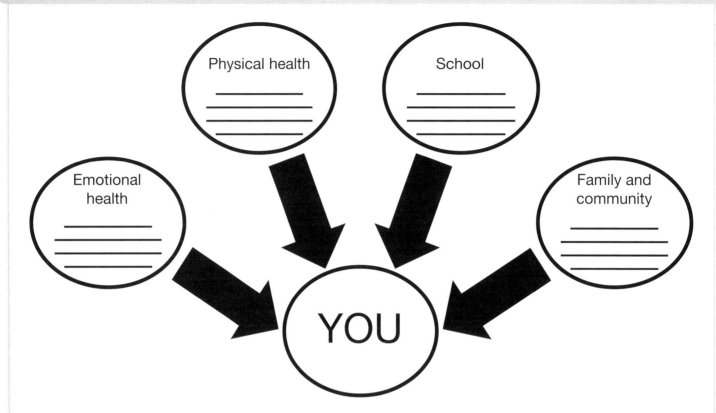

Examples and Nonexamples of Goal Setting

Situation 1 (nonexample—no goal and no action)

José daydreams every day about how his life will be after he makes the team.

Situation 2 (nonexample—no goal and ineffective action)

José draws pictures of basketballs and famous ball players while in class.

Situation 3 (nonexample—partial goal and action)

José makes a goal to find out when tryouts or practices will take place.

Situation 4 (example)

To increase his chances that he'll make the team and do his best, José makes a goal to spend at least 4 hours a week practicing until the day of tryouts.

Merrell's Strong Kids—Grades 3–5: A Social and Emotional Learning Curriculum, Second Edition,
by Dianna Carrizales-Engelmann, Laura L. Feuerborn, Barbara A. Gueldner, and Oanh K. Tran.
   221

Setting SMART Goals

SMART goals are *specific.* Specific goals speak about the exact part of something that we are going to fix. "I'm going to be a nicer person" would become "I'm going to be a nicer person by saying hello to someone new every day at lunch."

SMART goals are *measurable.* Measurable goals mean that we choose things or parts of things that can be compared to how they used to be to see how much they have changed. We can see the changes or we can keep track of them in some way. "I'm going to be happier," would become "I'm going do something that makes me laugh for 10 minutes every day after school."

SMART goals are *attainable.* Attainable goals mean that the goal is something that could actually happen by something you do. It can be a waste of our energy to be bothered by something we cannot change. "I'm going to get taller so I can play better basketball" would have to change to "I'm going to practice at least three times a week to get better at basketball."

SMART goals are *relevant.* Relevant goals connect with our healthy living domains. They are goals that connect to what we truly want and need to live healthier, happier lives. Getting a higher score on a video game probably won't do much to help us with our physical fitness and our need to meet new people, but setting goals to get outside and connect with our friends more could help.

SMART goals are *timely.* We need a time frame to achieve our goals. "I am going to get stronger by running 2 miles" may be specific, measurable, attainable, and relevant, but there is no time frame. "I'm going to run 2 miles by May 1" is a timely goal.

Merrell's Strong Kids—Grades 3–5: A Social and Emotional Learning Curriculum, Second Edition,
by Dianna Carrizales-Engelmann, Laura L. Feuerborn, Barbara A. Gueldner, and Oanh K. Tran.

Steps to Setting and Attaining Goals

1. Identify your goal area from the healthy living domains: emotional health, physical health, school, and family and community.

2. Create your SMART goal: specific, measurable, attainable, relevant, and timely

3. Implement your plan: What can help you? What might get in the way?

4. Check your progress: Are you on track to attain your goal? If not, investigate why. What changes do you need to make?

Personal Goal Organizer

Name (optional) _____

Directions: Complete this personal goal organizer for your activities at home, in school, and during your free time.

	Home	School	Free time
My SMART goal			
Evaluate my goal	○ Specific ○ Measurable ○ Attainable ○ Relevant ○ Timely	○ Specific ○ Measurable ○ Attainable ○ Relevant ○ Timely	○ Specific ○ Measurable ○ Attainable ○ Relevant ○ Timely
Did I implement my plan?	☐ Yes ☐ No	☐ Yes ☐ No	☐ Yes ☐ No
Is my plan working?	☐ Yes. What goal can I work on now? _____ _____ _____ _____ ☐ No. What changes can I make? _____ _____ _____ _____	☐ Yes. What goal can I work on now? _____ _____ _____ _____ ☐ No. What changes can I make? _____ _____ _____ _____	☐ Yes. What goal can I work on now? _____ _____ _____ _____ ☐ No. What changes can I make? _____ _____ _____ _____
How did it make me feel?			

LESSON 12

Finishing UP!

- Responsible decision making
- Self-awareness
- Relationship skills
- Self-management
- Social awareness

Teacher Notes

Purpose and Objectives

This lesson provides students with a review of major concepts and skills in the *Strong Kids* curriculum. In this lesson, students will

1. Review Lessons 1–11 content.

   - Comfortable and uncomfortable feelings and distinguishing healthy and unhealthy ways to express emotions

   - How thoughts, feelings, and behaviors are connected

   - The anger model and the problem-solving process

   - How to set and attain SMART goals

   - Common thinking traps and reframing them

   - Signs of stress and strategies for managing stress

   - Strategies for increasing habits for positive living

2. Develop an awareness of supports and safety networks.

   - Identify when more help and support is needed.

   - Identify where to go for more help.

   - Identify support systems that contribute to school and life success.

3. Enhance an understanding of resilience and persistence.

   - Identify ways to persist in adversity.

   - Understand the importance of social and emotional learning to healthy decision making.

4. Participate in the posttest (optional).

   - Complete the posttest assessment (provide additional time if necessary).

Materials Needed

☐ Supplement 12.1 (online download and handout)

☐ Supplements 12.2–12.4 (handout)

☐ *Strong Kids—Grades 3–5* Certificate of Achievement (optional certificate)

Running Short on Time?

Suggested stopping points: end of Activity A and the Closure activity. When continuing the lesson, begin with the Mindfulness-Based Focusing Activity found in the Introduction section, then Activity B.

Instructor Reflection

We have now come to the end of *Strong Kids—Grades 3–5*, and your students have gained essential skills for emotional, mental, social, and physical health. Think about the skills that you have taught your students throughout this program. How can you continue to reinforce these important skills so your students continue to practice them after the program ends? How can you encourage the development of these skills in your students' lives outside of this setting? Have you used any of these skills in your own life? If so, what experiences and outcomes did you observe? Did you learn anything about yourself, your strengths, and your weaknesses? What challenges in your professional or personal life might interfere with you reaching improved social, emotional, behavioral, social, and physical health? How might you address these challenges proactively? How can you prepare yourself to persist with your goals when you experience challenges? What goals do you have for yourself and your students moving forward? What steps can you take today to move forward and practice resilience when challenges come your way?

Note: If you have further concerns about how students may be coping with any social-emotional difficulties, consider talking to your administrator/supervisor, school psychologist, or school counselor. It is important to be familiar with your school's/agency's mental health referral process and community resources.

Preparation

Prior to teaching the Finishing UP! lesson, it can be helpful to review Lessons 1–11 to refresh your memory. Be familiar with names of those people at your school/agency who are there to support mental health concerns. Students will also be asked to identify resources and safety networks at the end of the lesson. As applicable, consider inviting your school's primary mental health practitioner (school psychologist, counselor, or other affiliated mental health provider) into your class to introduce him- or herself to your students.

Optional Posttest

If you conducted a pretest assessment before or during Lesson 1 and intend to conduct follow-up assessment of *Strong Kids—Grades 3–5* at the end of this lesson, you will need to reserve enough instructional time to do so. If you do not intend to conduct a follow-up assessment, see www.strongkidsresources.com for assessment recommendations. It is recommended that the same tests from the preassessment be used to determine the effects of students' participation in this curriculum.

Introduction

🕒 2–5 MINS. This is the final lesson of *Strong Kids—Grades 3–5*. This lesson reviews all the skills learned over the past weeks. Students may complete a brief posttest to measure what they learned. Emphasize that the skills learned from the curriculum are vital to students' social and emotional health, and there will be opportunities to use these skills throughout their lives. Help students engage in the final focusing activity of the program.

Sample Script

*Today is our last lesson of the Strong Kids program and we will review all the important skills we've been talking about for the past few months. We started each lesson with an activity to help us get started on the lesson and focus our minds. We also discussed how to understand our emotions and those of the people around us; ways to take someone's perspective; empathy, respect, and responsibility; how to practice a positive attitude; ways to reframe traps using evidence; ways to solve problems; how to set and attain goals; how to deal with anger and stress; and how to create healthier daily habits. These skills support us when we have to deal with adversity. They help us practice resilience and bounce back from problems we encounter and continue toward our goals.
We will use some time today to talk about what to do and who to talk to if we need help. We will talk about how to persevere toward our goals even when we stumble. We will end with setting a goal to keep practicing what we've learned so that we can continue to be emotionally and physically strong and healthy.*

Mindfulness-Based Focusing Activity

🕒 2 MINS. **Sample Script**

Let's practice settling our bodies and focusing our minds. Close your eyes or look at a point on the floor or on your desk. Rest your hands comfortably. Feel your feet on the floor or your hands as they rest. Pay attention to your breathing for three breaths. [Pause for three breaths.] *Let's take a moment to practice some of the focusing activities we've worked on. First, notice the sounds you hear in the room, near and far.* [Pause for about 15 seconds.] *Now, focus your attention on the feelings in your feet, legs, stomach, back, arms, shoulders, neck, and head.* [Pause for about 15 seconds.] *Next, with a curious and kind mind, pay attention to the emotions you are having. Notice how they feel.* [Pause for about 15 seconds.] *Now, focus on your thoughts. Notice how they change.* [Pause for about 15 seconds.] *Remember, whatever you are experiencing is okay. Now, let's focus on our breath for a minute.* [Pause for 1 minute to allow practice.] *Now, let's take two breaths together.* [Pause.] *When you finish letting out the second breath, slowly open your eyes.*

Activity A: *Strong Kids* Review and Discussion Questions

 11–14 MINS. Use Supplement 12.1 as a handout to guide this activity. Have students get into small groups to quickly review the lesson's main ideas. Then, have students share their thoughts regarding the discussion questions within their small groups. For each lesson, allow a leader to lead the discussion, then alternate to the next leader to lead the next lesson review. Continue to rotate for each lesson thereafter, allowing each student to be a leader. Allow a minute or two for each lesson discussion. In order to keep things moving, you may wish to set a timer that rings every 60–90 seconds per lesson to remind students to move to the next lesson.

Sample Script

We have learned so much by doing this program, so it's important to discuss what you remember and how you will continue to use these important skills. In small groups, identify someone in the group to be the first leader to review the topics and discussion questions for the first lesson. The leader will read the main ideas from each lesson in this handout. Then, the leader will briefly start a discussion based on the questions listed. We will only have about a minute to review each lesson, so you will need to be focused and efficient in your discussion. I will let you know when to move to the next lesson review and discussion, then the next student leader leads the lesson review. Within your groups, you will rotate to allow all students to be leaders. [Depending on the number of students in small groups, some may be a leader multiple times. The teacher may also choose to read the discussion questions aloud to the class.]

Keep students in small groups for the next activity.

Using *Strong Kids* Skills to Persevere Through Challenges

 15 MINS. Use Supplements 12.2 and 12.3 as handouts for this activity. Persevering through life's challenges helps to develop resilience. Encourage students to use the skills they've learned over the course of this program (e.g., positive thinking, coping strategies, making healthy choices) to persevere through adversity. Emphasize that there will be times when this will be difficult to do, but it's important to stay focused on healthy and helpful skills and choices to get them through challenges.

Activity B: Building Resilience

15 MINS.

Use Supplements 12.2 and 12.3 as handouts to facilitate a discussion on the importance of using strategies and skills to work through aversive conditions or situations based on the sample pictures. Be sure to cut out individual pictures in advance. Have students separate into small groups, and give each group a different picture from Supplement 12.2 to practice working through a difficult situation and how to persevere or overcome challenges (see pictures 1–6). You may also use situations that seem most relevant to your students. Use Supplement 12.3, Steps to Perseverance, and have each group write on the footprint, emphasizing skills and strategies and, in particular, *Strong Kids* skills that will help in the pictured situation. Allow time for large-group discussion of this activity when students are finished. You can post the steps next to the scenario picture and hang it on the wall as a visual reminder throughout the school year.

Sample Script

Sometimes, a situation will not always turn out the way you want, but how can you continue to use the skills you've learned to work through life's challenges? For example, if you don't make it on the basketball team, what will you do to improve your chances or learn something about this situation? Or if someone you like doesn't like you in return? Do you give up and not hang out with new people because you feel so embarrassed? Challenges are part of life and they can make us stronger and smarter.

Each group will get a different picture situation and a Steps to Perseverance footprint handout [Supplement 12.3]. Within your group, talk about skills and strategies you would use in that situation to practice resilience. Write your strategies on the Steps footprint. As you can see, each situation can be very different and the skills used will be different, too. In your small group, discuss 1) what the situation is, and 2) what you would do to practice resilience in that situation using Strong Kids skills. What might you need or do to get through a difficult situation? Remember to keep encouraging yourself and move through any discomfort. It might be helpful to keep your SMART goals in mind. Write your skills on the Steps footprint. We will come together and talk about your thoughts. We will also post the picture and Steps on the wall so that we can remind ourselves to continue working through challenges. [Allow time for discussion.]

Picture Scenario Examples:

Picture 1: Getting out of a maze

Picture 2: Stranded in the water

Picture 3: Getting teased

Picture 4: Failing a test

Picture 5: Not being chosen for the team

Picture 6: Your pet gets sick

Support Systems and Knowing When to Get Help

🕒 5 MINS.　Students may require additional assistance and support when faced with life's challenges. Encourage them to be proactive by knowing to whom they can turn in advance of any crisis. Ensure that they are able to identify the school personnel, personal safety networks, and community organizations that can be helpful.

Sample Script

We will talk about how to know when we might need help and things you can do if you feel like you need more help or support. There are resources available, and knowing who they are now, before you have any need for them, will help improve your chances of getting help quickly if you ever need it.

Activity C: When to Seek Help

🕒 2 MINS.　Explain to students that they have learned important skills during this unit but that these skills may not be enough help for all of the possible problems they might have. They may require other adults to be involved or professional help. Encourage a discussion of when to seek help. Emphasize awareness of their thoughts, emotions, and behaviors and the intensity of their problems by using the skills they have learned from *Strong Kids*. Encourage students to share their concerns with an adult they trust. In addition, encourage them to be aware of others' emotions and challenges so that they can suggest resources to their peers.

Sample Script

Sometimes, a problem can be too much for us to handle on our own, and sometimes our emotional issues can turn into serious problems. If a problem ever gets serious, there are people you can turn to for help. A problem is serious when it gets in the way of you being able to do the things you like to do or you need to do, like having healthy relationships and getting your work done. So, if you feel like life is feeling really difficult, you're having a hard time knowing what to do, some of the not-so-good or unhelpful ideas are coming to mind, and nothing is working to make you feel better, this is when you want to ask an adult you trust for help. For example, if you don't get asked to the school dance or feel rejected by someone, and you are sad for days and cannot eat or sleep or you don't want to leave the house, this is when you may want to talk to someone to help you feel better. It's also important for you to be aware of how your friends are feeling and what kinds of challenges they are going through. Remember, we talked about cues and paying attention to those cues so that you can be a support to your friends or encourage them to talk to someone. There are adults here at school who can help you and your classmates.

Activity D: List of Resources

🕒 3 MINS.　Use Supplement 12.4 as a handout. Have students think about and list the adults and other individuals they trust and can talk to at school, at home, and in the community. Help students generate names if they can't think of any (e.g., parent, other adult family members, a close adult friend or neighbor, clergy, principal, teacher, counselor, school psychologist). Have students also identify community resources or organizations that can be helpful when needed. Be familiar with your school's mental health referral process in case students have questions or if you ever need to make a referral.

Sample Script

Use this handout to discuss and write down the adults in your life whom you trust and can talk to when you need help. If you do not know anyone to contact, I will help you and give you some names of people who can support you. These people care about you, want you to be well, and can help you participate in life more fully. It is also important to know the resources within your community and to identify them before you ever need them [e.g., clergy]. *Can someone share what other resources are in our community?* [Allow time for sharing.] *When you are in a situation and you need someone to talk to or you have problems, look at this handout. Keep it in a safe place so that you can use it when it's needed.*

Optional Assessments

⏲ 15–20 MINS. If you administered pretests from the *Strong Kids* web site during Lesson 1, now is the time to administer these tests again so that you can determine how effective *Strong Kids—Grades 3–5* was at increasing students' knowledge and enhancing their emotional resilience. It will take approximately 15–20 minutes to take these tests.

Putting It All Together

⏲ 5 MINS. Reiterate the importance of perseverance and overcoming adversity. Encourage students to continue to reflect on the *Strong Kids* skills to help them through life's challenges.

Sample Script

Let's practice what we've learned by putting it all together.

Use Supplement 12.1 to review any last comments or questions from the lesson discussion. Facilitate discussion on which *Strong Kids* skills can be used to build resilience. Allow time to hand out certificates for participation in *Strong Kids—Grades 3–5* if you choose to give certificates.

Sample Script

Today, we reviewed everything we learned in this program and created a tree to help us remember what we need to help keep us strong. In the review activity we did earlier, were there any questions or comments about the key points from the lessons? [Allow time for students to share.] *Believe it or not, we will continue to work on these skills throughout our entire lives. You will make mistakes and that's okay. What's really important is that you learn from those mistakes and you keep trying. We also talked about when to talk to an adult to help when we need more help. Which Strong Kids skills would be helpful to build resilience when challenges arise?* [Allow time for students to share.] *As we have worked through the program, we have shared stories with each other. Remember that stories are personal, and even though today is the last day of the lessons, we will remember not to share each other's stories with anyone outside of the group. By keeping other people's stories to yourself, you will be respecting others. Congratulations on finishing Strong Kids! Your skills have built up your emotional strength, and they will continue to be valuable as you become an adult.* [Optional: Hand out *Strong Kids* Certificates.]

Closure

🕐 2 MINS.   Close the lesson using a brief breathing activity and a reflection on the lesson content.

Sample Script

Let's take a moment to regroup. Close your eyes and rest your hands in your lap. Feel your feet on the floor. Relax the muscles in your body and face. Relax and soften your stomach muscles. Counting to 3, take a deep breath in slowly. Inhale the air down into your lungs. Feel your chest and stomach expand like a balloon. [Pause.] *Now, exhale, counting to 4. Feel your chest and stomach collapse as all the air exits your body.* [Pause.] *Again, inhale deep into your lungs so that your stomach expands* [Pause.] *and exhale.* [Pause.] *Take a moment to think about something you learned today that was important to you.* [Note to instructor: Pause for a moment to allow time for reflection.] *Counting to 3, take one more deep breath in slowly* [Pause.] *and exhale, counting to 4.* [Pause.]

Tips for Transfer Training

Use the ideas and activities in the following section to practice the *Strong Kids* content with your students after completing the program. Also remember to pre-correct, remind, and reinforce concepts from the lessons in activities throughout the school week and to encourage students to use the skills taught in this lesson across settings including home, the bus, and the cafeteria.

Additional Activities

- Have students create a dream board of pictures or a word collage of their dreams and the ways the skills learned in this program can help them achieve their dreams, goals, and aspirations.

- Use *Strong Kids* language to reinforce skills throughout the school year.

Strong Kids Lesson Review and Discussion Questions

Lesson 1: About *Strong Kids:* Emotional Strength Training (introduction to the program, learning the rules of the group, and beginning to learn about emotions)

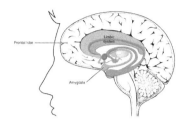

- Key terms: resilience, adversity, and perseverance

- We all have emotions, every day, and everywhere we are. Emotions are like signals that tell us something about our situation.

- There are different emotions that we all have, and we can experience more than one emotion at the same time (refer to list of emotions/faces).

Discussion questions

1. What emotions have you noticed and learned about by participating in this program?

2. Provide an example situation that brought out an emotion. How did you recognize your emotion?

Lessons 2 and 3: Understanding Your Feelings 1 and 2 (there are physical feelings that go along with our emotions; there are thoughts and behaviors or actions that go along with our emotions)

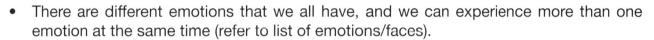

- Key terms: emotions, thoughts, behaviors, action, respect/respectful, disrespect/disrespectful, physical feelings, comfortable, uncomfortable, emotional intensity, resilience, adversity, and perseverance

- Emotions can be physical and are linked to thoughts, feelings, and behaviors.

- Emotions can range from comfortable (happy, excited) to uncomfortable (worried, frustrated), and we can gauge these emotions on a thermometer.

- We can respond to emotions in helpful ways to match our situation and our social needs.

Discussion questions

1. What emotions feel comfortable to you, and what emotions feel uncomfortable? What emotions feel both comfortable and uncomfortable?

2. How might you express emotions at home? In the cafeteria? With friends? With a teacher?

(continued)

Lesson 4: Understanding Other People's Feelings (noticing other people's emotions and showing empathy)

- Key terms: empathy, sympathy, social clues, and perspective

- How can we notice other people's feelings, try to understand other people's feelings better, and begin to see a situation from another person's perspective?

Discussion questions

1. What can you look for to give you clues about how someone might be feeling?

2. What kinds of information can help you take another person's perspective?

Lesson 5: Dealing with Anger (identify and manage angry emotions)

- Key terms: anger, aggression, anger management, perspective/point of view, response, and reaction

- Anger is a natural emotion that we all have, and it can be the result of a mixture of other upsetting emotions.

- When anger is unmanaged, it can lead to some not-so-good decisions, from holding it in to showing aggression.

Discussion questions

1. Do you think all people experience anger in the same way?

2. What are some helpful anger management strategies? Have you used any of these strategies? Which strategies worked best for you?

Lesson 6: Clear Thinking 1 (identify when your thoughts get stuck in thinking traps)

- Key terms: thoughts, self-talk, emotions, reactions, and thinking traps

- Thoughts can influence emotions and behaviors.

- We can develop an awareness of our own thoughts and identify common thinking traps.

Discussion questions

1. What are thinking traps, and why is it important to be aware of them?

2. How are thoughts, emotions, and behavior related?

Lesson 7: Clear Thinking 2 (strategies we can use to think about other perspectives in a situation)

- Key terms: evidence and reframing

- We can develop the ability to notice or observe our thoughts.

- We can learn how to spot and get out of thinking traps early, and we can keep thoughts from snowballing by reframing.

(continued)

Discussion questions

1. Think of a time when you or someone you know was stuck in a thinking trap. How did you know it was a thinking trap? What was the evidence? Did it snowball or grow and become a bigger trap?

2. Did you or the person reframe the thinking trap to get unstuck? If so, how? If not, how could you or the person have reframed it to get unstuck earlier?

Lesson 8: Solving People Problems (ways to solve problems and get along with others)

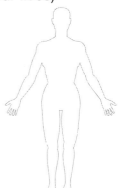

- Key terms: responsible, attitude, conflict, problem solving/conflict resolution, resolution, and resolve

- Conflict is an unavoidable part of life, so it's important to know how to deal with it effectively.

- We can use the four-step problem-solving model and examples and nonexamples of problem solving.

- We can make responsible and respectful choices in solving conflicts with others.

Discussion questions

1. Conflict is a natural part of life, but sometimes we try to avoid it. Other times we might overreact to conflict. How have you handled conflict, and how could you apply the four steps of the problem-solving model to the situation?

2. How might showing empathy or taking another person's perspective help you when you are in conflict with another person?

Lesson 9: Letting Go of Stress (strategies we can use to deal with stress in our lives)

- Key terms: stress, helpful or healthy stress, unhelpful or unhealthy stress, situational triggers, relaxation, realistic or unrealistic expectations, and common signs of stress

- There are ways to identify healthy and unhealthy stress and stress triggers before you feel stressed out.

- We can learn the difference between helpful and unhelpful options and techniques for managing stress, and we can learn to tell realistic from unrealistic expectations.

Discussion questions

1. What are your triggers and signs of stress in your life?

2. What are some strategies for managing stress early on, before getting too stressed out?

(continued)

Lesson 10: Positive Living (things we can do to live a positive and healthy life)

- Key terms: habit, moderation, attitude, and choice

- Our behaviors and actions can contribute to a healthy and positive life-style in the long term.

- We can learn the differences between examples (helpful) and non-examples (unhelpful) of life choices that can affect our lives at home, at school, and in the community.

Discussion questions

1. What are some activities or actions that energize us, motivate us, and make us happier in the long term?

2. What are some healthy living activities that you do now and healthier habits that you can create?

Lesson 11: Creating Strong and SMART Goals (setting goals and doing things that will help us lead a healthy life)

- Key terms: goals, goal setting, goal attainment, and healthy living

- It is important to increase and maintain positive activities.

- Set SMART goals and monitor your progress.

Discussion questions

1. What are SMART goals?

2. What are some ways we can identify areas of our lives in need of SMART goals?

3. How can we improve the chances that we will attain our goals?

SMART Goals

 S Specific

 **M** Measurable

 **A** Attainable

 **R** Relevant

T Timely

Resilience Scenarios

Picture 1: Getting out of a maze

Picture 2: Stranded in the water

Picture 3: Getting teased

Picture 4: Failing a test

Picture 5: Not being chosen for the team

Picture 6: Your pet gets sick

Steps to Perseverance

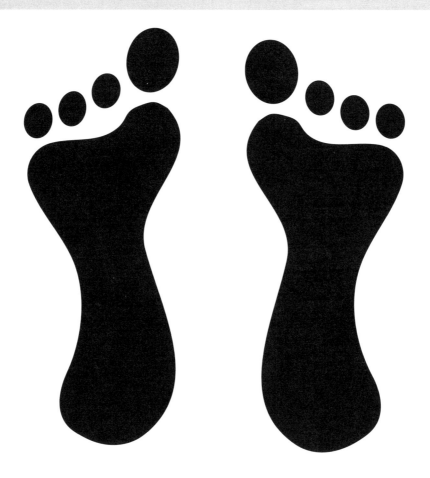

Helping Resources Handout

List the important resources that you can turn to if you need some help or someone to talk to. Include their phone numbers, too. If you do not have their numbers, try to obtain them within the next week or so. Having this information readily available can be very helpful. After you've completed this form, keep it in a safe place so that you can get to it when/if needed.

When I need help or someone to talk to, I will contact one of these people:

This person at home supports me and I can talk to him/her for help: _____

_____

This friend supports me and I can talk to him/her for help: _____

_____

This adult at school supports me and I can talk to him/her for help: _____ _____

_____

This person in the community supports me and I can talk to him/her for help: _____

_____

This is an organization/community resource in my area that I can go to for help: _____

_____

Remember that your school administrators, counselors, and teachers will know what to do or to whom you can talk if you need help.

Certificate of Achievement

Strong Kids—Grades 3–5 Certificate of Achievement

Awarded to

_____

for participating in
The *Strong Kids* Curriculum

Keep up the good work!

Instructor _____

Date _____

Appendices

Strong Kids Knowledge Test for Students in Grades 3-5

INSTRUCTIONS FOR TEACHERS/GROUP LEADERS

The *Strong Kids* Knowledge Test is a 20-item assessment tool designed to measure students' knowledge of social and emotional concepts and coping strategies; it is based on content from the curriculum. The Knowledge Test may be used to measure how effective *Strong Kids—Grades 3–5* is in increasing students' knowledge of social-emotional concepts and coping strategies. If you choose to use the Knowledge Test as a pre- and posttest measure, you should administer it before the first lesson (Lesson 1) and again after the last lesson (Lesson 12). Most students can complete the entire Knowledge Test in about 20 minutes. Some students (especially younger students and those students with reading problems) may have difficulty understanding the Knowledge Test and may require assistance (e.g., having the teacher read the items out loud or be available to answer questions about specific words) in completing it.

HOW TO SCORE THE KNOWLEDGE TEST

An answer key is included for the Knowledge Test. The key lists the correct answers for each of the 20 items, along with the lesson from which the question was drawn. To score students' tests, compare the students' actual answers to those in the answer key and place an *X* or other mark by every answer that is incorrect. Each item that has a correct answer should be given one point, and the final tally of correct answers can be converted into a percentage of correct responses. For example, if a student correctly answered 17 of the 20 questions, his or her raw score would be 17, and the percentage correct would be 85%.

HOW TO USE THE TEST SCORES

To compare posttest scores to pretest scores, subtract the pretest total score from the posttest total score for each of the two tests. The difference reflects how much change occurred from the beginning to the end of the curriculum. Ideally, participation in *Strong Kids—Grades 3–5* will result in an increase in knowledge from pretest to posttest (the posttest scores will be greater than the pretest scores).

Strong Kids Knowledge Test
for Students in Grades 3-5

PRETEST _____   POSTTEST _____

Name _____ Grade _____ Age _____

School _____ Today's date _____

On the next few pages, you will be asked to answer questions to see how much you know about feelings, thoughts, and behaviors. Read each question carefully and choose what you think is the *best* answer for each question. You may not know the answers to all the questions and you may not have heard some of the words before, but try your best. You will not be graded on your answers. If you have any questions, please ask your teacher.

TRUE or FALSE

Read each sentence. If you think it is true or mostly true, circle the word *True*. If you think it is false or mostly false, circle the word *False*.

1.   True   False   If someone's hands are in fists and he or she is shaking, it could mean that there is a problem that the person needs to stop and figure out.

2.   True   False   Emotions feel the same for everyone.

3.   True   False   Stress can sometimes happen if you compare yourself to other people.

4.   True   False   We can choose to be nice to other people.

5.   True   False   Feeling uncomfortable sometimes is normal.

6.   True   False   Some emotions can be felt in our bodies.

MULTIPLE CHOICE

Circle the letter that goes along with the *best* answer for each question.

7. An example of an emotion that feels uncomfortable for most people is
   a. Hopeful
   b. Frustrated
   c. Curious
   d. Excited

8. What is an emotion?
   a. A thought you have about a situation
   b. Your inner voice inside your head
   c. A memory you have about something that happened to you
   d. A feeling that tells you something about a situation

(continued)

9. Self-talk can be a way to calm down after you get angry. Helpful self-talk might include telling yourself

    a. I don't deserve this

    b. I should get angry when something like this happens

    c. I can work through this

    d. I hope I never see this person ever again

10. Which of these *best* describes empathy?

    a. Knowing how you are feeling

    b. Not knowing why another person is feeling sad

    c. Understanding how another person may be feeling

    d. Wanting another person to feel better soon

11. Your thoughts can become traps when

    a. You keep thinking of something that makes a problem worse, not better

    b. You see both the good and bad in each situation

    c. You think something different from your friend

    d. You think about how another person might feel

12. Reframing is a way to

    a. Make new friends

    b. Think about how you can ignore the situation

    c. Think about a situation differently

    d. Tell on another student

13. Why would you want to know how someone else is feeling?

    a. So you can leave that person alone when he or she is angry

    b. So you can do the right thing to help him or her if needed

    c. To tell other people about that person

    d. To act the same when you are together

14. Conflict resolution is *best* described as

    a. Discussing a problem until somebody wins and somebody loses

    b. Arguing with another person until he or she sees your point and gives in

    c. Problem solving so you can reach an agreement that is respectful and responsible for everyone

    d. Talking about the problem until something changes the other person's mind

(continued)

15. Which of these is a helpful way to handle being afraid when you have to tell someone about a mistake you made?

    a. Tell him or her why you are scared and that you will work harder next time.

    b. Hide the mistake you made and hope he or she will forget about it.

    c. Be sad and angry with yourself and stay in your room.

    d. Say that the mistake was not your fault.

16. Which of the following is a helpful way to deal with a problem when you are feeling worried and sad?

    a. Cry somewhere quietly.

    b. Talk about the problem with someone you trust, such as a friend or teacher.

    c. Throw things around.

    d. Ignore the problem.

17. Which of the following is a helpful way to handle your emotions in class when your neighbor's talking begins to annoy you?

    a. Yell at that person and tell him or her to stop.

    b. Call out to the teacher about the student.

    c. Stare at the person until he or she knows you're annoyed.

    d. Stop and breathe deeply.

18. If you're feeling tired, and you're having a hard time enjoying yourself even though things are mostly fine in your life, you could try

    a. Eating healthy meals

    b. Getting more sleep

    c. Spending time outdoors

    d. Spending time with friends

    e. Any of the above

19. An important part of getting what we want in life is knowing how to set SMART goals. Which of the following is the SMARTest goal?

    a. I want to be a faster runner next month.

    b. I want to start brushing my teeth after lunch.

    c. I want to be 10 feet tall when I'm an adult.

    d. I will read 5 pages from my favorite book 6 nights a week.

20. Your friend seems upset. You want to show your friend that you care about what he or she is feeling. The most helpful way to do this is to

    a. Talk about yourself or something that happened to you

    b. Listen and show that you are paying attention

    c. Talk about something else

    d. Look away and don't say anything

Strong Kids Knowledge Test for Students in Grades 3-5 Answer Key

Correct answers for each of the 20 items are listed below. The *Strong Kids* lesson to which the question corresponds is indicated in parentheses.

1. T (Lesson 2)
2. F (Lesson 1)
3. T (Lesson 9)
4. T (Lesson 8)
5. T (Lesson 2)
6. T (Lesson 3)
7. b (Lesson 2)
8. d (Lesson 1)
9. c (Lesson 6)
10. c (Lesson 4)
11. a (Lesson 6)
12. c (Lesson 7)
13. b (Lesson 4)
14. c (Lesson 8)
15. a (Lesson 3)
16. b (Lesson 9)
17. d (Lesson 5)
18. e (Lesson 10)
19. b (Lesson 11)
20. b (Lesson 4)

Basic Fidelity Checklist

INSTRUCTIONS For each section, check the box if the lesson component was completed. If no items were implemented, check "Not" for not implemented. If some items were implemented, but not all, check "Partial" for partially implemented. If all items were implemented, check "Full" for fully implemented. In the Notes column, record the reason(s) for incomplete implementation of the component. In the Lesson Notes row, describe conditions that may have affected the fidelity for the lesson overall. Include any modifications made to the lessons.

Lesson Component	Level of Implementation			Notes
LESSON 1	Start time:		End time:	
Introduction	☐ Not	☐ Partial	☐ Full	
Pretest	☐ Not	☐ Partial	☐ Full	
Focusing Activity	☐ Not	☐ Partial	☐ Full	
Lesson Topics	☐ Not	☐ Partial	☐ Full	
Key Terms	☐ Not	☐ Partial	☐ Full	
Activity A	☐ Not	☐ Partial	☐ Full	
Activity B	☐ Not	☐ Partial	☐ Full	
Putting It All Together	☐ Not	☐ Partial	☐ Full	
Closure	☐ Not	☐ Partial	☐ Full	

Lesson notes:

Lesson Component	Level of Implementation			Notes
LESSON 2	Start time:		End time:	
Review	☐ Not	☐ Partial	☐ Full	
Introduction	☐ Not	☐ Partial	☐ Full	
Focusing Activity	☐ Not	☐ Partial	☐ Full	
Key Terms	☐ Not	☐ Partial	☐ Full	
Activity A	☐ Not	☐ Partial	☐ Full	
Activity B	☐ Not	☐ Partial	☐ Full	
Activity C	☐ Not	☐ Partial	☐ Full	
Putting It All Together	☐ Not	☐ Partial	☐ Full	
Closure	☐ Not	☐ Partial	☐ Full	

Lesson notes:

(continued)

Lesson Component	Level of Implementation			Notes
LESSON 3	Start time:		End time:	
Review	☐ Not	☐ Partial	☐ Full	
Introduction	☐ Not	☐ Partial	☐ Full	
Focusing Activity	☐ Not	☐ Partial	☐ Full	
Key Terms	☐ Not	☐ Partial	☐ Full	
Activity A	☐ Not	☐ Partial	☐ Full	
Activity B	☐ Not	☐ Partial	☐ Full	
Activity C	☐ Not	☐ Partial	☐ Full	
Activity D	☐ Not	☐ Partial	☐ Full	
Putting It All Together	☐ Not	☐ Partial	☐ Full	
Closure	☐ Not	☐ Partial	☐ Full	

Lesson notes:

Lesson Component	Level of Implementation			Notes
LESSON 4	Start time:		End time:	
Review	☐ Not	☐ Partial	☐ Full	
Introduction	☐ Not	☐ Partial	☐ Full	
Focusing Activity	☐ Not	☐ Partial	☐ Full	
Key Terms	☐ Not	☐ Partial	☐ Full	
Activity A	☐ Not	☐ Partial	☐ Full	
Activity B	☐ Not	☐ Partial	☐ Full	
Activity C	☐ Not	☐ Partial	☐ Full	
Activity D	☐ Not	☐ Partial	☐ Full	
Putting It All Together	☐ Not	☐ Partial	☐ Full	
Closure	☐ Not	☐ Partial	☐ Full	

Lesson notes:

(continued)

Lesson Component	Level of Implementation			Notes
LESSON 5	Start time:		End time:	
Review	☐ Not	☐ Partial	☐ Full	
Introduction	☐ Not	☐ Partial	☐ Full	
Focusing Activity	☐ Not	☐ Partial	☐ Full	
Key Terms	☐ Not	☐ Partial	☐ Full	
Activity A	☐ Not	☐ Partial	☐ Full	
Activity B	☐ Not	☐ Partial	☐ Full	
Activity C	☐ Not	☐ Partial	☐ Full	
Activity D	☐ Not	☐ Partial	☐ Full	
Activity E	☐ Not	☐ Partial	☐ Full	
Putting It All Together	☐ Not	☐ Partial	☐ Full	
Closure	☐ Not	☐ Partial	☐ Full	

Lesson notes:

Lesson Component	Level of Implementation			Notes
LESSON 6	Start time:		End time:	
Review	☐ Not	☐ Partial	☐ Full	
Introduction	☐ Not	☐ Partial	☐ Full	
Focusing Activity	☐ Not	☐ Partial	☐ Full	
Key Terms	☐ Not	☐ Partial	☐ Full	
Activity A	☐ Not	☐ Partial	☐ Full	
Activity B	☐ Not	☐ Partial	☐ Full	
Activity C	☐ Not	☐ Partial	☐ Full	
Putting It All Together	☐ Not	☐ Partial	☐ Full	
Closure	☐ Not	☐ Partial	☐ Full	

Lesson notes:

(continued)

Lesson Component	Level of Implementation			Notes
LESSON 7	Start time:		End time:	
Review	☐ Not	☐ Partial	☐ Full	
Introduction	☐ Not	☐ Partial	☐ Full	
Focusing Activity	☐ Not	☐ Partial	☐ Full	
Key Terms	☐ Not	☐ Partial	☐ Full	
Activity A	☐ Not	☐ Partial	☐ Full	
Activity B	☐ Not	☐ Partial	☐ Full	
Activity C	☐ Not	☐ Partial	☐ Full	
Activity D	☐ Not	☐ Partial	☐ Full	
Putting It All Together	☐ Not	☐ Partial	☐ Full	
Closure	☐ Not	☐ Partial	☐ Full	

Lesson notes:

Lesson Component	Level of Implementation			Notes
LESSON 8	Start time:		End time:	
Review	☐ Not	☐ Partial	☐ Full	
Introduction	☐ Not	☐ Partial	☐ Full	
Focusing Activity	☐ Not	☐ Partial	☐ Full	
Key Terms	☐ Not	☐ Partial	☐ Full	
Activity A	☐ Not	☐ Partial	☐ Full	
Activity B	☐ Not	☐ Partial	☐ Full	
Activity C	☐ Not	☐ Partial	☐ Full	
Activity D	☐ Not	☐ Partial	☐ Full	
Putting It All Together	☐ Not	☐ Partial	☐ Full	
Closure	☐ Not	☐ Partial	☐ Full	

Lesson notes:

(continued)

Lesson Component	Level of Implementation			Notes
LESSON 9	Start time:		End time:	
Review	☐ Not	☐ Partial	☐ Full	
Introduction	☐ Not	☐ Partial	☐ Full	
Focusing Activity	☐ Not	☐ Partial	☐ Full	
Key Terms	☐ Not	☐ Partial	☐ Full	
Activity A	☐ Not	☐ Partial	☐ Full	
Activity B	☐ Not	☐ Partial	☐ Full	
Activity C	☐ Not	☐ Partial	☐ Full	
Activity D	☐ Not	☐ Partial	☐ Full	
Putting It All Together	☐ Not	☐ Partial	☐ Full	
Closure	☐ Not	☐ Partial	☐ Full	

Lesson notes:

Lesson Component	Level of Implementation			Notes
LESSON 10	Start time:		End time:	
Review	☐ Not	☐ Partial	☐ Full	
Introduction	☐ Not	☐ Partial	☐ Full	
Focusing Activity	☐ Not	☐ Partial	☐ Full	
Key Terms	☐ Not	☐ Partial	☐ Full	
Activity A	☐ Not	☐ Partial	☐ Full	
Activity B	☐ Not	☐ Partial	☐ Full	
Activity C	☐ Not	☐ Partial	☐ Full	
Activity D	☐ Not	☐ Partial	☐ Full	
Activity E	☐ Not	☐ Partial	☐ Full	
Putting It All Together	☐ Not	☐ Partial	☐ Full	
Closure	☐ Not	☐ Partial	☐ Full	

Lesson notes:

(continued)

Lesson Component	Level of Implementation			Notes
LESSON 11 Start time:			End time:	
Review	☐ Not	☐ Partial	☐ Full	
Introduction	☐ Not	☐ Partial	☐ Full	
Focusing Activity	☐ Not	☐ Partial	☐ Full	
Key Terms	☐ Not	☐ Partial	☐ Full	
Activity A	☐ Not	☐ Partial	☐ Full	
Activity B	☐ Not	☐ Partial	☐ Full	
Activity C	☐ Not	☐ Partial	☐ Full	
Activity D	☐ Not	☐ Partial	☐ Full	
Putting It All Together	☐ Not	☐ Partial	☐ Full	
Closure	☐ Not	☐ Partial	☐ Full	

Lesson notes:

Lesson Component	Level of Implementation			Notes
LESSON 12 Start time:			End time:	
Introduction	☐ Not	☐ Partial	☐ Full	
Focusing Activity	☐ Not	☐ Partial	☐ Full	
Key Terms	☐ Not	☐ Partial	☐ Full	
Activity A	☐ Not	☐ Partial	☐ Full	
Activity B	☐ Not	☐ Partial	☐ Full	
Activity C	☐ Not	☐ Partial	☐ Full	
Activity D	☐ Not	☐ Partial	☐ Full	
Posttest	☐ Not	☐ Partial	☐ Full	
Putting It All Together	☐ Not	☐ Partial	☐ Full	
Closure	☐ Not	☐ Partial	☐ Full	

Lesson notes: